T0366953

THE CAPE RADICALS

THE CAPE RADICALS

*Intellectual and Political Thought
of the New Era Fellowship,
1930s to 1960s*

Crain Soudien

Published in South Africa by:
Wits University Press
1 Jan Smuts Avenue
Johannesburg 2001

www.witspress.co.za

Copyright © Crain Soudien 2019
Published edition © Wits University Press 2019
Images © Copyright holders

First published 2019

http://dx.doi.org.10.18772/12019063177

978-1-77614-317-7 (Paperback)
978-1-77614-348-1 (Web PDF)
978-1-77614-349-8 (EPUB)
978-1-77614-350-4 (Mobi)

All rights reserved. No part of this publication may be reproduced, stored in a
retrieval system, or transmitted in any form or by any means, electronic, mechanical,
photocopying, recording or otherwise, without the written permission of the publisher,
except in accordance with the provisions of the Copyright Act, Act 98 of 1978.

All images remain the property of the copyright holders. The publishers gratefully
acknowledge the publishers, institutions and individuals referenced in captions for the
use of images. Every effort has been made to locate the original copyright holders of the
images reproduced here; please contact Wits University Press in case of any omissions
or errors.

Project manager: Pat Tucker
Copyeditors: Alison Lowry and Alison Lockhart
Proofreader: Judith Shier
Indexer: Margie Ramsay
Cover design: Hybrid Creative
Typesetter: MPS
Typeset in 11.5 point Crimson

Contents

Acknowledgements

This work arose out of a request by Charles Thomas, Usuf Chikte and Dihru Gihwala to write for their organisation, the New Unity Movement, a history of the New Era Fellowship (NEF). A version of this book was produced for the eightieth anniversary of the founding of the NEF. Charles, Usuf and Dihru are important interlocutors for the gestation and production of what has been developed into this book, but they gave me carte blanche. They bear no responsibility for the positions that are taken in it. I am deeply grateful for the opportunity they provided me.

Derek Gripper was central to the research process and assisted in locating and collecting some of the most hard-to-get materials that have been drawn on here. To Derek and his partner Jaqueline Yamey, and Diane Paulse, both of whom assisted Derek, I am sincerely thankful. They found what little there was to be found, and considerably enriched the base off which any work was possible.

And then I would like to thank my wife, Lyn Hanmer, for her willingness to read and reread my efforts at clarity.

Acronyms and Abbreviations

AAC	All-African Convention
ANB	African National Bond
ANC	African National Congress
Anti-CAD	Anti-Coloured Affairs Department
APDUSA	African People's Democratic Union of Southern Africa
APO	African People's Organisation
CAC	Coloured Advisory Council
CAD	Coloured Affairs Department
CAFEF	Cape Flats Educational Fellowship
CATA	Cape African Teachers' Association
CI	Communist International
CLSA	Communist League of South Africa
CPSA	Communist Party of South Africa
CPSU	Cape Peninsula Students' Union
CST	colonialism of a special type
FIOSA	Fourth International of South Africa
ICU	Industrial and Commercial Workers' Union
NEF	New Era Fellowship
NEUF	Non-European United Front
NEUM	Non-European Unity Movement
NLL	National Liberation League
NRC	Natives Representative Council
NUM	New Unity Movement

PF	Progressive Forum
SAIC	South African Indian Congress
SOYA	Society of Young Africa
SPEF	South Peninsula Education Fellowship
TLSA	Teachers' League of South Africa
UCT	University of Cape Town
WIL	Workers International League
WPSA	Workers' Party of South Africa

Timeline

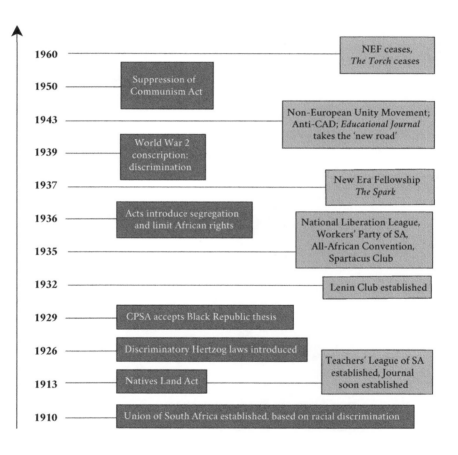

1960		NEF ceases, *The Torch* ceases
1950	Suppression of Communism Act	
1943		Non-European Unity Movement; Anti-CAD; *Educational Journal* takes the 'new road'
1939	World War 2 conscription; discrimination	
1937		New Era Fellowship *The Spark*
1936	Acts introduce segregation and limit African rights	
1935		National Liberation League, Workers' Party of SA, All-African Convention, Spartacus Club
1932		Lenin Club established
1929	CPSA accepts Black Republic thesis	
1926	Discriminatory Hertzog laws introduced	
1913	Natives Land Act	Teachers' League of SA established, Journal soon established
1910	Union of South Africa established, based on racial discrimination	

Introduction

In 1937 a small group of young Cape Town intellectual-activists made the decision to establish a cultural society for the purpose of, as they put it in their constitution, 'spreading enlightenment'. They called the society the New Era Fellowship (NEF). And so began an ambitious process of public education with the ordinary people of Cape Town. Their aim was to bring into being an organisation that would disrupt prevailing ruling-class thinking, which said that some people were naturally superior and others inferior. Integral to this disruption was making available to people the best thinking and opinions on a range of issues and subjects. 'We will discuss anything under the sun,' they announced to the people of Cape Town in 1937.[1]

A variety of forums were put in place: study circles, debating societies and cultural initiatives. These in turn were catalysts for new political formations, civic organisations and formative social organisations. Over a period of about 25 years the NEF introduced into the cultural life of Cape Town not only a sense of entitlement to dignity but also an awareness of new human possibility. In the process they made important contributions to the city on a local level. In rejecting out of hand the customs and practices of colonialism, a distinctive set of Cape cultural and political traditions, many of which live on into the present, were developed.

As innovative as the NEF was at the local level, on a much higher level it was groundbreaking. Its members were the first in South Africa's political history to locate the wider global discussions about 'race' and class in a larger discourse about the nature of domination. They arrived at the understanding – and this constituted the core of their global contribution – that the primary framing upon which the modern world was constructed, namely, race, was false. They developed a programmatic understanding of how hegemony – which is the complete domination of one group or power over another – can be constituted as a political and ideological project. They showed how the idea of race can be deployed to capture the cognitive and sense-making faculties of oppressed people, resulting in mental slavery. Not only did they seek to bring an end to mental slavery, they also committed themselves to building a new society in which all people could live with dignity. The means of effecting this, they came to understand, was education. As the ruling class used education to constitute the 'subjected' subject, it would be necessary to use the same powerful tool to produce new liberated human beings. This was their 'new era' vision.

Ultimately, the NEF did not become the mass movement its founders envisaged or hoped it would be. It did not produce the cultural revolution that would make every home, every school, every social and religious gathering, and every institution of the people a site and an opportunity for the formation of the new man (they had not yet come to the realisation that the term 'man' was problematic). It did not succeed in bringing the reproducers of hegemony – the institutions of the family, sites of learning, the ideological apparatuses of the courts, the police and the army, and places of worship – over to its side. But it was not for lack of trying. For some time, especially during the late 1940s and the 1950s, the NEF offered the people of Cape Town a vision of the ideal modern citizen. Leading by example, its leaders endeavoured to demonstrate the values, dispositions and attributes of a good citizen. A good citizen embodied core values: consideration for the marginalised and the oppressed, modesty and sensibility in tastes and manners, a deep desire for learning and an awareness of the need for self-effacement. In taking this path, the NEF influenced, and in some cases defined, how one entered and became a member of the professions.

Firstly, and importantly, they looked to the teaching profession. It was teachers, they believed, who carried the responsibility of role-modelling the new liberated people. Teachers were always to be available to the people but, simultaneously, they were to be the example of what it meant to be a citizen of a wider cosmopolitan world – humble, dignified, able to connect on a personal level, but never without a sense of their responsibility for breaking the shackles of oppression.

These imperatives carried over to all the professions. Few as there may have been, the NEF leaders worked hard to help those among them who were lawyers or doctors understand the attributes they should display. Interestingly, the ministers of religion and the imams in their midst were held to similar standards. The point is that they put in the minds of their followers the belief that a new way into the future was possible. They laid down the standards of comportment and personal responsibility to be emulated both within and outside of the professions. The impact was profound, and can still be seen today. Significant numbers of people, from generation to generation, adopted the behaviour and subscribed to these standards. They carried these forward in their lives.

As might be expected, it wasn't long before their public education work garnered the NEF much attention. With its members standing out in the places where they worked, the communities in which they lived and the public spaces where they began to appear, the efforts of the organisation stimulated admiration, respect and, sometimes, not a little envy. But there were also those who were less appreciative of the NEF's efforts to effect change and even some who regarded them with contempt. Despite noble intentions, over time and as conditions and circumstances changed, on both the local and the international stage, the organisation's ability to thrive faltered and its influence declined.

Many explanations have been proffered for why the NEF was unable to develop into a large cultural-political movement. One of them is the organisation's very reason for existing. It wished to break dominance – dominance in the social arrangements of South Africa, and dominance in the economic exploitation of the people of the world. It was, because of this, a threat to many. The establishment chose to ignore it.

If the NEF featured at all in various publications about Cape Town's history and its cultural life, it was usually in the footnotes. None of the major histories of Cape Town pays it any attention whatsoever. In more progressive histories, such as the two-volume 1999 publication *Cape Town in the Twentieth Century* by Vivian Bickford-Smith, Elizabeth van Heyningen and Nigel Worden, it merits only a small entry. When it is written about more fully, it is often in disparaging terms and, as a result, the NEF is hardly attended to. It is regrettable that the history of these intellectuals is scarcely known. This book is, in part, an attempt to go some way towards rectifying this.

Two authors who did, independently, give the NEF some attention were Baruch Hirson and Richard van der Ross. Both, in different ways, knew the people of the NEF. Hirson's book *The Cape Town Intellectuals* and the several articles he wrote, which were published in the journal *Searchlight South Africa* during the late 1980s and into the 1990s, constitute the most significant attempt to put together a considered narrative of the NEF's contribution.[2] His writing, however, shows an unintentional bias towards the white activists in this community. He was far more familiar and had more to do organisationally with the early political activists of the Trotskyist movement in South Africa – most of whom were white. He did not have much to do with the young leaders of colour in the organisation and so his accounts do not bring into full view the role they played.

The second attempt at a description of the intellectual activists of the NEF is to be found in Van der Ross's *The Rise and Decline of Apartheid*, which was published in 1986. Van der Ross acknowledges the brilliance of the leaders of the NEF but fails to engage with their conceptual contribution. In his political analysis of the central position of non-collaboration of the Non-European Unity Movement (NEUM) – their refusal to recognise or participate in the ruling power's 'separate development' political structures for 'non-Europeans' – he comes to the stinging conclusion, building on an assessment Gwendolen Carter made in 1958, that 'the Non-European Unity Movement has created more disunity than otherwise'.[3] This might have been so on certain levels but Van der Ross's dismissiveness is revealing. What it indicates is that he did not understand the objective of NEF and NEUM's intellectual analysis, which was to interrogate and explain hegemony and the discursive frameworks that surround and sustain it.

Both Hirson and Van der Ross failed to see what it was that made the leaders of the NEF so exceptional. In seeking to locate the local in the global and examining what underpins the ways in which ideas of dominance 'world' social space, the leaders of the NEF anticipated the subaltern movement, which originated in India, by almost 40 years. The NEF might not have had the terminology and they would not have called it 'worlding', but, intuitively, this was what they were doing.

The idea of worlding is important to understand. It is powerfully illustrated in an exchange in 2004 between two prominent subaltern historians, Dipesh Chakrabarty and Saurabh Dube. Dube distinguishes between what he calls ready-to-hand and present-at-hand categories of social description.[4] The first, he explains, is rooted in primordiality – ways of explaining the world before the rise of scientific rationality. In the second is the capacity for the analytic: 'Since, however, we cannot world our existence through "the present-at-hand", for the "present-at-hand" is indifferent to place; it is simply analytic, and if to be human is to dwell, then it follows that we cannot live by the "present-at-hand" alone either, that the "ready-to-hand" will also continually be called into being.'[5] The challenge, Dube insightfully tells us, is to understand 'ways of being' in the world and to acknowledge how the ready-to-hand, in ideas such as race, can inform that world.

It was worlding that the leaders of the NEF were attempting to frame in conceptual terms. As Phumi Giyose puts it in *The Return of Spartacus*, they looked around at both the ready-to-hand and the present-at-hand ideas of the world and found them wanting.[6] The NEF leaders took what they needed from dominant thinking and developed their own explanations. In the course of doing this they put forward theories of how consciousness is constructed and how it can be deconstructed. This was what made these leaders exceptional. This is what authors like Hirson and Van der Ross have missed.

That they were also exceptional people within their own families and communities almost goes without saying. Each of their immediate family histories would have been challenging. This as a subject by itself deserves attention. How individuals make lives for themselves in contexts of extreme hardship – adverse social conditions and harsh and repressive political circumstances – is sociologically significant. What made these leaders, the Cape Radicals, stand out was their ability to project and make sense of their own local sociological positioning against the global system of imperialism. Because they brought with them their personal experience of domination – that is, white and ruling class domination, the environment in which they had to operate – their approach came with a full sense of its totalising effect. They saw it, smelt it and lived it themselves, every day of their lives.

They rejected it. They wanted something new.

More importantly, they believed that something new was possible.

Just how critical this breakout thinking was, was something neither Hirson, writing from a somewhat inside-the-fold position of the NEF, nor Van der Ross, writing from outside, appreciated. Hirson's story is a story of the continuity of the Trotskyist imagination into the backwaters of the colonies and that story is certainly interesting. More interesting is the compulsion of the Cape Radicals to think their way from the local into a new, wider space and to begin to outline for themselves and for people around them what a new era could look like. The significance of this went considerably beyond the local. Van der Ross was not able to see this. What he saw, problematically, were simply misguided agents of Trotskyism and socialism. He described them as 'Coloured South Africans who absorbed the Trotskyist theories [and] saw themselves possibly as part of a world revolution (in rather unreal, starry-eyed terms) but also hopefully as the inheritors of power in South Africa'.[7] In this, Van der Ross displays not just his animus towards the people he was writing about but also an implicit contempt for their betrayal of their 'coloured' identity.

The members of the NEF, particularly the leaders, came to a point, historically, where they were able fully to disavow their racial identities. They were not blind to racism. They were not colour blind. What they rejected were the racial labels and the positioning imposed on all South Africans as dictated by these labels: white, 'coloured', African, Indian. How critically important this rejection was is seemingly lost on Van der Ross.

One cannot arrive at a proper sense of the significance of Cape Town as a global site of intellectual innovation without giving attention to the Cape Radicals. These intellectuals seeded into Cape Town and South Africa the idea that a new era was possible, even as the agents of racism innovated and came up with racism's last word – apartheid – as contemporary philosopher Jacques Derrida would say. They helped give the lie to the idea of apartheid as a total, or totalising, discourse. As apartheid unfolded in its enveloping complexity, the Cape Radicals fed into the everyday ideas of the self and the social that were profoundly disruptive. In doing this the hegemon – the ruling class and the whole order it had under its control – was incapacitated in slight but nevertheless impactful ways. Through these intellectuals' determination, their carefully designed programmes of education and the keen insight they brought to bear in debate and discussion, they were able to contain the hegemon's hubris. They claimed, and demonstrated, that the rules, habits and modalities of domination do not and should not define and contain the limits and possibilities of what the human spirit in all its expressive manifestations should be about.

This is not to say that the NEF and its members didn't have blind spots. Patriarchy was one. Only once, in the early 1940s, did leading theoretician Ben Kies open up the discussion of gender oppression. In the main the subject was ignored. In the post-apartheid period it would come up in the successor organisations of the NEF, but during the active life of the organisation it was only aired occasionally in informal conversation among the movement's women.[8] It is only in the current era that an awareness of gender has been fully assimilated and become a site of political mobilisation in its own right.

Another blind spot was the place of Africa in their analysis. The charge is that they underplayed their Africanness, that they could have been more attentive to questions of the cultural connectedness of the South African people. The theoretical opportunities were there for them to do so. One such opportunity was poignantly evident in Kies's 1953 *The Contribution of Non-European Peoples to World Civilisation*. The question of Africa and African pre-colonial history and colonialism did not animate internal debate, however. It was this omission that, in time, led to a schism within their ranks, from which they have yet to recover. An issue in this schism was the question of how the country – and this is the pertinent issue to keep in mind – should deal with African languages. The debate would later be taken on in the most productive ways by one of the Cape Radicals' most important products, Neville Alexander, in his study of language.[9]

The NEF's analysis of class, as Hirson's criticism suggests, was also open to question. It could be said that they did not pay sufficient attention to the changing political economy of South Africa in the 1930s. Van der Ross, in referring to the Anti-Coloured Affairs Department (Anti-CAD) movement, which the NEF launched in 1943, made this claim: 'Not one of the members had any appreciable background in sociology, and there was, therefore, little understanding of the nature, cohesion or interplay of groups, and an absolute refusal to recognise the need to speak of groups as having any cohesion.'[10] This is an interesting observation and Van der Ross would have known. He was a student at the University of Cape Town (UCT) at the same time as Richard (Dick) Dudley and Tom Hanmer.[11] Both men were leading intellectuals of the NEUM and the Teachers' League of South Africa (TLSA), the latter an organisation that the NEF almost undoubtedly instructed its members to enter and win over. However, his analysis fails to understand the NEF's interest in the psychology of oppression. Van der Ross did not appreciate the interesting analytic pathways they were opening up about how people come to both individual and collective consciousness and a sense of their identity.

When it came to discussions about class, the NEF's focus was largely on land and the role of the peasantry; this emphasis distracted its attention from the changes that were taking place in the South African economy at that time. Proletarianisation was proceeding at a rapid pace. They did not give sufficient attention in their analysis to the process of class formation.

These blind spots notwithstanding, the leaders of the NEF made, for the time in which they were operating, some of the most important contributions to social analysis. The most significant of these were their contributions to humanism. In strong contrast to prevalent thinking, through a process of intense intellectual deliberation, they arrived at the idea of the unconditional unity of the human race. Against the backdrop of the forces of domination preoccupied with racial classification and artificial levels of imposed hierarchy, supported increasingly by various forms of oppressive legislation, they were doing the opposite. They began to project the principle of unfettered possibility for all human beings. The principle was grounded in the oneness of people in the multiple syntaxes of their beings – their biologies, cognitive functioning and their spiritual possibilities. There was nothing about people intrinsically, they argued, that authorised and legitimated their separation into tribes, races and ethnicities. It was this insight these intellectuals brought into perspective. And it is one of the reasons why it is important that they be located in the country's wider history.

No one else was thinking or talking as they were. Their theory of the social was original.[12] The insight – the unity of all human beings – is powerfully relevant for the present. The dominant narrative of contemporary South Africa, almost a quarter of a century after the end of apartheid, enshrouds the country in a pall of pessimism. South Africa, in this narrative, is a failed experiment. Its phoenix-like ascent out of its long nightmare of apartheid is a lie. Nelson Mandela and Desmond Tutu's fabled rainbowism is shown to be, if anything, utterly chimerical. All there is, goes the explanation, is a heap of hate. In this narrative white people have learnt nothing. White people have failed to look into themselves and, as a result, have shown no indication whatsoever of taking responsibility for the horror of the last 300 years of the oppression of black people.

What's significant about this narrative of rainbowism and its denouement is its supposed incontrovertibility. This requires some explanation. Rainbowism is lodged in and and holds fast to the apartheid idea – the idea of South African identity only being available in racial terms. The effect is to condition how we come to conclusions about almost any aspect of South Africa's social, cultural and economic life. A critical dynamic in the process of assessing what is going on is how, in the narrative, the individual – the self – is positioned. In this dynamic, where the primary logic is race, it is through the prism of race that individuals (the self) will decide what is 'wrong' with the country. It is how they locate themselves with respect to their most important personal priorities, their family goals and objectives, their community interests and, finally, their national commitments. The self, in this process, is conjugated in a long historical algorithm of inevitability – racial inevitability. Race is the constant. It is the common denominator. The denominator has synonyms – 'our people' and 'our community', for example – but its basic function remains the same. It holds together and gives coherence to all social explanation. Everything in the social world, from personal desire and revulsion of feeling, to national aspiration and anxiety, takes its meaning from race. It is all that is needed for sense to be made.

Prefiguring this master narrative are a number of historical figures: Jan van Riebeeck, Cecil John Rhodes, Jan Smuts, Hendrick Verwoerd and, latterly, John Vorster, PW Botha and FW de Klerk. Authoring the narrative in terms of its construction, however, we can look back to George McCall Theal, South Africa's first major historian. In 1897, in his *History of South Africa under the Administration of the Dutch East India Company*, his reflections on the people and the environment around him were revealing. He wrote that the theme of black-white relations is 'not a pleasant subject to write of . . . but it is the subject that makes the history of the Cape Colony different from that of other British possessions, it is still, and must continue to be, a matter of vital importance to South Africans, and it is only a knowledge of past events that such great mistakes as were made can be avoided in the future'.[13] The 'great mistakes', as Theal would have it, were making 'agreements . . . with Africans . . . because Africans, being barbarians, were untrustworthy'.

The current narrative of South Africa rests on this basic algorithm of race. Its valences may have shifted somewhat – the numerators are more varied and of more substantial weight; racial terms are rendered positively – but it remains within the fundamental syllogism of race.

This book is part of a project to disrupt this discourse. Its purpose is to show that South Africa's history is not a long and predetermined story of either inevitable white triumph or a long-awaited black recovery. It is an attempt, as part of a larger set of articulated initiatives, to make the point that the country's history does not begin in race-drenched objectives and motives nor is its every turn and phase a response to this point of departure. Those beginnings are not explained here; the author has attempted elsewhere to show how much more open-ended they were.[14]

Race is, of course, absolutely central to the South African experience of the social, cultural and, ultimately, the economic. But it is not, in terms of its basic mechanics, always the determining factor in the country's experience of inequality. Race regularly stands in for other factors – religion and class, for example – and it tends to operate alongside class and gender. The argument here, in response to its essentialisation, is that race has been manipulated to function as the total explanation.

The position taken in this book, which was brought to a point of clarity by the NEF, is that race is not natural. The racial arises in relation to a complex set of economic and social forces. It is not independent of them. Theal's dominant narrative, the narrative that makes us think that race is natural, has the effect – the production of the pessimism – of lumping everything into race as the causal driver of South African history.

Beginning in the 1930s, the attempt by a group of young social-ist intellectuals in Cape Town, working separately from their Stalinist comrades (and sometimes opponents), to think outside of race, and the important intervention they made because of this, should be doc-umented. *The Cape Radicals*, by telling the NEF story, actively engages with the historiographical narrative of what is presented as *the* history of South Africa. It seeks, against the Theal legacy, to show that the coun-try's history is a great deal more varied and richer in its imaginations, and indeed lived expressions of itself, than the monotonic parable of racial inevitability that dominates our ways of thinking, talking and doing. It is intended to be not quite a deliberate companion, more an accompaniment, to a larger project on classification and regulatory frameworks. The purpose of that project is to expose the manufactured hegemon underpinning the imperial drive of the nineteenth and twen-tieth centuries.

This imperial hubris, hubris of almost unprecedented conceit, is approached in many analyses firstly, and correctly so, through its materialist manifestations. In these analyses economic interests are the drivers of history. The economic idea is deployed so mechani-cally, however, that the issue of how ideology evolves and operates falls by the wayside. The complex and often contradictory ways that ideology develops alongside economics are missed. Bringing the ideological into perspective has not been given the respect the subject deserves.

The point to be emphasised here is that the imperial order came to depend on all the trappings – the knowledge appurtenances and apparatuses, the systems of coercion – it brought with it, or allowed to develop, wherever it went and imposed itself in the world.[15]

Often, moreover, as Keith Breckenridge argues in his important book *Biometric State*,[16] it was the colonies that provided the metropole with its cues and prompts for how the economic and the ideological should be held together. At the heart of these processes were the deeply significant devices of classification and regulation. Many of these devices, although not all, were invented, practised and refined in the colonies and transferred to metropolitan centres of knowledge and knowledge production – often having gestated in profoundly contradictory ways in the satellite spaces of power.

Underpinning these frameworks were the algorithms of race. Race and its classification regimes were put to use in a range of sciences and fields of knowledge, from explanations of the body, through genetics, to ideas of hygiene and health, to accounts of the broader environment. They included domains of thought and practice, such as town and regional planning regulations, as well as culture and aesthetics. In fundamentally conditioning the everyday, these classifications determined lived realities.

It was within this environment, arising out of an awareness of how it worked, that the NEF began its work in 1937. It developed an understanding of how ideology was created by, sat inside of and fed the structures of domination. It would not have used the word 'hegemon' but this was, in effect, what it was fighting against and intellectually dismantling.

The NEF ceased to exist as an organisation in 1960 but the effects of its legacy remain to this day. It continues to influence social and cultural thought in the present. One could call it Cape Town's hidden history. If only for this reason, telling its story is important.

Populating the narrative are some of Cape Town's most talented scholar-activists, individuals produced directly and indirectly by the

NEF. The story begins almost monumentally in the figures of a handful of young men and women – Goolam Gool, Jane Gool, Isaac Tabata, Ben Kies, Willem van Schoor – and thunders into the 1940s and early 1950s in the examples of Dora Taylor, Sonny Abdurahman, Minnie Gool, Edgar Maurice, Joyce Meissenheimer, Helen Kies, Dick Dudley, A C Jordan, Phyllis Ntantala, Tom Hanmer, Polly Slingers, Ernie Steenveld, Cosmo Pieterse, Mda Mda, Victor Wessels, Gwen and Edna Wilcox, and Livie Mqotsi, to mention only a few. These men and women were responsible for producing, if not a golden age for Cape Town (the times were too oppressive), then certainly an age that was pregnant with possibility.

From these elders emerged a second generation of outstandingly creative individuals. Most of these were men – patriarchy being, and continuing to be, very hard to escape – many of them direct products of the NEF. Many would have been tutored in the NEF's study circles, while some would have been the fortunate beneficiaries of the organisation's networks; others grew, indirectly, out of the wide aura the NEF cast. These people would, in turn, produce the next layer of less visible but equally gifted young intellectuals, many of whom would, like their predecessors, end up in the high schools of Cape Town, especially Trafalgar, South Peninsula, Livingstone, Harold Cressy, Alexander Sinton, Athlone High and Belgravia.

Among the second generation were the great unsung luminaries of the city: Dullah Omar, Hosea Jaffe, Kenny Jordaan, Dulcie September, Albert Adams, Arthur Davids, Neville Alexander, Richard Rive, Bobby Wilcox, Hennie Ferris, Arthur Nortje, Vernon February, Kenny Abrahams, Benita Parry, Hassan Bavasah, Johaar Mosaval, Sedick Williams, John Erntzen, Veronica Williams, Johnny van der Westhuisen, Joe Rassool, Yusuf da Costa, Achmat Cassiem, Johnny Bosch, Sedick Isaacs, Dawood Parker, Jack Meltzer, Carl Brecker, Peter Meyer, Archie Mafeje and a host of less well-known names. Almost all these people, in more propitious times, would have been numbered among Cape Town's most lauded intellectuals and public figures.

A number of these people became famous as artists, politicians and academics. None, however, as agents of self-determination and as people making choices, found the space to venture where they would have liked. None, thinking more structurally, was allowed to take centre stage in the mainstream of Cape Town's social, economic and political life. Physical, practical and political constraints were in their way. Different commentators hold different views about these luminaries, but no one could deny that they exuded an intellectual radiance, which even the most oppressive of environments could not dim. None could deny how brightly they shone.[17]

Fakier Jessa, in his book *Echoes*, was ambivalent about them: 'Many of the teachers [at Trafalgar High] strutted around arrogantly, regarding their political knowledge as personal "shields of brilliance". These teachers were reluctant to allow scholars to question them: they were autocratic.'[18] Bill Nasson, on the other hand, saw them differently. They were, he said, 'mostly older men of towering personality and effective educational organization, they poured out a vivid freewheeling rhetoric . . . Above all, as socialists, they had an intuitive grasp of the primary value of "history" and of their own historical function.'[19]

Van der Ross conceded that it was 'true that the NEUM (Anti-CAD) included in its ranks some of the most brilliant intellectuals of the time', but he, too, noted their 'intellectual arrogance'.[20] This he attributed to the intellectuals' commitment to Trotskyism: 'This fitted in well with the Leninist-Trotskyist belief in the leadership of the intellectual in matters of revolution. It produced an intellectual arrogance which – despite protestations to the contrary – characterised the Anti-CAD movement, so much so that it often found itself criticised for this attitude in the non-white press.'[21] This press, it needs to be said, included *The Cape Herald*, of which Van der Ross was the first 'coloured' editor.

Many of the NEF leaders were students at UCT and many would, repeatedly, emerge as medal winners in their studies. Strikingly, with the exception of Johnny van der Westhuisen, whom the university somehow found a way to hold onto, none of the intellectuals was encouraged to stay there. Tom Hanmer, the medal winner for his course in Geography 3 in the early 1940s said: '[We were] three students doing third course in geography, and our professor was going to take us out for a meal. And he had to tell me that it wasn't possible for me to go along because they had to go into places where only whites were permitted.'[22] Peter Meyer, also in Geography, often told a similar story of his experience at UCT ten years later. A C Jordan was forced into exile in 1960.[23] UCT demurred repeatedly over Archie Mafeje.

Bringing these individuals of Cape Town's hidden history into view, providing a sense of who they were, is a necessary correction of the way in which the intellectual and cultural life of Cape Town is remembered and understood. Born in this movement was not just a South African version of the Indian subaltern studies project but an independent anti-hegemonic initiative, which – and this is the second dimension of this effort – developed its own distinctive frameworks in relation to knowledge and to the human state of being.

The most important product of this effort, to call it by its most meaningful description, was non-racialism. In its broader usage in the South African liberation movement, the term is wide and loose. In its most generic sense it equates to multi-racialism. But non-racialism in relation to multi-racialism is different. For the Cape Radicals non-racialism was a rejection of the very idea of race. Race was a fiction. Rendered as fact, it served as the ideological glue that made the imperial project possible. It took its significance directly from the fundamental character of capital. That race was indispensable for the production and reproduction of global domination was a given.

The engaged minds of the leaders of the NEF went further in their exploration. Their thinking was profound and transformative. Their analysis and insight took its most expressive form materially in the classrooms of Cape Town. 'Teach your children' was their strategy – and so they did. Generations of young people would emerge out of these physically inferior but academically charged environments inspired and forever changed.

The *Educational Journal* of the TLSA became the principal medium for this but it also emerged over the course of some years in the creative arts – in the writing of A C Jordan, Cosmo Pieterse and Arthur Nortje, in the little-studied but advanced literary criticism of Dora Taylor and A C Jordan, and in the art of Albert Adams and Lionel Davis. Outside of the literary and arts world it found expression in the politics of Frank van der Horst, Joe Ebrahim and Allan Zinn, as these individuals looked for and found other outlets for the message of non-racialism. It came to its most significant elaboration in the late 1970s and early 1980s in the writing of Neville Alexander.

In terms of this accounting, coming to a sense of non-racialism is vital for understanding the politics of colonialism and apartheid. It is also important to explain how such disjunctive thinking about alternative ways of being and of gaining and interpreting knowledge was able to arise in an oppressive and totalising environment. Demonstrating how everyday politics was constituted in tension and how that tension was managed intellectually and practically is equally important.

One needs to accept that on some levels the NEF's intervention was not altogether successful. Working out the reasons for this first requires a close engagement with the conceptual substance of their ideas. Many critiques of non-racialism and of the community of organisations in the NEF's orbit focus on their tactics and strategies. This is a fair move to make and this text does that, too, to a degree. Underneath those tactics and strategies, however, was critical intellectual thinking and meticulous analysis. How ideas are seeded into the public domain provides an important view of how hegemons work and, particularly, of their power. It can also give a sense of how, in response, that power is understood.

The inner logic of non-racialism is, by itself, worthy of deconstruction. Using what Steve Lofts calls 'a concept of a law', this book attempts to go some way towards doing this in the concluding chapter.[24] In his introduction to Ernst Cassirer's *The Logic of the Cultural Sciences*, and quoting Cassirer, Lofts explains how science works: 'Science is distinguished here from perception . . . only by the fact that it requires a strict determination . . . [The ideal at which all the sciences of nature aim is to express] the universal in the form of *a concept of a law* from which the individual "instances" can be deductively derived.' The point to work with in this text is to think of non-racialism as that counter-hegemonic logic for managing the translation of the general into the specific. It has as its object, as Cassirer explains, 'the ideal unity of signification'.[25]

Non-racialism's proponents in the NEF understood the necessity for coherence. They built, for themselves and for people around them, in a conscious and deliberate response to the dominating force, a counter-totalising world view. It had, in its production and delivery, a consistency and unity that held them to a fixity of principle. This fixity was often read from outside this counter-narrative as dogmatic, inflexible, intolerant and, in the last analysis, unrealistic. It began, however, from the empirical fact – a law, in Loft's terms – of the 'non-sense' of race. Race had no material, physical or biological substance. It was something that was made up.

The young products of the NEF would yield nothing in holding on to their fight for unconditional respect. Interviewing them has, for historians and social scientists, often been puzzling and sometimes frustrating. They kept to the 'line'. Looking for contradiction or variation in an explanation would yield almost nothing. Their vocabulary was characterised by the use of an uncontroversial and unproblematised 'we'. The sense of being part of a collective, to which they had ceded their individuality, remained with them all their lives – consistent in principle and in the expression of this principle. A colleague of Neville Alexander's, who had worked with him for many years, would say in exasperation of his tendency to speak last in a debate that 'one wondered which planet he came from'. How one makes sense of this 'unity of signification' of non-racialism is a task for the present. It is what the radical intellectuals of Cape Town bequeathed to us. Engaging with it is perhaps the most important way to honour their legacy.

* * *

The Cape Radicals moves in three major steps. In each of the three steps are distinct chapters. The idea of the steps is to hold the coherence of the sections in as discrete a form as is possible. As will be seen as the narrative unfolds, this is not always easily managed. Timelines and threads of continuity require separate discussions to take a relatively discursive form, which is not always strictly focused.

The first step contains three chapters: this introductory chapter, and chapters 1 and 2. The introductory chapter makes the argument for the necessity for the book. While it provides a brief synopsis of the NEF, its main purpose is to emphasise the need to tell the story of South Africa's social and cultural history more fully. It also outlines the approaches taken in the work to important theoretical issues raised and addressed in the text. The most critical of these is race. Chapter 1 sets the scene for the emergence of the NEF and contextualises the current discussion about the NEF. Chapter 2 begins with a discussion of the immediate backdrop to the NEF – the building blocks for its formation and the people who gave it its character and purpose.

The second step provides a narrative of the NEF in so far as this history can be pieced together. It is divided into four chapters, the first of which, Chapter 3, describes the first period of the NEF, its 'clearing of the ground' phase, from 1937 to 1942. This is the period in which one sees a relatively eclectic set of focuses arising inside the movement. The second, Chapter 4, describes how the NEF succeeds in clearing the ground and begins to clarify, in its agenda-setting phase, its position in relation to the big sociological and political issues of the day. The organisation becomes, for a time, the public face of the Workers' Party of South Africa (WPSA). Chapter 5, the consolidation phase, rounds off the narrative of the NEF and explains how the organisation's theoretical and strategic positions were consolidated between the 1950s and the beginning of the 1960s. The organisation is less visible in this period, but it is still the engine room behind the scenes in which the ideas and concepts of non-racialism originate and are refined.

In terms of this genealogy, this book is an attempt to develop a conceptual timeline of the way in which explanations of what South Africa is and how it can be understood and explained sociologically unfolded during the period of the NEF's influence. The timeline begins with the founders of the NEF in the mid-1930s. It then moves into its high-water-mark period in the late 1940s and early 1950s.

The third step is brief. Its purpose is to bring the work together around an assessment of the contribution of the NEF and its legacy. Chapter 6 outlines the important issues and ideas with which it grappled and shows how a split in the movement at a certain point was inevitable. Finally, Chapter 7 asks what lessons the contribution of the NEF has for the contemporary period in South Africa and the rest of the world.

Methodological note 1: Race

The use of the term 'race' is what much of this book is about. It is presented in inverted commas when it is used for the first time but for ease of reading has been used without the quotation marks in the rest of the text. What is important to be borne in mind when the word appears is the discomfort of the central actors in this history with respect to its use.

Two conceptual issues that arose in the writing of this book call for explanation. The first has to do with how one undertakes the task of 'doing' history – the approach to history, its basic points of departure for looking at the world of the social, and explaining how that world works.[26] The second, related, issue is about the very problematic with which the subjects of this history were preoccupied: the question of *the social*. The leading members of the NEF were driven to explain this social. What are we seeing in front of us, they asked. What is real and what is not? What is this place South Africa all about? What is South Africa? By 'the social' is meant how the everyday world of relationships between people is described and made sense of; it includes how they describe and label each other and, on the basis of these labels, treat each other. Explanations of the social are based on an implicit theory of power, the power to name and to use naming to allocate position and place – class, race, gender, religion, for example, or whatever other categories human beings use in order to separate themselves. Every historical, sociological, anthropological, political and psychological work of description and analysis is based on an understanding of the social.

This book is based on the understanding that the social *is* social. It is a way of understanding that is made up. It is not just out there. It does not explain itself. Each time it is observed it has to be explained.

Critically, it needs to be noted that this book is not a sociological analysis of the people who led the NEF. That is a study that still needs to be done. What is engaged with here is an analysis of the NEF's sociological reading of the social. To that extent it is a sociology of knowledge of the left movement of the 1930s to the 1960s. Van der Ross's observation that the thinkers of the NEF had no 'appreciable background' in sociology may well have been true and it should be held in mind.[27] Nevertheless, the Cape Radicals came up with an explanation of the social that deserves serious attention. How they got there and how they came to the conclusions they did is perhaps even more interesting.

A note on the approach taken in this book with respect to how one 'does' history is necessary. As Edward Hallet Carr tries to help us understand, this is not simply a matter of gathering a few 'facts'.[28] Carr is critical of dominant history, which consists of the assemblage of information for the purpose of producing an objective picture. Rejecting both pure empiricism and outright relativism, he argues for a middle path. 'History,' he writes, 'is a continuous process of interaction between the historian and his facts, an unending dialogue between the past and the present.'[29]

The Cape Radicals attempts to engage in a dialogue with a set of experiences that, for a number of people, including the author, were deeply formative. The dialogue is begun and undertaken with an acknowledgement of debt and, in these terms, it is a declaration of connectedness. This is, implicitly, the interest of this work. It is an attempt to put into perspective the intellectual history of the progressive community associated with anti-Stalinism in Cape Town. It does not pretend to be an objective and detached survey of 'things' that happened 'out there'. It is neither partisan nor hagiographic. It approaches the task with the hope and intention of making the significance of the experience of the NEF clearer to a broader audience.

The second methodological question relates to the social. This book is about people and organisations that inhabited and made their way in a social world. In that social world they had and took on subjectivity. They were given and performed identities. The approach taken in this work, as discussed above, is that those subjectivities are not natural. People are not born with race or class, or even gender. Identities and subjectivities are given to them through social processes. Race and class, both of which are social constructions, in this assemblage of socially imposed identities are the most revelant for this work.

Class is not a natural or a biological human attribute. It can be shown to function on the basis of material factors. Those material factors in Marxist terms are people's relationship to the means of production. The people either do or do not own the means of production. Class is endowed with features and characteristics that bring it close to the point of naturalisation. Class can be approached and understood in less instrumental terms. And this is what makes class status always something that needs to be unpacked and deconstructed. But class can be argued to rest on a relatively objective set of social realities.

Race is somewhat different. Race is a set of beliefs about human bodies based on physical appearance, mental capacity and other physiological features and characteristics. The point about beliefs about race, in contrast to class, is that they have no objective reality. Looks and bodies, we now know, have no significance whatsoever. They are insignificant. Human beings in their genetic makeup are almost exactly like each other. They share in common 99 per cent of their genetic histories. There is no such thing as an African gene, a European gene or a Chinese gene.

Race is something that is regularly called upon to do the work of other social factors.[30] It stands in for them. In so doing, it occludes complex social realities that have their origins in other factors, such as class, gender, patriarchy, language, religion and other dynamics. Race is also used as a synonym for racism. Race and racism are two different but related concepts.

Race is a concept of classification.[31] It is based on the idea that human beings can be divided into biologically or socially distinct groups of people, each with hereditable characteristics and features that definitively set them apart from others.

Racism is the process that invokes the idea of biologically and socially distinct groups of people for the purpose of assigning them positions of inferiority or superiority. In terms of this, white people or people who think of themselves as 'European' can believe themselves superior, either biologically or culturally, to people who are classified as African or negroid, or Asian or mongoloid. The clarification of how the idea of racism might be approached provided by Robert Miles, now almost 30 years ago, remains trenchant:

In order to [move beyond the conceptual conflation that has happened around the use of the idea of racism] an explanatory comment about the concept of ideology is necessary. The meaning of this concept is also widely contested . . . but in this [explanation] . . . it is used to refer to any discourse which, as a whole (but not necessarily in terms of all of its component parts) represents human beings, and the social relations between human beings in a distorted and misleading manner. Thus ideology is a specific form of discourse. The discourse need not be systematic or logically coherent, nor be intentionally created and reproduced in order to deceive or mislead, even though that is its consequence. Such a concept presumes an alternative epistemological position, from the occupancy of which it is possible to demonstrate the falsity of the discourse defined as ideology.[32]

Race, therefore, needs explanation. It isn't *the* explanation. It is an ideology about humanness. It presents itself as a natural state for and of being human. It contains and portends morphologically how cognition and sense-making function in human beings. Meaning is always imminent in and projects out of one's skin. Social descriptors such as 'a black person' are irredeemable markers of being. They are ontological fixities.

The transition to radicalism of the Cape Radicals who were involved in the process of unmasking this ideology is almost unique. How each of them personally evolved within the social complexities in the historical moment is not examined in this book, however. While this sociological unpacking is certainly necessary (and is alluded to), it is not brought to the front of the discussion. Explaining in detail how race and class forces worked in producing the people who feature in this history is important but that work would need to be explicitly and unreservedly psychoanalytical.

The psychoanalysis of racism has been begun by scholars such as Aletta Norval and Derek Hook and Garth Stevens, Norman Duncan and Derek Hook.[33] It has yet, however, to develop into a deep scholarly project around actual cases and actual subjects. Its empirical base has not been sufficiently developed. The potential for this work in South Africa is immense. The onus is on South Africa to take its place in the global community around the exploration of processes of coming to consciousness – I have described the country elsewhere as a global ontological hotspot.[34]

The focus of this work is not on the subjects themselves but rather on how this particular group of people began to describe, analyse and interpret these formational realities about and of their lives. It is about their ideas of the social.

Towards making the argument for seeing South Africa as a 'culture-bed' for thinking against race, I have also sought elsewhere to show how significantly the radical tradition needs to be understood not simply within a sociology *of* race, but a sociology *about* race.[35]

This distinction requires some explanation. In many discussions of race always at issue are the identities and the racial histories of the individuals in the discussion. The point that needs to be made is that those so-called realities, at any given time, are, in the end, treated as the explanations of whatever ideas are currently in circulation. The practice of describing a person in racial terms is often used to place the person in a social hierarchy of power but it then has the effect of completing explanations of his or her likely subjectivity. It is not being argued here that those ideas bear no significance for the conclusions to which people come in their heads about the meanings of these social questions. They would always feature in their thinking. But they are attributes of these individuals; it is the attributes themselves that need explaining.

The object of this exercise is the idea of race and the social construction of that idea. The task at hand, through exploring the history of the NEF, is to understand the evolution or the passage of the idea about race. The intention is to examine how the NEF constructed that idea for themselves, as opposed to its being imposed on them. Making sense of it requires a dialogue of time and space, a time of modernism with all its combustive multiplicity. This includes understanding, sociologically, new modes of communication, mobility and engagement with technology. A sociological analysis of this knowledge-making experience entails understanding how a space and its time come together – how they are configured with all their complex race, class, gender (and linguistic) affordances and encumbrances.

This work, therefore, is *of* race to the degree that all the individuals in a specific time and space found themselves positioned; but it is *about* race as they seized and made agency in relation to it. They acted. Sometimes they acted in contradictory ways. All of them, however, recognised the urgency of trying to gain an understanding of what it was about this thing of race that they needed to both manage and exceed. It was their decision to take charge of the knowledge process around them and to understand, in a proto-Foucauldian way, how to deconstruct it and then how to reconstruct it for a larger product of dignity, respect and inclusion. That is an important stimulus of this work. How race is made the object of a critical politics of the self – as a site of knowledge and consciousness – needs to be brought to the broader and deeper study of how South Africa is constituted and reconstituted.

Methodological note 2: Sources

A brief introduction to the secondary material available on the NEF has been provided above. An intense effort was undertaken to find primary material. The personal papers of a few of the major role players in its founding and functioning were looked at. These included the papers of Isaac Tabata and Dick Dudley, which are held at UCT. Little emerged from this examination. It is probable that this material, because of the apartheid regime's systematic pursuance and persecution of 'communists', was either destroyed or secreted away. Hopefully it will still be found.

Most useful for this work was a small archive of articles in the *Cape Standard* newspaper between 1937 and 1944 and Allison Drew's 1996 and 1997 collection of documents of the left movement in South Africa, *South Africa's Radical Tradition*, in two volumes. In the history of the independent political movement written by Sarah Mokone (the pseudonym of Victor Wessels) in 1982, 'Majority Rule: Some Notes', is a brief but invaluable account of the NEF.

The histories of the period and its people are also extremely useful. They include, relatively sequentially in terms of time, Van der Ross's (1986) *The Rise and Decline of Apartheid*, Ian Goldin's (1987) *Making Race*, Gavin Lewis's (1987) *Between the Wire and the Wall* and Mohamed Adhikari's (1993) *'Let us Live for Our Children'*. Honours and Master's theses written over between the 1970s and the 1990s have been useful sources, in particular, those of Farieda Khan (1976), Roy Gentle (1978) and Robin Kayser (2002); June Bam's 1993 Master's thesis was another. Equally valuable are Hosea Jaffe's (1994) *European Colonial Despotism*,

Baruch Hirson's (2001) *The Cape Town Intellectuals*, Ciraj Rassool's (2004) doctoral thesis on IB Tabata, Yunus Omar's (2015) doctoral thesis on Alie Fataar, Alan Wieder's (2008) biography of Richard Dudley, and Corinne Sandwith's (2014) *World of Letters*. This book has also benefited from Peter Abrahams' (1982, originally published in 1954) *Tell Freedom*, Ralph Bunche's *Travel Notes*, collected by Robert Edgar (1992), Doreen Musson's (1989) *Johnny Gomas*, an essay written by Richard Dudley (1990) on the forced removals in District Six, an essay on the role of Hosea Jaffe by Joe Rassool (1993), Jaffe's own (1992) 'Signposts of the History of the Unity Movement', and outline notes for a family history by Selim Gool (undated).

This book was also significantly advanced by two products of the NEF, Neville Alexander, writing as No Sizwe (1979) in *One Azania, One Nation* and Jaffe (1980) in his *The Pyramid of Nations*.

Archives of the NEF do exist outside the public domain. When these become available it is anticipated that they will considerably enrich the record of the NEF in its nuance and particularity. The archive, however, is fragmented and so what is brought together here is, it is acknowledged, partial and incomplete.

What is significant about much of this material is the politics surrounding its production. Implicit in these politics are issues and anxieties about how South African history has been produced.

In engaging deliberately with dominant historiography, a continuous pipeline of students has been doing important research – Gentle, Khan, Kayser, Drew, Rassool, Omar, in the main; their work is a response to their own intellectual histories and an attempt to engage critically with the larger history of struggle in the country. Almost all these scholars would have had an association of one kind or another with the individuals, cultural societies or schools associated with the NEF. Many of them, for example, had an association with the South Peninsula Education Fellowship (SPEF), led by Dawood Parker. SPEF was one of the NEF's most visible offshoots. Its success and influence were based on the person and leadership of Parker and the substantial organisational library he was able to put together in his home in Wynberg in Cape Town.[36]

While Hosea Jaffe might not have thought highly of Baruch Hirson, Hirson's work, and his long commitment over many years to documenting the history of Trotskyism, is nevertheless extremely important. It arises out of an awareness of the absence from the South African story of the progressive left movement. In *Abandoning Imperialism* Jaffe dismissively calls Hirson 'an old collaborator with "white anti-apartheid socialists" against whom I had written *Fascism in South Africa in 1946* and who had been in prison for a terrorist act by the "whites only" anarchist group he belonged to, whose bomb killed an innocent woman bystander during the so-called ANC-led "armed struggle" after Mandela's arrest.'[37]

Drew describes him as 'a Johannesburg-based socialist who entered politics through the Hashomer Hatzair, a Jewish youth group, worked in the Trotskyist WIL (Workers International League) in the 1940s, and in the 1950s, with the PF (Progressive Forum), a Non-European Unity Movement affiliate. He broke with the NEUM over the issue of how to fight the extension of apartheid to universities.'[38] It was Hirson who was responsible for the publication of Tabata's *The Awakening of a People* and his own *The Cape Town Intellectuals* is an important resource for recovering a sense of who these early radicals of South Africa were.

While the source material may sometimes appear sparser than ideal, it has provided a rich bed of information and insight.

1 | A Battle of Ideas

Just how significant South African colonialism was in the global rise of white supremacy has not been fully acknowledged or understood. It was in South Africa, in circumstances that are very different from those in the United States, that other global laboratory of race-making, that science and politics were yoked together to produce for the world the narratives and strategies it would use to explain and legitimate the great 19th- and 20th-century conceit of white supremacy. Keith Breckenridge, in *Biometric State*, describes the country as a 'culture-bed' for the imperial project.[1] The discourses and policies of eugenics and the practices and procedures of oppression and exploitation were a demonstrably powerful combination.

The science was pioneered by Francis Galton, the founder of the eugenicist movement. In the 1850s he had travelled through South West Africa. His observations of the Herero people there allowed him to conclude that he had the proof to show that black people were the cognitive inferiors of white people. The politics came through a battery of laws, policies and practices evolved by the governments of the Cape Colony and the republics of the Transvaal and the Free State to regulate and control black people. The Glen Grey Act of 1894 was an early indicator. Its purpose was to force able-bodied men off their land and it did this through the imposition of a poll tax. Subsistence lifestyles, which was how people in the rural areas survived, did not place in people's hands the money required to pay the colonial government's taxes. The only way they could get the money was by submitting themselves to the formality of low-paid employment in the mines. The early 1900s saw techniques of labour control being developed on the Rand as the mining industry grew.

Through these developments, South Africa presented itself to the world as an important focal point for the British Empire's imagination and realisation of its class and race mission.

At the same time as this mission was taking shape, a number of developments came together to make South Africa also one of the most important global culture-beds for thinking *against* the imperial project. This thinking, as the country's oppressed people fought for their dignity, took many forms. Its most dominant was expressed in essentially liberal, assimilationist terms. The struggle for equality was based on European notions of citizenship. Much of the struggle of early nationalism in South Africa – the African National Congress (ANC) provides the clearest example of this – was founded on the principle of the inclusion of African people in the existing social and political architecture of South Africa.

A series of Africanist struggles did emerge, most specifically in what was the Natal area, around the turn of the nineteenth century and several uprisings took place. The most notable of these was the Bambatha rebellion in 1906.

Most pertinent for this book, however, is what was happening within the socialist movement in South Africa. A number of different analytic thrusts began to present themselves in disruptive cadences, vocabularies and frameworks. Political activists began to open up the possibility of the making of what they called 'the new man'. This thinking, constructed around alternative ways of being human – in opposition to the dominant themes of superiority and inferiority – took dramatic flight towards the end of the 1930s in Cape Town. Dora Taylor, in her 1974 introduction to Isaac Tabata's book *The Awakening of the People*, described it as a 'battle of ideas . . . amongst the intellectuals'.[2]

The ideas to which Taylor was referring emerged in inchoate form with the establishment, nationally, of a range of influential political organisations, beginning with the Lenin Club in 1932, the Workers' Party of

South Africa (WPSA) and the All-African Convention (AAC) in 1935 and the National Liberation League (NLL) in 1937. They would come to flower a decade and a half later in the philosophy of non-racialism. The engine room for these ideas in the Cape was the New Era Fellowship (NEF), which was formed in 1937.

Dick Dudley, a former president of the New Unity Movement (NUM), in writing about the destruction of District Six, described the NEF as having been 'the single most influential training ground for students and workers in those early years . . . the Stakesby-Lewis Hostel in Canterbury Street was the centre of some of the most fruitful developments in the new ideology that was to sweep South Africa after the second world war.'[3]

NUM intellectual Hosea Jaffe labelled the NEF as the 'only Jacobin-Cordelier type "club" of its kind in the country'.[4] The reference was to the radical political clubs that were formed during the French Revolution, attracting to their membership like-minded activists who gathered regularly for discussion and debate. In the 1930s the NEF attracted the attention of the major anti-Stalinist theoreticians in the world. C L R James, for example, the influential Caribbean social theorist, was aware of and in communication with his comrades across the Atlantic. Several of the actors around the NEF and its antecedent organisations, the Lenin Club and WPSA, as Baruch Hirson recorded, became 'leading cadres of the Trotskyist movements in China, India, the USA and Great Britain'. He described where these leaders came to find themselves:

Internationally, in the first decade of the movement's existence, Frank Glass (LiFu-jen/Furen) moved to China and then the US, Murray Gow to India, Ted Grant, Max Basch (Sid Frost), Charlie van Gelderen, Ralph and Millie Lee, Heaton Lee, Ann Keen and others to Britain. There were also persons who joined, or were associated with Trotskyist groups and received later acclaim for work in their specialities. Among these were Peter Abrahams, the novelist, Frederick Bodmer, whose work in linguistics was widely acclaimed when his *Loom of Language* was published,

Dorothea Krook, an acknowledged expert on the later writings of Henry James, and Joseph Sandler, currently president of the International Association of Psychoanalysis.[5]

They also, at great personal sacrifice, kept the most significant Marxist journals and broadsheets going in South Africa. One of these, still to be studied properly, was *The Spark*. Produced weekly between 1937 and the 1940s, it was an extraordinary publication, which contained a steady stream of high-quality popular writing, polemic and social analysis. As a journal it provided a model for critical writing for several of the young socialists who emerged during this period. One of these was Helen Kies who, with her husband Ben Kies, was also responsible for the publication of eight editions of the *Educational Journal* per year between 1943 and the turn of the century.[6] The *Educational Journal* was not a samizdat publication but it was certainly closely scrutinised by the state and, as a result, frequently banned. That it appeared regularly and reliably for more than 60 years places it among the most important examples of resistance journalism. The leaders of the NEF translated and published the *Communist Manifesto* in Afrikaans.

The NEF was started in the early moments of the rebirth of the socialist movement in South Africa. Soon after its establishment it began to organise lectures and discussions at the Stakesby-Lewis Hostel as well as other venues (a hall in Primrose Street was one) around District Six and these continued and expanded over many years. In 1939 the *Cape Standard* described its activities: 'Among the amenities to make evenings in the hostels agreeable and instructive, the New Era Fellowship [held] frequent meetings, at which subjects of topical interest [were] discussed. The organization has had some of the most outstanding men and women to lecture to it since its inception.'[7] In 1940 it summarised: 'At Canterbury Street, the Coloured boarders spend interesting and instructive evenings, generally on Saturday, when the New Era Fellowship arranges for lectures and discussions on topical subjects and visitors are welcomed.'[8]

These gatherings quickly became a feature of Cape Town intellectual life. Although the NEF's regular advertisements presented it as
an open debating space, it served as a clearing house for progressive
socialist thought, effectively replacing earlier vanguard forums such
as the Lenin and Spartacus clubs. (The latter was formed by the WPSA
in 1935.) Out of this came two distinct South African contributions to
the world: a range of progressive anti-Stalinist organisations, principal
among them the Non-European Unity Movement (NEUM), but encom-
passing, too, almost all the strains of progressive Marxism that came
to exist on the South African political landscape. Some of these would
identify as Trotskyist. Many, while open to Trotskyism, would refuse
that label. They were simply socialists.

The NEF was responsible for generating some of the most seminal thinking on socialism, social thought and social analysis for the
1940s and 1950s to be found anywhere in the world. Its contribution
to the discussion on race and class, much of it either unnoticed or
ignored, was new and, at the time, so different that it was dismissed.[9]
One of the country's foremost historians, Leonard Thompson,
expressing himself with undisguised indignation, described its contribution as polemical.[10] In his view its members were offensive intellectual poseurs.

Seeing more clearly than Thompson, Christopher Saunders argues
that the contribution of the NEF constituted a serious Africanist historiographic innovation. He makes the point that 'their work together
embodied an Africanist intervention more radical than Roux's', referring to Eddie Roux, author of the well-known and influential text *Time
Longer Than Rope*.[11] The NEF's contribution also preceded the rebirth of
contemporary Marxist analysis, to be called neo-Marxism, which made
its appearance in the 1960s, much of it following the mid-1960s uprisings of the anti-Vietnam movement, the Paris student revolts and the
American Civil Rights struggle. Jaffe made the comment, with respect
to a Cape Flats Educational Fellowship (CAFEF) lecture in 1955 on the
French Revolution, that 'the firmness of the theoretical foundations on

which our anti-racist, anti-imperialist and real democracy liberation movement was, and continues to be constructed . . . was more than a decade before the works of A. Gunder Frank and Amin Samir [sic] made world-system theory fashionable'.[12] Critically, in South Africa, it preceded the wave of neo-Marxist South African revisionism writing of the 1970s by more than two decades.

Reflecting on the contribution of the anti-Stalinist socialist movement, historian Christopher Joon-Hai Lee suggests that this work constituted an organic, counter-hegemonic body of thought that revealed new ways of thinking about the interplay between politics, culture and consciousness among subaltern subjects and communities.[13]

The NEF's contribution, however, remains largely hidden. It is hidden in two senses. The first comes through the diffusion of the work and influence of the NEF into the structures of the radical movement. After the 1950s, when it became a support structure to the NEUM, the NEF was active but not easily distinguished from the multiple organisations and forums with which its members were associated. It is hidden, secondly, because of the dominant historiographic presence of the Congress tradition. The history of resistance in South Africa has morphed into a history of the ANC.[14] The effect of this has been to displace alternative narratives. As a result of this marginalisation the NEF, regrettably, has little historical visibility.

The NEF was propelled by the dream of a better life for all South Africa's people, but the conditions surrounding its beginnings and the journey it had to travel were never propitious. The enormity of what it was chasing after was almost too demanding. At every step of the way it had to deal with the weight of ruling-class thinking – ruling-class thinking from the ruling class itself and ruling-class thinking reproduced from within the subordinate community as well. But by the time this intervention had reached its climax in the 1950s it had opened a window to an alternative for how to be human in a capitalist and racist world.

Sitting outside the academy as the NEF did, and without either the acknowledgement or even the curiosity of the academy, it came to depend on a small handful of intellectual-activists to spread its message. These breakers of new ground, wherever they found themselves, and they were largely in the teaching profession, were admired and respected, but also regularly ridiculed and derided. They were called, among other things, out-of-touch, armchair politicians.

They understood the implications of swimming against the tide and this made their commitment even stronger. As a result, their responses were (and still are, it needs to be said) burdened with the complexity of holding fast to the belief in the possibility of *another way*. Another way was one that did not depend on the hegemonic thinking of race and its complex conceits of white superiority. The NEF provided the country with its first deep organic intellectuals. Theorists had, of course, arisen from the oppressed before but none had worked with the question of consciousness and modernity with the comprehension demonstrated by the members of the NEF intellectual community. They attempted to understand South Africa in its productive and reproductive socialities in a way no one else was doing.

How these socialities were put in place, instantiated in the everyday and rendered ordinary was the political focus of the NEF's work. Suffusing people with a certain view of themselves, one that permeates all areas of their lives, is what shapes their consciousness. Intense socialisation experiences, such as those developed by a ruling class for a subordinate class, are so totalising that they are internalised and reproduced over and over again. This results in particular orientations and outlooks among the oppressed.

The leaders of the NEF understood this. They understood that what was needed was a counter-force to this totalisation. They fixed their focus on providing one and on breaking the cycle. This they saw as their most important practical objective. To achieve it, they realised, the nation had to be taken to school. In that great task they saw teachers as the vanguard force. Teachers were the 'awakeners'. Their job was the production of good education, an education that would place in the hands of young people the capacity to discern the difference between a defensible right and an indefensible wrong.

Reason and its cultivation were the leitmotifs that guided and shaped their sense of who they were and could be. Out of this, Isaac Tabata, a leading NEUM theoretician, argued, would come a new human being: 'In all this a new man [sic] will be emerging, capable of tackling the problems of society. And a new cultural renaissance will accompany this development. Man must increasingly unravel the secrets of nature, conquer its forces and harness them to his needs.'[15] The significance of this new line of thinking, as Ben Kies would say in 1945, was the making of a 'whole outlook, a new outlook, for the majority [of the people]'.[16]

At the core of this thinking was a complete rejection of race as any sort of signifier. These radical thinkers believed that a fundamental recuperation of the dignity of people who had been positioned by global whiteness was possible. It could be attained, they claimed, through the simple correction of history and how history had been put to use ideologically for racial supremacy. It went beyond recuperation, however, beyond appeals to ontologies of race that depended on the inversion of white supremacy with black supremacy, or indeed any other form of ethnocentric supremacy. As Tabata explained it, there were new possibilities for understanding humanity, which did not only not take race as the starting point, but excluded race altogether. In this progressive thinking the Cape Radicals anticipated the current discussion taking place in the broader humanities regarding the making of a post-apartheid sensibility.[17]

In nineteenth-century France the Jacobin-Cordelier intervention was extinguished in the complex dynamics of the French Revolution, but it is undeniable that it had changed the course of modern history. It put liberty, equality and fraternity on the agenda of social and political struggles everywhere. In twentieth-century South Africa the NEF ceased functioning in 1960, 23 years after its birth. It was stifled out of existence by the apartheid security apparatus in the heat of the Sharpeville uprising. The groundbreaking work it did, however, in the formation of political, social and cultural thought in the country cannot be discounted.

Joe Rassool would say of the time: 'The screws of oppression were being tightened by the Herrenvolk so that it became almost impossible to recruit new cadres into the movement. In 1960 *The Torch* ceased to be published. The NEF closed shop soon afterwards.'[18]

Although this book is about the NEF, it also touches on the associated organisations that came after it – principally the NLL and the NEUM. But it is not, it needs to be emphasised, a history of those organisations. The focus of this work is the NEF itself. It deliberately does not engage with the larger discussion about the 'failure' of the NEUM. In that discussion is an ongoing debate, on the one hand about the grand strategy of the NEUM and its distance from the people,[19] and on the other hand, its practical difficulties in managing debate and dissent within its ranks.[20]

Eighty years after its birth in 1937 it is important that we reflect on the significance of the NEF and try to fairly evaluate its contribution to knowledge of the social. What did this African Jacobin interruption signify? What, in the course of its 23 years, did it achieve? What did it bring to an end? What did it inaugurate? What new ideas did it seed into the South African and global political discussion? In order to try and answer these questions, we need first to understand the context of South Africa and the world in the 1930s.

Let us begin.

2 | Planters of the Seed

In a review of the events of the political history of South Africa, essayist M M Herries, writing in the *Educational Journal* in 1961, commented that the 1930s was a 'tumultuous' period for South African politics. He reflected on the protests against the Hertzog Bills, the bills that had been designed to legislate against people who were classified as African and gave rise to the Natives Representative Council (NRC). 'Like the pass campaigns,' wrote Herries, 'and multifarious *ad hoc* activities inspired for decades by certain political tendencies, they were – at the highest – fast-burning and quickly burnt-out fires.' Much more significant, 'was the formation in 1937 of the New Era Fellowship, [which] initially started out as a sorting-house of ideas and later developed into a political force which played a major part in changing the whole basis and outlook of the liberatory movement'.[1]

It is not possible to describe precisely how the New Era Fellowship (NEF) came into being because not only are its founding documents not available, there are also no records of its meetings or testimony of those present at its establishment. Traces of the beginnings of the organisation have been found, however, and these are helpful. A significant find was a copy of its revised (in 1939) constitution. From this it is clear that the NEF was the product of an extraordinary conjuncture of forces, events and individuals. The forces were, on the one hand, the global schisms playing out in the community of communists, and particularly the fight between Stalinism and Trotskyism; on the other hand was the rising tide of struggles for independence around the world on the part of people who were not white: the Abyssinian repulsion of an invading Italian army, the Indian independence movement and China's civil war and the growth of its Communist Party.

In South Africa, the events were the immediate struggle around the accelerating colonial-racial project of stripping away the residual franchise rights of people classified as non-white, the majority of whom were people deemed to be coloured. The focus of the first of the Hertzog Bills was on 'Africans'. This was followed by the attempts of the Hertzog-Smuts government to similarly disenfranchise people who were classified coloured.

* * *

South Africa in the 1930s had just come out of the Great Depression and was going through a rapid phase of economic and social development. The five years after 1933 were especially important for the country's development. Between 1932 and 1937 gross domestic product increased from £217 million to £370 million. As Hobart Houghton stated in his contribution to the *Oxford History of South Africa*, rates of inflation were low, making the gains in growth meaningful.[2] Foreign capital flowed into the country and employment rates increased. The white labour force grew by 100 000 and over 300 000 people classified African, coloured and Indian were drawn into employment.

When the Second World War broke out in 1939, economically South Africa was in a strong position. Politically, at that time, the country was led by what was called the fusion government, an alliance between the National Party and the South African Party. This alliance led to the breakaway of conservative Afrikaners and the build-up of strong ethnic sentiment around the plight of the Afrikaner people. Nigel Worden, in the 1994 publication *The Making of Modern South Africa*, writes about this drive by the National Party: 'After 1934 a conscious effort was made by the National Party to capture power by mobilizing Afrikaners across divisions of region and class. This was marked in three main ways. Firstly, Afrikaner culture was further defined and propagated through the Afrikaner Broederbond, the FAK [Federasie van Afrikaanse Kultuurvereniginge/ Federation of Afrikaans Cultural Organisations] and Christian Nationalist Education.'[3] In this period the Poor White problem was given serious attention, initiating a long phase of white affirmative action.

Simultaneously, the urgency was growing in white political circles to accelerate the processes of segregation and achieve greater control over the black working class. R B Hatting, speaking for the fusion government, in relation to these issues, confirmed: 'We want a white South Africa. We want to solve the Native Question and we want to get rid of the Native vote.'[4] Thus the Hertzog Bills were put forward for adoption in the white parliament. Their objective was to strip first African and then 'coloured' voters off the voters' roll in the Cape and to complete the process of dispossessing the African people of their land, which the 1913 Land Act had put in motion.

* * *

Cape Town in the 1930s was a relatively small and contained city. The population in 1936 was approximately 350 000. Of this number, almost two-thirds, 205 000, were people classified non-white, the majority of whom were people deemed to be coloured.[5] The majority of the non-whites resided mainly in and around the centre of Cape Town in the suburbs of District Six, the Bo-Kaap and Woodstock. The rest lived in varying degrees of hardship along the major arteries leading away from Cape Town, along Main Road out of the city towards Simon's Town, and Voortrekker Road running towards Bellville. People were crushingly poor. The Great Depression had bruised the economy badly and many workers had lost their jobs. In 1926, of the 70 000 non-Europeans living in Cape Town, '77,5% were living in overcrowded dwellings'. Their accommodation was often poor. By the 1940s 'tenant farming' was firmly established in the poorer sections of Cape Town – '90% of District Six housing being landlord-owned'.[6]

Ralph Bunche, an African-American visitor to Cape Town in 1937, looked around the city and discovered that the number of professionals in the 'coloured' community, other than teachers, could be counted on just two hands. Cissie Gool, the daughter of Abdullah Abdurahman, told him that in the 'coloured' community there were only about 'ten doctors (mostly Abdurahmans and Gools), architect – one (and not well qualified . . .), lawyer, one (and he's in jail), law student – one, minister, many'.[7] Most of the 'coloured' people were employed in the clothing and textile industries. Women were mainly in the clothing factories while, predictably, men dominated the building and construction sectors. Domestic service provided many women with employment. Critical about these areas of work was that they were close to people's homes: 'Thus, the breadwinners of households in Hanover or Horstley streets in District Six would walk to the south east corner of the city (Barrack, Commercial, Buitenkant and Roeland streets) if they were employed in the clothing industry or Pontac Street to nearby Sir Lowry Road if they were employed by leather, or food and drink concerns.'[8]

Schools at this time were sites of extreme inequality. Education had been made compulsory in 1905 in the Cape for children classified white. Communities of colour could petition the authorities for schools for their children. In the 1930s there were only five non-denominational schools for 'coloured' children in District Six and not many more in the suburbs. Amelia Lewis described the context in the following way:

The 1930s saw the earliest attempts by the Cape Education Department to dilute the influence of the British educational system on which syllabuses, teaching methods, text books and reading matter were based. The medium of instruction at virtually every school in the area in that period was English. At a primary school like Zonnebloem the standard 'Beacon' and 'Blackie's Systematic' Readers, beautifully illustrated with many reproductions of famous paintings, provided the pupils with a wealth of literature – prose and poetry – covering a range of subject matter featuring the Old World and the New, the Ancient and, for those times, the Modern. In those days boys in the schools of District Six were amongst the many who were inspired to the point where they ran away to sea, joined the British Navy and returned home after some length of time, fully fledged AB's, to visit their old school and be proudly paraded before the envious juniors by their former headmaster![9]

Children struggled to get into and stay in school. In 1931 there were 77 000 'coloured' school pupils in the Cape Province.[10] The bulk of them, 94 per cent, were enrolled in 626 schools. Of these schools, the majority were denominational. In 1931 eight schools offered secondary education to coloured children. Such schools, in the whole country, held 632 pupils.[11] In 1933 only 233 students passed either Standard 8 or Standard 10 (today's Grade 10 and Grade 12, respectively).[12] Jackie Loos tells the story of Janet Jackson, an African-American woman who started her own school in Caledon Street, District Six in 1939.[13] In 1941 she had 192 children, 'many of whom had failed to gain admission to other schools'.

At the same time that the Cape Radicals were beginning to gather in 1937 an education conference was held. It was convened by Professor Ernst Gideon Malherbe and took place over the whole month of July, moving between Johannesburg and Cape Town. At the time Malherbe was the director of the National Bureau of Educational and Social Research, an organisation established by the government in 1929 (in 1968 it would change its name to the Human Sciences Research Council). The conference was held under the auspices of the New Education Fellowship, which had as its objective the challenge of coming 'face-to-face with the general problem of the function of education in modern society'.[14] Two tasks presented themselves to education, the gathering was told: reproducing the 'type' (the people and their culture) and of 'providing for growth beyond the type'.[15] Malherbe, explaining his own thinking, urged an awareness of the dangers of neglecting the second task: 'The fact that the world is fast becoming a neighbourhood owing to the rapid developments in the means of transport and communication demands mental attitudes which are capable of transcending the more limited needs of the smaller group.' This was the raison d'être, he explained, of the New Education Fellowship. Leading the intellectual charge at the conference was the world's foremost educational philosopher, John Dewey.

What significance this conference would have had for the NEF is unclear. They would have certainly been aware of it. None of them participated in this New Education Fellowship, but their teachers certainly would have.

Obtaining a degree for a person of colour was in these times a highly significant event. When Alie Fataar obtained his Bachelor of Arts from the University of South Africa the matter was reported in the *Cape Standard*: 'Mr Fataar has obtained the B.A. as an external student of the University of South Africa. He is on the secondary staff of the Livingstone High School. Mr Fataar is a former Livingstone student, where he passed both the JC (Junior Certificate) and the SC (Senior Certificate) examinations in the first grade.'[16] It had not been an easy journey for him, however. His first application was to the University of Cape Town (UCT) where, despite having a first-class pass in his matric, he was turned down. The reason he was given was that he did not have mathematics as a matric subject.[17] (Ben Kies, on the other hand, who did not obtain a first-class pass but who did have mathematics, was offered a scholarship.)

Individuals such as Alie Fataar came from difficult backgrounds. Yunus Omar's transcription of an interview with Fataar describing the way that he managed his life in the 1940s is illuminating. Two years into his teaching career at Livingstone High School, and newly married to Rita Davidson-Saban, he shows how powerfully agency was at work:

We were working on two fronts: your home, and the political . . .
it was daily: afternoon, evening, weekends, holidays. There wasn't
a week when we could say that there was nothing to do politically.

Day and night, because you are also a teacher: you had to prepare lessons, you had to mark marks and you had to attend meetings. Then there was the political: meetings, conferences, correspondence, reports, all sorts of things. Then there was at one time still my studies . . . I did three courses a year. And so you start the day at four o'clock studying.[18]

* * *

This was the context in which the individuals who led the development of the NEF lived and worked. That they were gifted intellectuals is not in doubt. That they were enabled by both large and small privilege – the privilege of social class or the privilege of forceful parents and mentors – and inspired by high ideals is also not in dispute. But in terms of understanding the class-race nexus in which these people found themselves the issue is contentious.

An important explanation of the NEF's leaders' transition into radicalism in the 1930s is provided by Mohamed Adhikari in *Let us Live for Our Children*. It is worth quoting him at some length:

> The radical movement which challenged the moderates' domination of coloured politics in the 1930s and 1940s did not arise in isolation from its moderate antecedent; nor can radical ideology be represented as a simple antithesis of conventional values within the coloured elite. This movement was also not entirely exempt from the ambiguities and contradictions that came with the baggage of coloured identity and status. Rather, the radical movement was firmly rooted within the moderate status quo from which it grew and shared substantial common ground with its predecessor, especially before the establishment of the Anti-CAD movement in 1943. However much the radicals may have prided themselves on their principled stance on non-racism and on their egalitarian values, they nevertheless

had to come to their own accommodation with their marginality, the tenacity of racial identities within their society and their structurally ambiguous position of the coloured bourgeoisie . . .. Indeed, it would not be difficult to show that many modern-day radicals who dismiss coloured identity as a creation of the 'racist-capitalist' state and the refuge of 'collaborators' and 'opportunists', themselves often in the same breath acknowledge the reality of coloured identity . . . One cannot ignore the fact that there were substantive similarities and continuities in their responses to white supremacism and to their predicament of marginality.[19]

Richard van der Ross, in attempting to explain what he describes as the naivety of the NEF, ascribed their attitude, interestingly, to their colouredness. It was the fact that they belonged to this group, he avers, that made them so unaware of the depth of racial feeling in the country. This group, he claims, 'had the least conscious[ness] of any group feeling, and [was] a marginal group, most eager to divest itself of any "group label"'.[20] Paradoxically, Van der Ross argues, it was exactly their racial marginality that was most productively at work in the way in which they approached questions of the social makeup of the country.

It would be naive to ignore or minimise these racial explanations. It has to be remembered, as Adhikari described them,[21] that the Gools, the Abdurahmans and the Kieses were 'the scions . . . of Cape Town's most prominent coloured families . . .' and that 'Ben Kies'. . . father had served for many years on the African People's Organisation (APO) Executive'. These individuals' subject positions were consequential, therefore, in both their discriminatory and empowering effects.

The Kieses, perhaps less so the Gools and the Abdurahmans, would have been painfully aware of how their positioning as people labelled 'coloured' would have caused them severe prejudice. They were denied the opportunity to live, learn and love as people of human dignity. The pain of this must have struck deeply.

Nevertheless, the Kieses and the Gools were, and this is always necessary to keep in mind in thinking about social actors in any time and space, *relatively* privileged. They had opportunity, power and capacity that the poor within their immediate ken would not have been able even to imagine. The Gool brothers were distinctly privileged in this regard. For a time the family was sufficiently wealthy for Goolam Gool's father to send his sons – and the gender privileging must not be ignored – to finish their education in England. But they also experienced hardship, some of it due to their father's predilection for gambling, some of it a result of the Great Depression.

When Goolam Gool's sister Minnie was in her teens, in the 1930s, family circumstances deteriorated to the extent that 'Minnie had to find employment to assist in providing for the family's living requirements'.[22] Goolam Gool, in theorising this relationship between privilege and disadvantage, argued in 1937 in a debate about 'coloured professionals', which was reported on in the *Cape Standard* on 8 November, that there was 'no intellectual class among the non-Europeans'.[23] He argued that this elite was emerging as an organic-intellectual stratum, and in this demonstrated an awareness of how subject positions were formed. They were not fixed human attributes. Life was on the move.

Adhikari's explanation, which focuses on the racial dimensions of the transition to radicalism that these individuals made, is useful to a degree. Political discourse at the time, as Gavin Lewis writes in *Between the Wire and the Wall*, was dominated by the deliberate efforts of the state to draw a dividing line between Africans and 'coloureds'.[24] The 1930s saw the emergence of the first national discussion between groupings within the oppressed community about 'non-European' unity. Abdurahman himself played a central role in these discussions.

Three attempts at unity talks were made between 1930 and 1934. 'For moderate black leaders,' Lewis writes, '. . . the Non-European Conferences offered a rallying point both to oppose the Pact regime and to muster support for their strategies of compromise and appeals to the ideals of the Cape liberal tradition.'[25] These initiatives were important, and would have been known to the Cape Radicals. The talks broke down over questions of the role of white people and the leadership of the oppressed people. Leaders of the African National Congress (ANC) were anxious about the possible exclusion of white people and their own precedence over everybody else. The struggle was essentially to be led by the ANC. There was also in the air, and especially in the 'coloured' community, a suspicion about making common cause with African and Indian people. The African National Bond (ANB), a grouping that emerged in the late 1920s around 'coloured' interests, made the point that the Hertzog Bills gave, for the first time, a sense of acknowledgement of 'coloured' interests. Intriguingly, Lewis says, 'Abdurahman privately claimed to have knowledge of a concerted attempt by leading Cape Nationalists to ensure that the ANB took the stand it did.'[26] Abdurahman's own brother, Dr I Abdurahman, campaigned on this ticket for the nationalists in the 1929 election.

The point to take away from this is that 'coloured' separatism as an idea was very present. The ANB would die a quick death, but, as Lewis notes, the suggestion of an exclusive 'coloured' way forward was attractive to the 'coloured' elite.[27] The leader of the ANB, W Le Grange, said: 'We want to build up a race that the Europeans will be proud of.'[28]

Undoubtedly at this time a great deal of race consciousness existed in the broader social and political environment. The idea of 'we Coloured' people, as against more inclusive terms such as 'we Africans', was gaining traction. In the political debate about social mobility it was positively alluring. It made sense. In some ways it was all that people knew. It was the only way in which they could express a sense of themselves and their connectednesses and responsibilities.[29]

The point that this book seeks to make, in acknowledgement of an explanation such as Adhikari's, is that it sociologically runs ahead of itself. It presents the social topography, that which is there to be seen in people's language and self-description and in their affiliations and distantiating strategies, as the explanation of itself, rather than a social situation that requires explanation. It naturalises, both corporeally and psychically, the idea that racialised bodies have within them explanations for their subjects' behaviours, desires and preferences.

In response to this, what, arguably, a racially inflected explanation such as Adhikari's does is constrain the examination that needs to be undertaken about the complexity of what emerged out of the tumultuous 1930s. That examination is critical for the dialogue suggested above. Racial naturalisation, against this, as Corinne Sandwith argues, 'reif[ies] Coloured identity' and 'corroborat[es] the mistaken view that the NEF and the NEUM [Non-European Unity Movement] were organisations of exclusively Coloured membership, confined to the Western Cape'.[30] It underplays the complexity of both the social and the cultural and the deeply important ways in which the space of the political is informed and created out of a multiplicity of factors.

Cape Town at this time was a very cosmopolitan place. Its sociality provided to everybody who lived there, whether they liked it or not, a lesson in living with and managing difference. The description of what District Six was like in the 1930s provided by Esther Wilkin demonstrates this rather well:

In our midst in District 6 were coloured and Malay families. I became friends with a number of girls. In some cases the fathers were white and the mothers coloured and in a few isolated cases the fathers Jewish and the mothers coloured. The fathers of some of these girls were Remittance men. They were in the main Blacksheep members of the British Aristocracy sent to the colonies and money was remitted to them on a monthly basis – enough to live on but not enough for a ticket back to Britain. My Malay friends the Gadidas', Chalimas', Mymonmas', Fatimas' and Asas' were amongst those many years later who had to leave District 6 because of the Group Areas Act. The girls in those families who passed for white became my classmates, their dark-skinned brothers and sisters had to go to the De Villiers Street school. So a group of us aged between 6 and 11 years walked from the Chapel Street area to Buitenkant Street where the William Fehr Museum is located.

Our route to school took us down Wicht Street and it was here that we Jewish children had our first taste of anti-Semitism. A poor white Afrikaans speaking family lived in a dilapidated terraced house in the street. The children pelted us with rotten fruit and other garbage when we passed their house calling out 'Bloody Jews, Christ killers, Kaffir lovers' and made our lives a misery. Help however was at hand. At the end of Wicht Street, corner Mount Street, lived the daughters of Dr. Abdurahman with his Scottish ex-wife. The sisters saw what was happening to us and became our escorts. Whether the Van Wyks had respect for Warradak's uniform [she was the district nurse] or Cissie's threats, the harassment ceased. Cissie subsequently married Dr. Gool and became a town councilor, always ready to help the underdog. From those early days of my life a friendship developed between the much older Cissie and myself which lasted until she died.[31]

The men and women in the NEF may have come to the moment of the 1930s suffused with racial thoughts and predispositions but, critically, they had in both their lived experiences and in their intellectual stimuli a wide range of other ways of seeing and being in the world. And so they did not stay in their racial universes. They were subjects of their time, but they also sought to make their time. This was the idea of the 'new era', a springboard into something different. They took agency. They made decisions about themselves that explicitly disavowed, and did not take personal advantage of, the small privilege they brought to their situations. That they did this, over and over, and in contradictory ways, needs to be acknowledged. Race as a mind-set followed them. It permeated the ether. But it was against race that, later, they set their whole beings in their cognitive assessment of how the social came to them and how they should manage their personal lives in relation to it. Describing them, then, as 'coloured' intellectuals and even as the 'coloured' elite, does them a severe injustice. It is an affront to the very project they built up and attempted to implement as the basis for imagining themselves anew.

Explanations using race do not help us understand their routes to agency and political choice. Using race as a rubric to explain the subjects of this book, the individuals who passionately led the NEF, is to underplay the quite extraordinary ways in which these human beings came to a sense of their own identity and their own self-awareness.

In this dynamic the influence of the global is visible. Cape Town in the 1930s was a small provincial place, despite being the capital of South Africa. It did not have the affordances of metropoles like Paris, London and New York. It was relatively quiet and self-contained. Even more extraordinary, then, was how it was able to attract some of the most provocative progressive intellectuals floating around the globe. And in Cape Town these intellectuals found, equally extraordinarily, a small gathering of insatiably curious local activists. They were almost ineluctably drawn to them. The NEF turned a small provincial centre into a global intellectual hotspot.

In terms of this larger picture there is another story to tell. It picks up a different genealogical thread from that of a race-worlded universe. This alternative goes back to the innovative thinking of Olive Schreiner.[32] Her contribution was made when the South African imperial culture-bed was already beyond its seedling stage, when its shoots had matured into sturdy plants. One sees in this imperial laboratory the propagation of racially predatory organisms and its results – an array of social, political and economic institutions thriving in the hothouse of a rampant modernity.

South Africa constituted itself as a white Union in 1910. Between the turn of the century and the early 1920s the mining political economy refined the structural mechanisms and the practical techniques for managing its race-class project – the racial division of the working class and the recruitment of white workers behind a white supremacist agenda; and the nascent higher education system, despite the presence of dissenters within it, settled into its role as the training ground for white civilisation.[33] On the sidelines of this rapidly evolving political and economic laboratory stood Schreiner, sister of Will Schreiner, the eighth prime minister of the Cape Colony. She was the author of *The Story of an African Farm* (1883), the first South African novel and also one of the world's first feminist novels.

As a result of her participation in the Suffragette movement in England in the closing decades of the nineteenth century, Schreiner developed a clearly articulated anti-determinist view of gender and also, although admittedly less so, of race. She was the first critical theoretician on social difference in South Africa, taking essentially what we would in contemporary terms describe as a 'social constructionist direction'. Her seminal work, *Women and Labour*, written partly in response to Karl Marx's work, rejected the idea that women were biologically different from men. She introduced the idea of gender as something that was made up. Her thinking on race was less developed but intuitively fed off the thinking she had developed on gender. She was, extraordinarily, given where she was in the world at that time, profoundly influenced by the writing of Toussaint L'Ouverture and W E B Du Bois. Writing to her brother Will on 2 May 1911, she described the world she desired: 'A society which according to its carefully drawn up principles, which each member would have to subscribe [to], would be in favour of the doing away with all the <u>artificial</u> restriction of sex, & which would seek the good of <u>all</u> women quite irrespective of race and creed.'[34]

Schreiner died in 1920. During her life she had touched a number of people deeply. One of these was a young British-American woman living in Cape Town named Ruth Schechter. Schreiner and Schechter had developed an intense relationship over a period of about a decade. The younger woman, the product of an intellectually and politically progressive Jewish family, initiated in the twenties a kind of salon, to which she invited Cape Town's small but influential group of young progressive intellectuals. Invoking the memory and thinking of Schreiner, she used the freedom of her home deliberately to promote the cause of social justice. She set up a social circle of activist intellectuals who engaged with the ideas of progressive thinkers from around the world, including those of Mohandas Gandhi and, critically, those of Schreiner. She took from Schreiner her 'great love of her fellow-human-beings'.[35]

Into her house would come Ben Farrington, a classics professor at UCT and an Irish Republican activist (for whom she would leave her husband) and Lancelot Hogben, a young biologist and also a professor at the university. Farrington is described by Baruch Hirson as follows: '[He] was not only part of her circle, he complemented her in bringing it to life. Ben was a remarkable man who towered over his contemporaries as thinker and author, and as a personality.'[36] He helped Schechter transition into a critical socialism, which gave her the conceptual tools with which to think about the future of South Africa. Hogben, who would go on to become one of the world's path-breaking socio-biologists and a leading opponent of eugenics, was a hugely influential presence. Eddie Roux, a leading member of the Communist Party, said he 'had a galvanising effect on the radical members of the university staff'.[37] Of the gatherings at Schechter's house and the people who came and went he said:

> The most exciting of these was Lancelot Hogben ... at the height of his intellectual powers and in his most iconoclastic phase ... He had become the centre of a group of intelligent and charming people.
>
> Hogben combined his leftist position in politics with strong opposition to religions, nationalist and all such. He disliked flags and national anthems and did not care at all whom or how he annoyed by his gestures of iconoclasm.[38]

In the 1920s there was a climate of downswing for 'non-white' politics. The two major political structures in the country, the ANC and the

Industrial and Commercial Workers' Union (ICU), were in a state of decline. Schechter created a platform for keeping radical thinking alive and thus was of seminal influence for the whole left movement in the country. Politically her intervention was slight. She had no intention of starting a new political organisation. But what she stimulated was immensely productive. People like Hogben revelled in this environment. He was no dilettante, however. His purpose was deadly serious. The questions he asked of the social determinants of race were by any means and measure extraordinary. That he was raising them in a community of people, small as it was, who were asking questions about rank and privilege was possibly fortunate happenstance, but it was, in ways that might not properly be accounted for, enormously generative.

A separate study should be undertaken of how these new ways of thinking were generated. It raises many more questions than are broached here. One issue for future consideration is the question of Jewish vulnerability and how the theorising of this question stimu-lated and connected with other forms of vulnerability. Its coincidence with the stirrings of race awareness in a creolised space such as South Africa is in some senses a historical accident. But it produced a distinct intellectual sensibility which, in one dynamic eruption, was framed by the global but insistently grounded in the local. Global ways of seeing passed through the analytic optics that offered themselves for mean-ing-making to the communities of Jewish refugees and South African subalterns. Together they began to originate perspectives that were entirely new.

The horror in the 1930s of the experience of the pogroms across Europe, before and during the rise of Hitler, influenced the direction of theorising around race in immediate ways. To illustrate the point, there was Claire Goodlatte, who consciously gave up her anti-Semitism and begin to take into her social analysis the ways in which race as a con-struction was used for promoting the imperial project.[39]

The young intellectuals in the oppressed community might have been in the presence of the full complexity of tragedy, but they had astonishing intellectual vitality in their midst to buoy them up. Hogben and Farrington, at that point two of Cape Town's foremost thinkers, provided them with a group of public intellectualism that would have been impressive in any part of the world. That these people were in Cape Town was of immense historical significance. From these sources they were able to access a rich body of writing and scholarship concerning 'the Jewish question' and they could see race accounted for in the elegant analysis of their communist interlocutors. Being demonstrated in Europe, in the hands of the supposedly best exponents and bearers of advanced civilisation, was barbarism on a scale never witnessed before in history. Not a Europe of civilisation. A barbarous Europe.

There was also powerful learning to be had in the lived examples of these interlocutors. How did their experiences of both having to think and live through social difference impact on the choices and decisions they made? How did they begin to explain themselves in their own lived spaces? These critical questions resonated strongly with their Cape Town comrades and the relationships they formed among the members of this unusual mix of people in a small community of intellectuals. Schechter would leave her husband Morris for Farrington. Isaac Tabata and Jane Gool would be married. Cissie would divorce Hamid Gool and move in with Sam Kahn.

In his thesis on the life of Alie Fataar, Omar throws useful light on the relationship between the personal and the political, as well as the complex issue of religion.[40] That he and Fataar shared a common Muslim background made him ponder the question of how this might have influenced how Fataar related to him in the interviews he did with him. It also arises in his description of Fataar's relationship with Goolam Gool, who was Fataar's first mentor. Fataar makes the observation to Omar that despite the fact that Gool was an atheist, possibly their shared Muslim background was a factor in allowing them to get on as comfortably with each other as they did.

Who these Cape Jacobins were had a great deal to do with their own social contexts. The politics of their immediate pasts would have loomed large in their lives. D F Malan, Jan Smuts and white domination were names and issues that would have featured regularly and frustratingly in their daily comings and goings. Against this context, events on the international stage would no doubt have catalysed their development. The First World War and the threat of a second, together with the struggles for independence in different territories around the world, had the effect of connecting people and their issues at a deep level.

Ruth Schechter had planted a seed and after she left South Africa in 1933 her role was taken over by others. Among these Claire Goodlatte was a central connector and Yudel Burlak, a Polish exile, was another; and there were the Gool brothers, Abdul and Goolam, both of whom were medical doctors. Among them they nurtured the seed and began to survey, mark out and make ready a greenhouse of another kind. Its ecological ethos was not of conquest and predation. It was of co-existence, inter-dependence and generativity.

As the seed grew, it sprouted its own organisms. The constant threat, relentlessly hovering, was the toxicity of hegemony masquerading almost everywhere in racial form. The cultivation in this greenhouse called for a clear-eyed perspective of the broader conditions within which the growth of discourse needed to happen – the hold of capitalism in the world and the ways in which it penetrated and took control of the spaces and places where it grew. But it demanded, also, a sensitivity to the related conceits of inferiority and superiority, to the ways in which power operates at the micro-level to produce advantage. Examples abound: access to English produced social inequality; cultures of masculinity reproduced deep oppressions inside the confines of the already disadvantaged; colourism, the desire for whiteness, produced within oppressed and disenfranchised communities visible hierarchies of privilege and unfair opportunity.

The new intellectuals of the 1930s had to have within their interpretive repertoires the capacity to intuit and respond to the complex ways power was produced and reproduced. They forged new paths for making sense of the workings of power. Imagining how an alternative set of frameworks, against the full panoply of dominance, might be made to work was what made their approach and thinking groundbreaking.

Goodlatte, Burlak and the Gools, the founding agents of this movement, all kept open houses, especially over weekends. A wide spectrum of Cape Town's intelligentsia, including the leading young intellectuals of the day, drifted in and out of their homes. Eddie Roux, a biologist at UCT, was one. Another was Jean van der Poel, an educationist and historian; the artist Gregoire Boonzaier was a regular visitor. They were of all colours and backgrounds, but distinctly left wing in their orientation. Some of them were from the small émigré community of socialists, political refugees from the European pogrom. Hirson writes: 'Some followers of the Trotskyist movement gathered at the house of Y Burlak . . . and there was also a gathering at the house of Dr Abdul Hamin [sic] Gool, Cissie's general practitioner husband.'[41] Some were from the small handful of black students who could gain admission to UCT or who were taking their degrees by distance learning through the University of South Africa.

UCT, at that time, had fewer than 100 black students. Ben Kies came from a prominent APO household. Tabata had come to Cape Town from a village near Queenstown in the Eastern Cape, having left the University of Fort Hare where he was a student. He became a truck driver and joined the Lorry Drivers' Union.[42] Roux was a member of the Communist Party of South Africa (CPSA) and a major proponent of the Black Republic thesis, discussed below. In later years they would sit at opposite ends of the table of communism in Cape Town.

Bernhard Herzberg described how he had befriended Abdul Gool in 1934 at a musical concert in the Cape Town City Hall and walked home with him:

I shall never forget our walk through the non-White District Six to save money. We were both received with open arms not only by the doctor but also by the diverse company. Every Saturday, Dr Gool and his wife Cissie held open house. It was the only dwelling in this racially divided city where folks from all walks of life, and kind of origin, met, in defiance of ingrained custom. Assembled there was a veritable League of Nations. We met . . . Frederick Bodmer. Next to him sat Sam Kahn, a leading Stalinist Communist. Painters were there too: Gregoire Boonzaier . . .. Cissie presided over this gathering with her husband. She was sitting next to her father . . . busy berating him, calling him an Uncle Tom, for his lack of radical opposition to the prevailing political and social system in South Africa.

I spotted an African intellectual, [I B] Tabata, a prominent member of the Trotskyite Spartacus Club, in earnest conversation with Dr Eddie Roux.[43]

Tabata and Roux in conversation was indicative of the mood and spirit of what Schechter had begun. In what they represented, the gatherings were social experiments in themselves. Cape Town was not the hyper-racialised environment that places such as Johannesburg had become, but it was acutely sensitive to rank, religion and, increasingly, the concentration of one's pigmentation. How dark or how fair one was, was at that time of rising racial awareness either an irreversible disability or the pigmented passport to social mobility. Class, race, gender and culture were, as single issues and in their fusion, combustive elements.

In this friable universe the homes of people such as Goodlatte and the Gools were highly unusual places and would have attracted a great deal of curiosity. But the Gools, the Goodlattes and the Burlaks – and this point cannot be made strongly enough – were not representative of the population. They were exceptional in all kinds of ways.

Burlak, about whom very little has been written, was a brilliant theoretician. He came to South Africa in 1930 as an exile from Poland. The General Secretary of the Workers' Party of South Africa (WPSA) in 1936, presumably Goodlatte, wrote to the International Secretariat of the International Communist League in July of 1936 saying, 'Our unity is based theoretically on the common acceptance of the principles contained in the theses written by Comrade Burlak.'[44] Allison Drew describes him as having 'played a major role in formulating the WPSA's draft theses' and says he 'continued to exert a powerful but behind-the-scenes intellectual pull over younger WPSA members through the 1950s'.[45]

Goodlatte was a central figure in these developments. She had been a nun (she was known as the 'red nun') living in Grahamstown when she was converted to socialism. She took her religious fervour into her commitment to socialism and would be a major nurturer of its counter-culture possibilities. She saw her role as a prober of the question of what it meant to be a new transgressive subject. Ciraj Rassool expands on this:

> In the detail of this narrative, it was Claire Goodlatte, the 'Red Nun' who had been Gool and Tabata's WPSA mentor and trainer in political theory, who had granted 'responsibility of leader-ship' to Tabata and Jane Gool. Jane Gool recalled this moment in Goodlatte's house in York Street, Woodstock in about 1935 in solemn terms: 'I got such a shock that the hairs on my skin rose, I got cold . . . [Tabata] stammered, 'I never thought of myself as a leader . . .'. It was like a tidal wave had hit us. Both of us grew pale with shock . . . We knew then that we were going to be burdened with the responsibility of leadership.'[46]

Tabata later told Rassool that Goodlatte was one of the people who 'helped to mould' him. It was she who 'showed us how to live'.

The Gools, for their part, were complex people. Their socio-economic location was unusual, but more complex was how they functioned politically. Cissie was the daughter of Dr Abdullah Abdurahman, the leader of the APO. She actively challenged her father and his movement and this would feature prominently in the dynamics of the radical movement during this period. She would make and break alliances with her more left-leaning brother-in-law, Goolam, several times. As Fataar said of her: 'The community had a great respect for her, because she was a woman and no other woman, non-white, was a member of the [Cape Town City] Council. In that respect she was a pioneer.'[47]

The APO had peaked as a political formation in the first decades of the twentieth century. Its reputation – that of a moderate 'coloured' political group – hung by a thread. Its leaders and followers had the image of 'respectable' coloured petitioners, nothing more. Abdurahman's personal reputation was, it needs to be acknowledged, greater than that of his party. Cissie Gool's husband had trained as a doctor in England. His younger brother Goolam, who became one of the leading left figures of the late 1930s, had also qualified as a doctor in England; he returned to South Africa in 1932 at age 29. In 2003 Selim Gool, wanting to explain his parents, Halima and Goolam, described his father as a 'majestically tall . . . large and athletic man . . . With a heavy "British" English accent . . . with a proud bearing'.[48] The characters in this space in the 1930s, he said, were a 'bohemian, artist[ic] and intellectual set', 'the politicos of the time and the coming generation of socialist militants (Goolam, Jane, Tabata, Kies, who form a core of the Non-White anti-Stalinist Left)[49] and the "liberal" bourgeois elements [who] all partied at the home of Cissie and A.H. Gool.'[50] Peter Abrahams, who became a celebrated South African writer, said of Goolam Gool: 'He seemed absurdly relaxed and aloof. He wore his fine clothes with the casualness of those born to wealth.'[51] Marcus Solomon recalled an encounter he had with Gool that reinforced the impression he conveyed to people around him of unrelenting fixity of purpose:

I met Goolam Gool at Minnie's [Gool; they were siblings] one Saturday. Kader was there, Enver, Ravi Pillay. Goolam held Saturday afternoon meetings at Minnie's house. He gave us an impromptu lecture. In his heyday he was Ben's [Kies] teacher. He said, 'Who built the country? To learn you don't need to go to university. Just look around you.' . . . It was a lesson on Marxism on the spot. When you read that poem, he said, remember that life is in front of you. Says 'Good afternoon chaps', and buggers off. Imagine if he had the mass struggle, as bolsheviks tried to do. He brings it down to simple things, makes a derisory comment, but he left something deep.[52]

Accurate or not as these characterisations may be, it is important to emphasise that these people were not cut off from the world around them. What was especially striking about them, at this delicate time of heightened class, race, religious and gender awareness, was that they deliberately cultivated the desire and inclination to cross the boundaries of their histories. Abrahams would say to Goolam Gool: 'Of all the Coloureds I've met, you are, most completely, most naturally, free of the slightest hint of prejudice, upwards to the whites, or downwards to the blacks, and that is important.'[53] Halima Gool, also quite unusually, developed a gender analysis of patriarchy in 1937. It would offend today – it was intoned in racial adjectives – but it was for her time significantly in advance of anything anybody else around her would come to an understanding about. People formed relationships in a free and open way. Their mind-sets and demeanours were socially transgressive. They were, as Selim Gool would say, bohemian to a degree. But they were more than that. They were the organic intellectuals of their time and space.

* * *

While it is necessary to acknowledge the social complexity of these planters of the alternative seed bed, it is equally important to emphasise how conscious they were of their own privilege. Goolam Gool, Jane Gool and Isaac Tabata were completely attuned to the ways and seductions of conceit, superiority and social hauteur, and the insidious ways in which they bred and reproduced inferiority and self-disregard. Bunche said of the National Liberation League (NLL) that they were 'too high-brow and above the masses'.[54] This was not entirely correct. A sense of their privilege there may have been, but their complete obsession was with how to break the web of rank and class in which they found themselves enmeshed.

They did not come to this moment directly. It came via the larger schism that was taking place within the global communist movement – the attack by Joseph Stalin on Leon Trotsky and what he stood for and the whole Soviet apparatus.

The appeal of Trotsky for the South African radicals was not only a response to the excesses of Stalinism; it was Trotsky's consistency of principle they admired. This consistency was evident as the Comintern swung dramatically from the late 1920s to the middle of the 1930s from what Isaac Deutscher described as rightism to ultra-leftism. Trotsky offered the view that the 'whole epoch opened by the First World War and the Russian revolution was one of the decline of capitalism, the very foundations of which were shattered. This, however, did not mean that the edifice was about to come down with a crash.'[55] He was developing his theory of Permanent Revolution. The decay of a social system was not a single process. Its end would not come in one climactic burst, heralded by either an economic slump or an uninterrupted succession of revolutionary events. 'It was therefore preposterous to announce that the bourgeoisie had "objectively" reached its ultimate impasse', as the Comintern was telling its followers around the world. What was needed, he argued, was a constant analysis of the balance of forces. It was this analytic compulsion, accompanied by a deep respect for intellectual rigour, that attracted the Cape Town radicals. They found in Trotsky an élan that many among them would emulate.

This shift towards Trotskyism had its origins in the global struggle in the socialist movement. When Trotsky finally made the decision to establish the Fourth International in 1938 in opposition to the Comintern many among the radical left in Cape Town followed developments with great interest. The establishment of the Fourth International of South Africa (FIOSA) would follow. It was the pronouncement of the Comintern on the tactics and strategies of struggle in

South Africa, however, that was decisive for Trotskyism in South Africa. The Comintern adopted a resolution on 'the South African question' at its executive committee meeting following its Sixth Congress in 1928. It brought to a crisis all the issues that divided the socialist community in South Africa. Most critically it put into stark perspective the explosive question of how to analyse and explain the struggle in South Africa, and on the basis of this, how to prosecute it.[56] How, to be precise, should the social of this place, South Africa, be understood? What were superiority and inferiority all about?

The Resolution of the Comintern Executive came out of a discussion about national liberation between the executive and the CPSA. Until then the majority view in the CPSA was that a nationalist struggle was reformist. The intervention of the Comintern overturned this. The resolution said that white people constituted a national minority in South Africa and that while it was correct to call for 'full and equal rights for all races', the correct principle to work with was that South Africa belonged to the 'native population'. It said explicitly that it could not confine itself to the general slogan of 'let there be no whites and no blacks'. Communists, it insisted, had to understand the revolutionary importance of the national and agrarian questions:

> South Africa is a black country, the majority of its population is black and so is the majority of the workers and peasants. The bulk of the South African population is the black peasantry, whose land has been expropriated by the *white* minority . . . Hence the national question in South Africa, which is based on the agrarian question, lies at the foundation of the revolution in South Africa. The black peasantry constitutes the basic moving force of the revolution in alliance with and under the leadership of the working class.[57]

After much disagreement inside the CPSA, the Comintern resolution was accepted, under the colonialism of a special type (CST) thesis, which, essentially, came to inform the position of the Communist movement in South Africa. An intense debate inside the country had been set in motion, out of which was to come a response from communists outside of the Communist International (CI), largely led by Trotsky's followers in South Africa. The CI, established in 1919 after the Russian Revolution, brought together the world's Communist parties. A central contention in the debate was whether the struggle was primarily a class or a race struggle. The Trotskyists prevaricated on many issues. One of these was the question of land. Like the Stalinists, they were very aware of the role of the peasantry and accorded to the peasantry a leading role in the return of South Africa's dispossessed physical space.

It was a different question, however, that gradually brought into perspective race as an idea.[58] This was the question of the two-stage revolution: a national bourgeois revolution in which racial equality was sought, or a working-class revolution in which all the problems of capitalism were resolved in a single process. Trotsky's supporters in South Africa objected vociferously, and bluntly so, to Trotsky, about the CST approach, on the grounds that it was nationalist. They argued that 'a national revolution, with its unavoidable blocs, etc., is here in South Africa more than anywhere else doomed beforehand . . . A national revolution on purely racial slogans of black against white, and that is all the CP does here, excludes the possibility of the proletariat as the vanguard of the revolution, because these *purely racial slogans draw a fatal line through the ranks of the proletariat*.'[59]

The issue in the social and political gatherings in Cape Town, such as the one Herzberg saw being played out between Tabata and Roux, was whether the problem of South Africa was one of race or one of class. In raising it here it is important, in attempting to give a sense of the texture of the times, to note how open-ended these early beginnings of the left's debate about these issues were. There was not, as yet, a clear, defined and ready-to-hand approach to the question of the social. The general understanding of race, within both the CPSA and the anti-Stalinist movement, was essentially that people belonged 'naturally' in racial categories. As Adhikari has argued, race was an extremely tenacious idea.[60] There was not, at that time, the theoretical understanding of race that would keep these two socialist camps in a state of visceral opposition to each other. This meant that while socialists gravitated towards and did indeed belong to either the Stalinist Comintern grouping or the Trotskyist opposition alternative, they nevertheless continued to engage with one another. Their vocabularies of the social were indistinguishable. Words such as 'Bantu', 'European', 'coloured' and 'Indian' tripped easily off their tongues.

This willingness to engage saw them come together in a number of different political structures and alliances. In all of these initiatives debate raged around the nature of the country and its economy and the kind of political programme it required. Sometimes the CPSA held to the CST line, other times not. During the 1940s, for example, even though African Communists played a significant role in organising the 1946 mineworkers' strike, the CPSA put nearly all its efforts into organising the white working class, at the expense of black workers.

Socialists in the anti-Stalinist grouping similarly equivocated. While they acknowledged that foregrounding the role and place of the African community was necessary, at the same time they didn't want to lose the possibility of winning back the support of the white working class. They argued that 'South African capitalism was heading to a crisis which would force the bourgeoisie to break its historic pact with the white working class . . . and that it was incumbent on socialists to organise poor whites rather than let them succumb to fascist ideology.'[61] These questions would remain open-ended and even be cause for ambivalence right into the 1950s. They would continue to pit the anti-Stalinists against each other.

Hirson, writing many years after the debate was first opened up, criticised his comrades for having misunderstood the social formation of the 1930s:

When the WPSA programme was first drafted in 1934 the great depression was lifting in South Africa and the new industrialism that followed . . . had barely commenced. Many of the newly urbanised workers were fresh from the country and were not viewed as a potential base for socialism. Nor did the authors see any place in the coming struggle for the Coloured workers, despite their long history as artisans and workers in light industry. Long afterwards members of the WPSA – now leading members of the NEUM – looked exclusively to rural conditions and continued to speak of the workers as if they were only peasants temporarily in the towns or the mines.

Even more erroneous was the continued description of the Africans in the Reserves as peasants even though they did not produce commodities for the market . . . It was only Trotsky's criticism of the WPSA's programme that led to their re-examination of the role of workers in any future struggle, but this was a concession that was not reflected in their activities.[62]

In assessing the Cape Radicals' grasp of the social this criticism is powerful. It raises questions of their appreciation of the material and political conditions in which they found themselves. What is critical is the understanding they were building the country's political economy and the class character of the social formation. There was a recognition (and this is the particular clarity they brought) of how racism worked. There was also a sense, especially among the white members of the anti-Stalinist movement, as was to be seen in the example of older leaders such as Goodlatte, that they should be making way for their black colleagues. This issue continued to be a cause for debate within the liberation movement as a whole into the contemporary period.

What was happening at the international level between Stalinists and Trotskyists had a strong and divisive influence on their South African followers and their various organisations at the time. Both the Stalinists and the Trotskyists splintered and regrouped. Contrary to the perception that was being created, and which remains, that the Trotskyists were fractious and inclined to doctrinally-inspired factions, much the same was playing itself out, and still is, among the Moscow-aligned socialists. People took theoretical issue with each other and moved off on their own. The two groups came to treat each other with deep suspicion.

Although the CPSA remained organisationally relatively intact, it blew hot and cold, writes Drew, around the question of the place of black workers and white workers and where the vanguard of the working class was located. In the early 1940s, for example, the dominant grouping in the CPSA would 'make no mention of a native or Black Republic', but they remained within the Stalin camp.[63]

The anti-Stalinists, on the other hand, very influenced by Trotskyism in the 1930s, struck out in their own distinctive political organisations.[64] The first of these was T W Thibedi's Communist League of Africa, formed in 1932 on the Witwatersrand. What was distinctive about the league, and influenced by communication between the league and Trotsky, was its essentially African membership. When this initiative petered out, the Bolshevist Leninist League was formed. In the Western Cape Trotskyists started the Lenin Club in 1933, which split in 1934.

The Lenin Club, brief as its existence was, was profoundly important for the establishment of the left-wing radical movement in South Africa and the subsequent emergence of the Cape Radicals. The majority of its members were people who had been expelled from the CPSA. Hirson describes it as being born 'not in blood but in confusion'.[65] Before its split it projected itself as a deliberate counter to the CPSA. It was dominated by Yiddish speakers from Eastern Europe, many of whom had personal experience of the split between Stalin and Trotsky. It set itself up as a 'forum for serious socialist discussion [and] soon [attracted] wider interest from UCT radicals, itinerant socialists and political activists, including . . . Tabata, Goolam Gool and Jane Gool'. It held 'regular meetings on Saturday nights, [and] club members participated in a weekly socialist Sunday school . . . [and] studied the history of socialism'.[66] As a site for the induction of instinctive social rebels into deep analytic thought it was exceptional.

One of the most important features about the Lenin Club, and which is little reflected upon in South African history, was its proximity to the experience of the pogroms that were playing out in the heartlands of the so-called civilised world. The Jewish question was not simply a theoretical issue of which Marxists everywhere had to have some grasp. It was visceral. People in the Lenin Club had personal experience of it. It was what essentially brought Goodlatte around from being an anti-Semite, said Hirson, to being a deeply worldly human being conscious of her privilege and positionality.[67] The Lenin Club was where Dora Taylor and Tabata met; many other members built up long-lasting comradely relationships.

When the split happened, the majority merged with the Bolshevist Leninist League to form the WPSA in 1935. The others formed the Communist League of South Africa, which would later call itself FIOSA.[68]

The differences between the WPSA and FIOSA, explains Drew, 'boiled down to one of emphasis on the nature and degree of peasant consciousness amongst the rural population and the degree of black proletarian development'.[69] The debate between the two groups pivoted on the relationship between consciousness and social structure. Interestingly, in both camps there was a privileging of class over colour. What divided them was the issue of how to work with the different manifestations of consciousness evident within the oppressed; uniting them was their commitment, in the beginning, to a two-stage theory of revolution. First there needed to be an anti-imperialist struggle; the socialist revolution would follow.

Following their engagements with Trotsky, both groups would shift.[70] The WPSA modified its position over the next decade towards a permanentist revolution approach based on a transitional programme. In this transitional programme land was central. Both groups, however, continued to argue for the inclusion of white workers in the struggle for the realisation of socialism. As Drew explains, neither side followed the Trotskyist International's recommendations for unity.[71] They collaborated in the attempt to build united fronts in the experience of the NLL and again with the Non-European United Front (NEUF), but they worked independently of each other, setting up parallel structures and forums. Significantly, it was the WPSA that would advance the debate around race. The FIOSA group would continue to work with the idea of race, right up until the 1950s, in its hegemonic register.

A leading figure in FIOSA was Moshe Noah Averbach, who came from Europe via Palestine. He owned a grocery shop in District Six and started out as a member of the CPSA. He joined the Lenin Club in 1932 and when it split was influential in establishing the Communist League of South Africa (CLSA) and then FIOSA. In 1944 he wrote the 'Historical Basis for the Programme of the Fourth International organisation of South Africa', which provided a detailed explication of the political and social analysis of FIOSA. Central to this document was the theory of 'Uneven Development', but more pertinent for the purposes of this analysis is its implicit acceptance of race. It referred to 'tribal divisions', but did not suggest that there was an interest in questions of race formation.[72]

Also in the leadership circle, Hirson notes, were Charlie van Gelderen and, later, Jack Meltzer, Max Blieden and Bernhard Herzberg, 'who edited the group's paper . . . When the League reassembled . . . several younger persons joined . . . Arthur Davids was an early recruit, Zeid Gamiet entered at a later date and Hosea Jaffe joined in 1939. The younger members, together with Averbach, were the mainstay of the group during the war years.'[73]

FIOSA had passing through it some of the most gifted organisers in South Africa's history. Among them was Ralph Lee (originally named Raphael Levy and sometimes called Raff), who established the Workers' International League in 1944, which was largely responsible for what was, possibly, the upsurge of black trade union militancy in 1945–1946.[74] From its ranks would come, later, significant theoreticians such as Kenny Jordaan, who was born in 1924 and who became a member of the NEF. They established the Forum Club in the early 1950s after the Suppression of Communism Act was passed in 1950.[75] Relationships between the CPSA and other communists in the 1930s rallied around the necessity to challenge the Representation of Natives Bill and the Native Trust and Land Bill.

It was in response to the proposed four Hertzog Bills that the first attempts in the country to forge alliances around the principle of a 'united front' were made. The bills were designed to remove people classified African from the voters' roll in the Cape, to establish a natives' representative council, to develop the provisions of the 1913 Land Act, and to abolish the access of people classified 'coloured' to the franchise.

The All-African Convention (AAC) and the NLL were set up in 1935 and then, in a later attempt at a united front, in 1939 the NEUF was formed. The AAC and the NLL were both multi-class and multi-party alliances. There were two streams of thought in the AAC – the boycott-ers, led by the WPSA, and the negotiators, who sought some form of par-ticipation in the structures proposed by Hertzog. The AAC foundered on the basic question of participation in the Native Representative Council. The CPSA, by 1937, supported this orientation.

The NLL brought together Stalinists and anti-Stalinists, who were more radical. What differentiated them, which became determinative, were their views on collaboration with the instruments of the ruling class. It distinguished Stalinists from those with Trotskyite sympathies and Trotskyite relationships. The anti-Stalinists, following a line taken in the WPSA and influenced by a 1935 letter from Trotsky, decided that the AAC offered 'an opportunity to apply the method of work-ing class struggle'.[76] They deliberately entered the AAC with the idea that they could influence its direction. As Lewis has argued, they 'tried unsuccessfully to urge a policy of non-collaboration on the AAC'.[77] This was the first articulation of the strategy of boycott: 'The coin-cidence of class and colour suggested to South African Trotskyists that black united fronts could form the basis for a revolutionary alli-ance of workers and peasants. In this racial society, where the white bourgeoisie prevented the extension of full democratic rights to all, many socialists, especially Trotskyists, argued that the struggle against class collaboration would take the form of non-collaboration and political boycott.'[78]

The entry into the AAC was deeply important for the Cape Radicals of the NEF. It offered them the first real opportunity, outside of Cape Town, to explore the significance and challenges of working in a united front. Tabata was delegated as the WPSA's major representative, supported by Goolam Gool. They soon found that they had to struggle against entrenched nationalism inside the AAC.[79] Trouble came to a head when the leadership of the AAC, led by the ANC, was 'to interview the Government, and the "Compromise", as it was called, was hatched. This "compromise" was to have "Native" voters elect three "white persons" to parliament, there to represent "the Natives" in the House of Assembly of 152 members.' This the NEF's colleagues described as the beginning of 'dummy parliamentary representation'.

The NEF did not completely abandon the AAC but, their position having been defeated and their attempt at entry having failed, a period of wariness followed. They worked hard to turn the NLL into a political alternative to the existing conservative structures such as the APO and the ANC. The trouble was that the CPSA had the same intentions for the NLL and as a result the NLL foundered. It fell apart over a dispute between the Stalinists and the anti-Stalinists about ways of engaging the working class. The Stalinists, led by Johnny Gomas, wanted to take a populist line while the anti-Stalinists, led by Goolam Gool, argued that education 'was a precondition for the development of popular political consciousness'.[80] It was this position, that of educating the masses, that caused the NEF-aligned members of the NLL to be criticised as being purists.

At moments, particularly in 1937, when Goolam Gool and Gomas were able to lead the organisation, the NLL contained elements of what a left-wing popular party could become. It was instrumental in the establishment of a number of trade unions. It published a popular newsletter, the *Liberator*, which urged black working-class unity and attacked imperialism. It focused criticism on the APO. It was the eclipse of Gool and Gomas by the CPSA, led by Cissie Gool and supported by Sam Kahn and Harry Snitcher, that took the NLL into the collaborationist trajectory and saw members of the NEF walking away.

Naz Gool Ebrahim attributed the split in the NLL to ideological divisions between Cissie Gool and James La Guma and Goolam Gool. Ebrahim said that they 'were expelled for removing documents, files and records from the League's offices. La Guma explained that his section of the League wanted to debar Europeans from holding office in the group. Cissie opposed the idea. Later, the expelled members became the chief instigators for the foundation of the Non-European Unity Movement in the 1940s.'[81]

In the NEF's view, the NLL was no different from the APO. While it continued to promote boycotts and strikes – in March 1939, for example, the NLL and the NEUF mounted one of the largest protests Cape Town had ever seen when it mobilised almost 15 000 people 'for the emancipation of all non-Europeans' – it also continued with the APO tradition of leading deputations to the authorities, gathering petitions and putting its weight into the local elections.[82]

In bringing the significance of the backdrop against which the NEF operated into perspective it is important to recognise the core issues of contention between the socialists. One of these was populism versus more challenging ways of engaging the working class. The criticism of this position was its implied suggestion of superiority. Lewis says that this earned the NEF the pejorative label 'the purists'.[83] He referred to an article in the *Sun*, which, inaccurately it turns out, generated the observation that members of the NEF saw their work as being that 'of the more advanced members of the community, [doing work] for the benefit of those less mature'.

Underpinning this debate was a deeper question: the nature and character of hegemony. The approaches taken were not worked into clear positions during this period, but they were already beginning to take form. In understanding the NEF and what it would become, it is important to note that there were individuals in this early discussion who were beginning to ask questions about class and how class worked. Why, they were asking, did the white working class not understand the objective reality of their own oppression?

The question of 'consciousness' was central in the evolving thinking in the left movement around understanding the social. It was an issue that saw Goolam Gool take one position and Johnny Gomas another. An entirely new approach to race was beginning to germinate. Gomas intuitively rejected race, but was less interested in how it worked. Gool, on the other hand, was stimulated by the question at a profound level. He was beginning to understand how racial consciousness worked and coming around to the view that it was a social construct, something that was produced deliberately to divide people for the purposes of maintaining hegemony. Race was a construction of capitalism. But, and this is important to emphasise, neither he nor the people around him connected the idea of race as a social construction with the urgency of explaining how race as an idea was actually implemented. He and his colleagues could see that it was a divisive move on the part of the ruling class. Now they had the insight that it was artificial, a thing, something human beings had made up. What they were not yet able to do was elaborate it conceptually. It was not yet a proper theory of how society came to produce and reproduce it. The full complexity of the social eluded their grasp.

So here were the two most critical organic intellectuals of their day beginning to outline the positions that would emerge a great deal more clearly among the intellectual-activists who would come in their wake. Gomas, as Doreen Musson says, chose the path at this moment of remaining inside in the CPSA. Anxious as he was about a shift to the right in the CPSA with its support of the Natives Representative Council, he believed it offered greater opportunity for building the unity of oppressed.[84] It was Gool who was opening up the hegemony discussion much more clearly. The stance he took was signalled in a statement the NLL made at its founding in 1937:

> The National Liberation League of South Africa identifies itself with the convictions and aspirations of the South African peoples, more especially the non-Europeans, and determines to realise those convictions and aspirations.
>
> It declares in direct opposition to all assertions concerning an alleged 'civilizing' mission of the imperialist nations.
>
> In opposition to all assertions concerning the alleged superiority of certain races and peoples.
>
> It declares that no natural or social superiority or subordination exists within the human race and that any such superiority or subordination is inadmissible.[85]

This NLL statement was written in the racial discourse of the time, but in and of itself it was extremely important. It referred to 'certain races' and was in this respect reflective of what one might call a 'multi-racial' perspective. What it succeeded in doing in the process was to open up the question of race through the invocation of the idea of the 'human race'.[86]

The documentation that is available is not sufficiently strong to find direct genealogical lines of descent, but it can be surmised that the the rise of racial theorisation in Nazi Germany was the backdrop to this statement. This discussion was taking place in the socialist movement at that time. A report by Johnny Gomas in the *South African Worker* of 17 April 1937 on the NLL's activities indicates this: 'Bearing in mind the atrocities committed upon the people of Africa by the imperial nations, and in particular the sufferings of the non-European people under [the] former German colonial Government, and *in view of racial theories propagated by the Hitler Nazi regime*, this Congress is in determined opposition to any intention . . . to return mandated territories or colonies to the German government.'[87]

The issue was about the mandated territories but it is also evident from this extract that there was in the NLL a realisation that the racial question needed to be theorised to counter the thinking that was dominating European political life and intellectual thought. An antecedent had come from Abdurahman: 'In 1926, APO President, Abdullah Abdurahman . . . had denounced the Pact government's policies as based on unscientific race theories.'[88]

Material in this thinking in 1937, and many of the statements of the left into the 1940s would show this, was the idea of human beings belonging to distinct groups. South Africa, the NLL stated in a document on 'how to work among urban Africans', consisted of 'three distinct groups: the Coloured, the Indian and the African'.[89] It went further: 'The three of them differ in custom, tradition and cultural development. The African, the least developed of the three, is by far the largest.' In this it is apparent that the thinking was still some way from being clearly articulated. Bunche was obviously not aware how people such as Gool and Gomas were thinking against the grain when he made this note: 'The National Liberation League is not yet clear in its thinking – much of membership still thinking in terms of special status for coloured. Many now hope for development of non-European business as a way out.'[90]

As this NLL statement indicates, the differences between groups within society, 'races', as they might be described, were social and cultural, but they were all equal: 'It [the NLL] declares that no natural or social superiority or subordination exists within the human race.'[91] Powerful about this moment was its instinctive antibiological logic. It was a moment of extraordinary precocity. Cedric Dover's book *The Myth of Race*, which Gomas would come to know, would appear two years later, in 1939.[92] In it Dover would provide, cogently, an argument against the idea of race.

The NEF's leaders might not have been articulating the point about race with clarity yet, but almost nowhere else in the world at that time was there anything rivalling the insight the drafters of that statement displayed. This historiographical fact cannot be emphasised enough.

From the mainstream of science two of the world's leading thinkers on the question of race were Julian Huxley and A C Haddon. In their book *We Europeans* (1935) the idea that 'Europeans could be divided meaningfully into distinct races' was considered.[93] Haddon pushed the argument harder and introduced the idea 'of the pseudo-science of racial biology', but demurred when it came to thinking of differences between white and black people. Huxley said, in 1932: 'There is also certain evidence that the negro is an earlier product of evolution than the Mongolian or the European, and as such might be expected to have advanced less, both in body and mind.'[94]

Where Gomas and Gool were taking their thinking from cannot be definitively determined but, as Bruce Baum tells us, there was Hogben in 1931, just some months after having left South Africa because he could no longer tolerate the racialised environment in which he found himself, explaining: 'Geneticists believe that anthropologists have decided what race is.[95] Ethnologists assume that their classifications embody principles which genetic science has proved correct . . . We have very little justification for assuming a close approximation to genetic purity when we define a group of human beings by a large and heterogeneous assemblage of physical traits.'[96]

The point is that the intellectual environment of the Cape Town left, spearheaded by the formidable personage of Claire Goodlatte, a missionary to her core, and the talent of the Gools, who were profoundly aware of how racism had affected their own lives, had available to it the most advanced thinking on race and genetics at that time. Hogben had left already, but his anti-eugenics theories had lit a fuse among these Cape Town intellectuals. It took them the next 20 years to translate Hogben's social biology into political theory. In the course of getting there they first had to find the evidence and also the appropriate platform. The space provided by the NEF would make that possible.

3 | 'Anything under the Sun': The Formation of the New Era Fellowship

The precise origins of the New Era Fellowship (NEF) are, to all intents and purposes, lost in time. The records of the inaugural meeting that gave rise to the organisation are not available. If there were minutes taken at the meeting, unfortunately these have not been located. Who was present, what they said and what they intended is not known to us. There are, however, a few documents and oral histories that give one a sense of the beginning years. These can be tracked, largely, through announcements and reports that appeared in the *Cape Standard*; we also have the personal testimonies of people such as Dick Dudley and Alie Fataar.

According to Allison Drew, the NEF was 'a radical discussion and debating society which was formed by Goolam Gool in 1937 which ran until the late 1960s. It met at the Stakesby-Lewis Hostel and in the Fidelity Hall on the edge of District Six in Cape Town.'[1] Dudley, who was not present personally at the establishment of the NEF, but who would have arrived on the scene shortly afterwards, described the NEF's origins as being in the National Liberation League (NLL): 'The Goolam Gool, Tabata and Kies branch [of the NLL] started the New Era Fellowship in 1937.'[2] Baruch Hirson puts it more directly, writing that the NEF 'was formed in 1937 by Gool', who 'was a member of the All-African Convention (AAC), and was associated together with other members or sympathisers of the Workers Party of South Africa

(WPSA), with the New Era Fellowship.'[3] He describes it as comprising a 'nucleus of students and members of existing Cape organisations'. Names mentioned as early members in various sources include Sidney George Maurice,[4] a teacher and, at one time, principal of Trafalgar High School, Ben Kies, Hawa Ahmed (the pseudonym of Halima Gool), Willem van Schoor and Solly Edross.[5] By 1940, when Dudley first came to NEF lectures, Gool was the chairman, Kies his vice and Hawa Ahmed the secretary. Yunus Omar has an insightful description from Fataar of the role that Goolam Gool played:

> I learnt from him . . . in the very instance because he was the kind of person who would find the individual, the young person that he wants to work with, and I happened to be one of them. There were others around but he didn't get through . . . they didn't get through to him or he didn't get through to them. But that group of six were all Goolam Gool: Ben Kies; Solly Edross, who was a teacher at Trafalgar . . . he had a marvellous brain; he was a teacher of math – he came from Cape Town University; then Winston Layne, primary school teacher at Chapel Street . . . he and Frank Grammer at Livingstone, Solly Edross and Ben Kies at Trafalgar, and then afterwards Fowler who came from Kimberley to Livingstone, he was one of them. And then we had George Meissenheimer who was also at Trafalgar.[6]

Sarah Mokone provides a useful contextualisation of some of the debates that were circulating about the establishment of the NEF: 'This open forum was the form finally agreed to after an initial suggestion that the Non-European students at the University of Cape Town should form their own Non-European organisation had been effectively criticised and rejected as a voluntary acceptance of segregation.'[7]

What is less clear is exactly where the direction for the establishment of the NEF came from. It could have been from Gool himself, one of the 'Three Musketeers', as he, Jane Gool and Isaac Tabata were at times referred to ('all for one and one for all'). It could have come from the NLL, although the likelihood of this is small, given its united front nature. The WPSA presents itself as a more likely source, given its nature as a vanguard party, holding its members to a code of conduct and expecting of them a commitment to a regime of intellectual rigour. Interestingly, Drew, in *South Africa's Radical Tradition*, has a letter from the WPSA written in the first person by an unnamed author.[8] The letter, dated 4 March 1937, is to Goolam Gool and in it Gool is told how he could conduct himself in the NLL: 'We must distinguish between members of the Party and members of the Club, the former being under stricter obligations than the latter ... we who are members of the Party do not bind ourselves to any action taken by the Liberation League. But we leave you a clear field in the League, hoping that you will work within it for the Fourth International.' It is probable that Claire Goodlatte was its author; at the time she was secretary of the WPSA. The reference to the Fourth International is itself interesting, signalling that the break between the WPSA and the grouping that would become Fourth International of South Africa (FIOSA) had not yet hardened. That the writer refers to the 'Fourth International' and not the WPSA suggests that the name the 'WPSA' had not yet solidified.

Another document, undated, from the WPSA says: 'Comrade Dr Gool was permitted by the Spartacus Club to accept the Presidency of the Liberation League.'[9] Driving the WPSA at that time, according to Hirson, were Yudel Burlak, Claire Goodlatte and Paul Koston, who owned a bookshop called Modern Books. Goodlatte was its secretary until late 1937.[10]

A small curiosity about the ways in which these structures worked might be referenced here. Where the locus of authority for the discipline of the comrades lay and where decisions were actually taken is somewhat unclear. This has some significance in thinking about the reasons behind the establishment of the NEF and how it would operate. In the pen of the unnamed writer cited above, Goodlatte it must be assumed, Goolam Gool was given permission by the Spartacus Club to go into the NEF. The Spartacus Club, as a successor to the Lenin Club, was a structure for 'political debate . . . and intense theoretical discussion'.[11] It was not the WPSA itself. Given the small numbers of people involved and their common membership and participation in different organisations, it may be that what in contemporary parlance is described as 'mission drift' had taken place. Or it may have simply been that the comrades wearing their multiple organisational hats took a decision in one forum, which they allowed to stand for what should have taken place in another. This was evident, for example, when a political decision was taken in a Spartacus Club meeting, which, properly, should have been taken in a meeting of the WPSA. The minutes of the WPSA for 24 July 1936 in Johannesburg read as follows: '. . . a small group discussed in the Spartacus Club the agitation for equal franchise rights for Africans. Those present formed a committee to meet on Saturday week.'[12]

Why the NEF was established when there was already a Spartacus Club is also an interesting question. The reason may have been that the Spartacus Club was strictly under the leadership and direction of the WPSA. The Johannesburg branch of the WPSA drove the Spartacus Club intensely. The minutes of a meeting held on 3 April 1936 reported that 'attendance at the Spartacus Club was improving. Com Gosani would lecture next Wednesday evening on "Bantu Woman's Place in Politics". It was decided that Dunbar be invited to lecture on "War", also Findlay, Danchen, B. Sachs (on "Trotsky, man, thinker, revolutionary"), Ballinger (on the Future of the Native Worker), FAW Lucas, De Moore.'[13]

The WPSA decided what the Spartacus Club would and would not do. It also had responsibility for the publication of *The Spark*, which was produced on a monthly basis and was unmistakably the propaganda outlet for the WPSA.[14] The Spartacus Club, in these terms, was a direct political arm of the WPSA. It belonged to the WPSA. When it came to the NEF this appeared to be less the case.

The 1939 constitution of the NEF is helpful in understanding this possible difference. The first significant feature is what it stipulated in relation to membership: 'Membership: Shall be open to all persons satisfying the Fellowship as their sympathy with aims specified under clause 3 (i)'.[15] This clause stated: 'Members shall be pledged to fight, both within the Fellowship and in their private capacity, for (a) the spread of enlightenment with regard to matters political, educational and religious; (b) the unity of the oppressed peoples of South Africa, both European and Non-European, for the removal of racial and class prejudices.'[16] The constitution went on to say that the scope of the fellowship would 'include lectures by competent members or non-members, debates and the formation of Study Circles, public meetings, social events such as dances, social evenings, musical evenings, smoking concerts and sporting activities.'[17]

With respect to its formation, as opposed to where it may have ended up, the NEF clearly saw itself as more than simply an arm of a political movement. Its first membership requirement was a commitment to 'enlightenment' in 'matters political, educational and religious'. The constitution or standing orders of the Spartacus Club are not available but the objectives of the NEF, while clearly political, were not those of a political party. Members were not required to be card-carrying members of the WPSA.

One needs to be aware of the distinct cultural politics of Cape Town in the 1930s for an understanding of why the NEF came to be. The idea of fellowships and cultural societies – forums for social and cultural development – in the broader society was very popular at the time and social and cultural clubs were springing up all over the area. An example was the Cape Debating and Literary Society, which was formed at the Stakesby-Lewis Hostel in 1932.[18] In 1939 the Archbishop of Cape Town presided over a celebration to mark the hostels' 25th anniversary and to recognise the important part they played in the social life of Cape Town.

The pervasiveness of the culture of both segregation and racial identity can be demonstrated in that the Stakesby-Lewis hostels in Canterbury and Harrington streets, buildings alongside one another, had two entrances, two sections and two managers – 'Coloured' and 'Bantu'. Public meetings were held in the larger restaurant in the Canterbury hostel, which could seat 100 people and was ideal for meetings, lectures and discussions. In the 1938/9 year, as reported in the *Cape Standard* on 14 November 1949, '306 Coloured people had received accommodation at Canterbury Street and 506 Natives at Harrington Street where Tabata stayed. Prof. Jabavu and other well-known leaders would lodge there when visiting town.'[19] Segregation at the hostels was taken for granted. That this practice prevailed and was simply accepted, even as the NEF grew, indicates how entrenched it was.

Just how controversial the question of the cultural life of the subordinate classes of Cape Town was during the 1930s is also relevant here. Within the political community there was a great deal of disquiet with respect to popular and everyday social and leisure practices. Much of this centred on the question of what was appropriate behaviour and what appropriate forms of recreation and leisure activity for the working people of Cape Town should be. The question of the minstrels, for example, was a heated issue. So, too, was sport, especially soccer, rugby and cricket.

Sport was a central part of the cultural life Cape Town. It was a major outlet for people's recreation and many traditions ran deep. Some of the oldest football clubs in the country were established in Cape Town during the period immediately after the First World War.[20] Teams such as Young Men's Own, Sea Point Swift and East End were set up through religious networks and by influential families and individuals. In 1918 the Church Lads Brigade Football League was established.[21]

A number of associations were formed and competitive leagues grew and strengthened. In the middle of the 1930s these associations were beginning to experience the first signs of the deep segregation that was to come in the next few decades. In 1936 the City Council of Cape Town refused black people permission to use playing fields they had used for many years. Green Point Common was one of these, a ground that had been used by black people from as far back as the late 1800s. They were forced to play at a field allocated to them at Rosmead grounds in Kenilworth.[22]

It is pertinent here to acknowledge how racialised attitudes were to playing and organising sport. Clubs organised themselves in accordance with the dominant discourse of the time, which facilitated the emergence of whites-only leagues and associations into separate African, coloured and Indian leagues. From about 1950 these associations' racial characters were challenged, largely as a result of the prompting of intellectuals associated with the NEF. They would later move even further and take the lead in the establishment of the South African Council on Sport, which had non-racial sport as its first order of business.

The Cape Radicals recognised how important sport was to social development. Marcus Solomon, a Robben Island prisoner, recalled how Cosmo Pieterse, his teacher at Trafalgar High School, insisted that his students should build both their mental faculties and their physical talents: 'It's not just about education. It's about socialisation. Cosmo made me run at school. These chaps . . . they realised what was significant in a person's life.'[23]

The world of aesthetics was a great deal more contentious. While sport was recognised as a social necessity, music, drama and art were approached with more seriousness. The young members of the NEF, as socialists, took the arts deeply seriously. They mattered in terms of the development of consciousness. What one did in one's leisure time preoccupied them intently. A significant event of the WPSA, for example, was the performance, in Cape Town, of a play entitled *The Spark* at the Oddfellows Hall in Loop Street, on 6 November 1937.[24] The script of the play indicated deep Brechtian influences, and it spoke directly to the political situation in the country. The struggle for the land and issues of race and identity featured strongly. As in the international socialist genre of popular theatre, music underpinned the performance. Inevitably, *The Internationale* brought the production to a close.

It was not strange, as a consequence then, that the leaders of the socialist movement watched cultural developments around them with a beady eye. They were aware of the large role and presence of music and performance in people's lives. They were aware of the different and multiple forms and genres of singing and performing – the Christmas bands, the Malay choirs and, of course, the minstrels. It was the latter that disturbed them most. The Coons, as the minstrel culture came to be described, was, for them, offensive. The New Year Carnival was an especially controversial feature of this history.

Several letters and columns appeared in the *Cape Standard* during the late 1930s and early 1940s criticising the minstrels. In 1940 a letter appeared written by a person who described himself as 'Coloured Student'. He said:

> 'Don't I like Coons?' you ask. No. Positively and emphatically not. I dislike them. If the term is not too strong, I detest them. How any body of persons can spend weeks, perhaps months, preparing costumes, rehearsing songs, organising on a large scale in order to appear at a certain date, and for the benefit . . . of the general public, perform a series of gyrations and other writhing and threshing movements more suited to a snake when its head is firmly held . . . is beyond me.[25]

'Coloured Student' continued to express his disgust with the hermaphroditic – 'moffie' – intimations of the minstrels' performance but raised most forcefully the question of their degradation of 'coloured' people's dignity. They were presenting themselves in 'primitive' forms. The white people watching, he said, 'inwardly I am sure . . . feel disgusted at the coloured people's primitiveness – and those who don't feel disgusted at it feel pleased with it . . . so many Europeans do not wish the Coloured people to grow out of the Coon stage of primitiveness.'[26]

The New Year events were extremely popular all the same. Shamil Jeppie points out that 'at two venues in 1942, more than 15,000 people turned up to watch the coon troupes perform. The hardship of the war years did not inhibit the spontaneous participation in and admiration of the troupes.'[27]

It was exactly this grip on the popular imagination that led the members of the NEF to work extremely hard to provide alternative stimulation for the people. Amelia Lewis, talking of District Six, says that the intellectuals took their efforts into structures such as the Liberman and Marion institutes, and the Bloemhof and St Mark's community centres: 'The Liberman Institute with its library, crèche, discussion groups, physical education and dancing classes was the nursery for much of the cultural activity which thrived in the area.'[28] Later, into the 1940s and 1950s, 'cultural and intellectual activity' initiatives continued to be seen in the Children's Art Centre and the St Philip's Church Drama Centre. Out of these emerged many of Cape Town's most accomplished musicians, singers and actors. Through these initiatives, as Lewis says, they sought to cultivate the whole child, mentally and physically.[29]

It was not only the socialist cultural workers who inhabited this space, however. Many well-meaning liberal groups were active too. The most visible to emerge in this time was the Eoan Group of opera singers. It had been established in 1933 by Helen Southern-Holt exclusively for 'coloured' people. It came out of her conviction, as Denis-Constant Martin explains in *Sounding the Cape*, that 'coloured' people could realise 'the dawning of a new cultural expansion in themselves and a new understanding of well-being, physical, mental, for their race'.[30] The Eoan Group was racially exclusive. It had 'joyous service', 'middle-class sensibility' and 'purity' as its aims. Southern-Holt had become aware that many coloured women spoke a language she felt was not intelligible to ordinary English speakers and so she laid on elocution classes for them. She was joined by her daughter, a trained ballet dancer, who offered dancing classes to the girls of District Six. They performed with the Cape Town Municipal Orchestra in 1937 and in 1938 a group went to London to take the Royal Academy of Dance examinations.[31]

The Hyman Liberman Institute was established in 1937 as a 'result of a donation by a former Cape Town mayor. It was a centre for "social and cultural upliftment" and a place of "mental recreation" which targeted the working class.'[32] The librarian there was Christian Ziervogel, 'a self-taught man who had originally begun a library for coloured people with his own collection of 3 000 volumes. He complained to Ralph Bunche that the board of the Institute would not let him keep his collection on the shelves of the Institute library because he had "too many dangerous" books.'[33] Ziervogel himself 'was a member of the radical discussion circle, the Fifteen Group'.

All these structures were underpinned and activated by liberal ideals of 'harmonious race-relations'. They were propelled by the Joint Council idea initiated in Johannesburg for building relationships between Africans and Europeans. Joint Councils were needed in Cape Town, it was felt, for relationships between Europeans and 'coloureds'.

In this context of competing influences the NEF and its members gradually began to take for themselves a distinctive role. They felt it was their task to develop and provide forms of education and stimulation that would make no concession to either race or class. Culture was universal. It did not belong to anybody. It could not, in its content, project itself as the distinct legacy or property of any particular group. Opera was not 'white' or the preserve of 'white' people. Neither could it be used, in the ways in which it was pedagogically mediated, to teach racial lessons. Betterment was not, as the liberals of the African People's Organisation (APO) or from the white community were presenting themselves as exemplifying, a process through which racial improvement could be effected.

Access to culture, at its highest levels of expression, was the unconditional right of everybody.

* * *

Critical about this period of cultural societies and discussion forums was
the conjuncture of various elements: Trotskyist ideas about Permanent
Revolution, suspicion of liberalism and a distinct hostility to 'coloured
civility' and its 40-year-long Abdurahmanism all came together in
a tumultuous awareness of what collaboration with the forces of
domination meant. The members of the left-wing community in Cape
Town understood the need for a social and cultural movement that
would proceed from a different set of values and intentions to liberalism.

As Corinne Sandwith insightfully explains, the younger generation
of intellectuals 'took exception to the Eoan Group and to the liberalism
of the emerging cultural societies'.[34] They refused to accept the 'civilisation test' of the liberals. They would come to describe those who collaborated with them as 'quislings' (a term they learnt from the struggle
against Nazism in Norway), and as 'sell-outs' and 'collaborators'.

But this language was yet to come. In the mid-1930s they were still
working these ideas out. As shall be seen, into the late 1930s came people
such as Margaret Ballinger, a person whom they would have treated with a
great deal of suspicion. Ballinger began her political career as an associate
of Clements Kadalie, the pioneer of African trade unionism. She went on to
become a representative of the Natives Representative Council (NRC) in the
middle of the 1930s. What the young leaders of the NEF had a strong sense of,
in the three years before 1940, was that their elders, people such as Ballinger,
had let them down. This was very evident in a key lecture Ben Kies gave on
4 June 1938, 'The Revolt of the Youth'. It embodied the thinking of the
founders of the NEF:

Defeatism and despair are not necessarily the unanimous characteristics of the present day Coloured man, despite the assertions of

the novelist Sarah Gertrude Millin, the statements of the Coloured
Commission Report, and the tacit admittance of all the Coloured
leaders . . . More than anything, [what] is dividing the teacher from
his people is his spurious cult of respectability. His pride in his profession and his new-found dignity and culture make him ashamed
of [the] rough, untutored parents who made his education possible.[35]

The kind of education people were receiving, Kies continued, had only
produced the physical health and discipline necessary for successful ser-
vitude, 'turning out a regular supply of "wages slaves"'.[36] Kies and his
comrades roused a sense of dread in the minds of the older 'coloured'
leadership, who described them as loud, vulgar and uncouth. Helen Kies
recalls the man she first knew as a teacher:

There was one special teacher, whom I married. He didn't teach
me, fortunately. But he was at the school, at Trafalgar. He had one
hell of a reputation as an activist, politico, atheist and all sorts of
things that at the time stamped one as a monster. My father told his
friends that I was going to Trafalgar. They came in a deputation.
'You can't send your daughter to that school. She's going to come
under the influence of Ben Kies. He's an atheist, a Communist.'
I mean all the most shocking things you could think of, you know.
And I married him.[37]

Sandwith, describing the reaction of the conservative members of the
Teachers' League to the young radicals, said they were unsettled by the
young people's bad manners: 'The young radicals shout . . . as if they are
on the verge of nervous breakdowns.'[38] They might have been loud and
vociferous in their passion, but these youths understood the urgency of
re-educating themselves and their elders.

A distinctive feature of the NEF was its structure. It organised lectures and debates but also established what it called 'study circles'. While
these study circles were not the disciplined reading groups the WPSA

would have run, they operated with not much less discipline. Young people, at least in the 1940s, had to be considered for membership of a study circle. Dick Dudley was himself sponsored by an older member. The study circles usually took place on Sunday mornings and lessons were structured. Dudley's description of a lesson by Kies is particularly descriptive:

> Ben Kies walked in with a copy of a newspaper called *The Sun.* There was an announcement that the government was going to set up a special commission to deal with the affairs of the coloured people. He gave us this article and then asked what we felt about it. We made comments, I suppose, which were inconsequential, and then he pointed out the significance of this for us. Now that showed me that if you don't have a system of analysis you can actually read a newspaper and miss completely the actual importance. And well, from that point on, I would say that I don't really know how many stages there were of being made politically conscious, but that was one of the things that I'll never forget that made me leap into this kind of action in understanding things and then deciding what needed to be done These study circles met regularly. It was there that the younger members were taken through a process of intense reading and preparation for the lectures themselves . . . In the study circles there was a structured process of teaching people histori-cal analysis. I think that went through the ways in which history was approached, not merely by the well-known academic, classical Marxists, but we went through the approaches of the seventeenth century English writers, the eighteenth century. And we went through, for example, the work of Hobbes, *The Leviathan*. And then we went on to learn about the teachings of the Hegelians and then Marx.[39]

Senior members of the NEF provided the organisation with its cur-riculum. Reading lists included analysis and critique of capitalism, imperialism, inequality and racism: 'If you were serious then you attended specific study groups with meetings on Sunday mornings, with speakers and discussions from the likes of Goolam Gool, Jane Gool, Isaac Tabata, Saul Jayiya and Alie Fataar who spoke on *Das Kapital*.'[40] Not only were the young participants tutored during these study circles, but they were also subjected to a kind of training in the broad arts of life. Those selected to give talks were taken through practice runs in the study circles. Young scholars and inductees into the thinking of the movement were required to cast their intellectual imaginations as widely as they could but to focus their analytic attention on the explanation of the local. Importantly, at the heart of this analysis was the character of South African society. Rehearsal was not just about getting the content right; it was also about modelling deportment and style. Young members remembered how they were encouraged to speak – the importance of their vocabulary and cadence.[41] Dudley is again an invaluable informant here:

[In] my second year in the study group I was given the chance to speak to the study group. My task was to examine the position of native labour in South Africa. Now we used to sit in a horseshoe shape . . . . And the person who was due to speak would be in the centre so that you faced everybody there. And so you go along there full of yourself and full of this information and so on. You feel that you've done a good job. And then the tutors start taking you apart. You go there thinking that you're Gulliver in Lilliput. You shrink in size but you learn an important lesson, and that is analysis.[42]

The NEF both complemented and countered what the students were learning in their formal experiences at school and university. It became an intense learning space where participants were made both self-aware and socially conscious. This countering feature of the NEF was one of the things that made it unique. While it was intent on countering what students were being taught formally in school, its focus was broader.

It included what people were imbibing informally through the 'uplift-ment' societies like the Eoan Group, which continued to emerge around them. It was the obligation of the educated intellectual, Ben Kies argued in the middle of 1938, to study history, and to make 'objective analysis and, above all, avoid the uncritical acceptance of conventional wisdom (looking with as much suspicion upon a University Professor or a Bishop, as upon a parade monger)'.[43]

The NEF adopted an entirely utilitarian attitude to the University of Cape Town (UCT). It was a place to which its members had to go but they also understood its limitations. Their full and proper education they would find outside in the forums established by the NEF.

The NEF had its beginning as a consequence of the heightened political awareness of the global situation, a discomfort with the existing political leadership and a rapidly evolving preoccupation with consciousness, with the formation of thought. Its essence – which set Goolam Gool apart from Johnny Gomas, leader of the Stalinists in the NLL – was the question of thought. How people understood the world and particularly the world of South Africa was critical for Gool. The consciousness of the person in the street was the NEF"s foremost object of engagement. If it was going to make any difference in the complex setting of social inferiority and superiority it had to make sure that its members were exemplary in their own thinking and bearing. Neither superiority nor subservience was acceptable. Their own consciousness had to manifest that heightened sense of self-awareness they were seeking through the work of the NEF.

The NEF's agenda, as became evident in its lectures, talks and debates, did not suddenly arise and take shape fully formed. It took a number of years for it to develop what became a formidable programme of public education, which had thinking deeply and thinking critically at its heart. This focus was not there at the beginning. It would come. It came through an intense process of clearing of the ground. Keith Breckenridge's metaphor of the 'culture-bed' is apposite here.[44] What was obvious to the founders of the NEF was that a seed bed had to be prepared. How it should be prepared and what should be cultivated in it, however, was by no means clear. That it should sustain a new world was understood. But what would sustain this new world – what would be good for it – was still to be worked out.

The NEF went through three phases. The first, after its establishment in 1937, can be described as the clearing of the ground phase. The next five years, from about 1943 to the end of the 1950s, saw a period of intense thinking around strategy, tactics and analysis. This was the period of conceptual clarification inside the NEF. The third, from the 1950s, was a phase of theoretical consolidation.

4 | 'Honest, Sincere
and Fearless', 1937–1940

The first few years of the New Era Fellowship (NEF) were self-consciously experimental in their form and substance. Phumi Giyose, a New Unity Movement (NUM) theoretician, describes it, in relation to the role of Ben Kies, as 'an experimental period from 1935 onwards when the upcoming leadership of the Non-European Unity Movement [NEUM] was looking in a rich mine field of political experiences for a theory and organisation praxis'.[1] M M Herries has described it as a 'sorting-house'.[2] This experimentation and 'sorting out' took all of its stimulus from the particular character of the conjuncture – the onset of the Second World War, and the intentions of the South African government to take the franchise away from people classified as 'coloured'. The conjuncture precipitated an intense crisis of social analysis – how to hold together what was going on internationally with what was happening in South Africa. The thesis of the 'Black Republic' was, by itself, inadequate, but it was not immediately apparent what to put in its place. The ground first needed to be cleared. Giyose says that 'maximum programmes from Europe were tried out and got rejected in favour of a minimum programme of democratic demands. Vanguard party formations offered their candidature. These were put aside in favour of a broad national front. Liberalism, Gandhism, nationalism – all these put themselves on offer. They were pushed aside.'[3]

One sees in this experimentation the NEF giving its attention to a wide range of issues in the beginning. The organisation arose in response to the need for clearing the ground with respect to the immediate issues of the socialist struggle and the tactics and strategies of the South African revolution. At that time, as Sarah Mokone explains:

> . . . very many political currents flowed through [the NEF], contributing a wide diversity of political outlooks, attitudes and approaches . . . There was the initial nucleus – the group of UCT [University of Cape Town] students – and then there were people from every political grouping: These included young members of the TLSA [Teachers' League of South Africa] dissatisfied with the Van der Ross-F. Hendricks bureaucracy. There were also elements from around the APO [African People's Organisation] increasingly sceptical of Abdurahmanism. And even Abdurahman himself on occasion went to the NEF to teach youngsters their place.[4]

What made the period so experimental? For a start the ground-clearing phase was in itself politically challenging. The founding of the national Workers' Party of South Africa (WPSA) had been an important organisational development. That it did not have a real public presence was a matter of some contention. Some members noted: 'The Workers Party in Cape Town was highly, if not overly selective, maintained a tight discipline, and was secretive in many of its inner party activities.[5] There were rules as to what documents could be read at branch meetings, and what was to be read only by Executive members. It was a regime that led to derisive comments from members of the League.'[6]

The Cape Town members of the WPSA came to this position through some debate and taking prevailing conditions into consideration. They judged, perhaps incorrectly, conditions on the ground to be too hostile.

Taking a public presence as Trotsky advised, they believed, was not appropriate under conditions of political crisis: 'A certain part, and by the way a very important part, of the work cannot be carried out openly, that is before the eyes of the class enemies . . . Nobody, of course, is proposing to create an illegal apparatus for such functions as in the given conditions can be executed by legal organs.'[7] The NEF was one such legal organ. The question that absorbed the WPSA's attention – how to prepare South Africa for real revolutionary struggle – was the challenge that would come to define what the NEF would define as its programme of work. Many members of the NEF, at least those who were operating under the clandestine aegis of the WPSA, would have had ringing in their ears the implicit admonitions of the International Secretariat of the Communist League about being careful about the founding of a revolutionary party. The remarks of Comrade Du Bois (the pseudonym taken by Ruth Fischer) in a 1935 letter to the Communist League of South Africa and the WPSA were trenchant and, indeed, as Hirson said, controversial – he described the criticisms as 'crude and insensitive'. But the central message of this correspondence with Du Bois was that serious theoretical work had to be done.[8] This was to stay with the NEF – theory, theory, theory.

The correspondence between Trotsky and the founders of the WPSA is deeply interesting. It would lead, many years later, to Hosea Jaffe posing questions about Trotsky's positions on race.[9] He would, on more than one occasion, remark that these positions were deeply problematic. Trotsky's support for the Black Republic thesis, South African Trotskyists would argue, was flawed. It was based on the same argument that Trotsky would make for an independent Black Republic in the middle of the United States of America. He was criticised for understanding neither the state of capitalism nor the sociology of race and ethnicity.[10] Jaffe was unsparing in his criticism of Trotsky who, in his letter to the WPSA of 20 April 1935, wrote of 'the relations between the two races' and of the struggle 'to help the Negroes to catch up to the White race in order to ascend hand in hand with them to new cultural heights'.

These concepts, said Jaffe, were 'quite alien to the pre-NEUM New Era Fellowship founded in 1937 in Cape Town'. He declared that Marx, among the Marxists, was an exception: 'Race-blind, [Marx] merely used "race" for "nation", as was common usage.'[11]

* * *

The NEF's leaders would have recognised that they were venturing into a demanding minefield. Not only were they attempting to break new ground theoretically, but, simultaneously, they were building a movement. The times were fraught. In the immediate foreground was the declining health of Claire Goodlatte. Until then, Hirson says, 'almost all the work [in Cape Town] was conducted by Burlak, Koston and Goodlatte. They handled the mail with the groups in the US, UK and Australia . . . It was an overwhelming load, but there were no full time party workers, and no indication that other members assisted in any substantial way.'[12] Almost in the blink of an eye, then, the leadership of the movement was passed on to the younger generation of black leaders – the most prominent of these being Goolam Gool, Ben Kies and Isaac Tabata.

Not all the resources, material or intellectual, the NEF needed in order for it to develop its own agenda were readily to hand. Comrades would have had the words, as Giyose points out, of established revolution theory, and these would have helped.[13] But at the same time much more thinking was needed. The issue for the WPSA, following an interchange of letters with Trotsky, was, as Trotsky put it in his 'Remarks on the Draft Theses of the Workers' Party', 'not . . . with the programme itself but rather with the ways and means of carrying this programme to the consciousness of the native masses'.[14] How to understand and work with consciousness became the central question for the young activist-intellectuals of the NEF.

Clearing the ground required the new leadership to think both globally and locally. Responding to the global was, in some ways, easier. There were frequent messages and words of advice from comrades in the Fourth International about what was going on around the world. Herman van Gelderen gave a lecture on 'The Invasion of Poland' on 18 November 1939.[15] For its inaugural lecture the NEF chose an address by Willem P van Schoor on the subject of 'Imperialism'.[16] With the assistance of international colleagues, the NEF would return regularly to issues and challenges for socialism on the global front.

Van Schoor and his comrades had access to and engaged in the publication of *The Spark*, which had begun with the establishment of the WPSA in March 1935 and, by the time the NEF was established in 1937, it had put together and published over 200 articles on the global struggle against capitalism. Although it did provide some commentary on the 'Native Bills', its focus was largely on the international situation. It carried incisive description and analysis of what was happening in fascist Spain and the Stalinist Soviet Union and offered the latest commentary to be found on the liberation struggles in China, India and elsewhere in the world. As a source for the history of the NEF *The Spark* is surprisingly empty. There is almost nothing in it for the period between 1935 and the end of 1937, when the NEF was established, relating either to the NEF or the debates it hosted.

Because of the strong emphasis on the global, the NEF had less to work with with respect to the local situation. It would have to develop its own distinctive approach and theory. The advice of the international theoreticians, including Trotsky, was not always entirely appropriate. As Jaffe has remarked: 'One side of Trotsky's thinking was rejected by the [All-African Convention's] AAC's "Trotskyists" – his acceptance of the existence of races and hence of the "Black Republic" (and equally of a separate "Negro State" in the USA, which was also CI [Communist International] policy).'[17]

Working out what was successful and what was not might have been one of the NEF's starting points. Characteristic of this early approach was that it did what it knew. It provided a diet of the kind that would have been in evidence in many of the other clubs that were in existence in Cape Town. Many of the early regular Saturday night events could as easily have taken place under the auspices of any of the other clubs and societies where lectures on all kinds of topics flowed. These events would have been watched with a keen eye by the rising community of intellectuals in Cape Town as the NEF began to host its own. It would not have got its initiatives right every time, of course – as is shown by an anonymous letter written by 'Bored' to the *Cape Standard* in March of 1939: 'The level of the New Era Fellowship discussion last Friday night was far below their average. Interruptions and personal remarks were many.'[18]

Nevertheless the meetings elicited a great deal of interest and were attended by a cross-section of political figures. At an early meeting of the NEF in June 1938 it hosted, for example, the presidential address of the TLSA. Present on that occasion were leading members of the APO, including Dr Abdurahman, Mr Carlier, Mr L Morley-Turner and Mr D Maurice, all of whom used the opportunity to voice their opinions. That meeting was chaired by a young Ben Kies, still only in his mid-twenties. In the presence of his 'worthy' elders he closed the meeting with the following invocation, which was reproduced in the *Cape Standard* of 7 June 1938:

[We are] appeal[ing] to all thinking young men and women to join the New Era Fellowship, one of the only organisations where they can put forward their views, and have them seriously dis-cussed by men and women as sincere as themselves in a search for a solution of their problems. An organization where graduates, undergraduates, teachers, non-teachers, high school and college students, Native, Coloured and White [meet] on an equal footing. The progressive ideas of the New Era Fellowship should be spread abroad to help clear the muddled thinking of so many of our edu-cated people and break down the many barriers within our ranks. Eventually a practical policy will be reached and practical men and women will be produced, honest, sincere and fearless, who will nail their colours to the mast and keep them there.[19]

These early events were of a diverse nature and the NEF leadership continually tried new things. One of these was the development of the study circles. These – which were not reported on regularly in the newspapers – were the spaces where the intellectual muscle of the NEF was deliberately cultivated. They involved, as is seen below in the sessions run by Dora Taylor and Ben Kies, intense engagements with texts. They constituted opportunities for exposure to the most significant fiction and reference works that were available and the modelling of how one worked with a text critically. They combined polemic and scholarship. Much later, in the 1950s, Taylor would use the opportunity to show how problematic dominant Leavisite decontextualised English literary criticism was and what alternative approaches to critical reading could look like. In the early days patterns for consciousness development were being trialled in these settings.

The *Cape Standard* on 16 May 1939 announced the formation of the NEF Literary Circle and carried the first review (by Kies) of George Bernard Shaw's *Black Girl in Search of God* and one by Mr S Stoddard on Sarah Gertrude Millin's *God's Stepchildren*.[20] Stoddard was the first chairman of the circle and Mr Z Gamiet was its secretary. Kies was a committee member. This announcement also emphasised: 'Membership is open to all interested. Non-members of the New Era Fellowship are also eligible . . . The policy of the circle for the next few months is that members read papers upon various books, fictional and otherwise.'

This experimentation involved a deliberate engagement with the questions of how ideas could be mediated. It was obviously political but it was underpinned by an educational clarity. Consciousness was a learnt quality. It brought to the young leaders of the NEF a clear sense of what it was that they needed to concentrate on.

What did this eclectic programme in these early years look like? For one thing, as suggested above, it was extremely diverse – the 'all things under the sun' description given to it by Jaffe is apt.[21] Topics varied widely in their scope and range. Initially people came together as progressives, communists, liberals and interested parties. They seemed determined to hear each other out and to chart a new way forward. Some were from abroad. While the liberals wanted to build bonds in the community, the members of the NEF wanted their ideas to be spread more widely. Dr Abdurahman was still active at this time and he attended many NEF lectures.

The first lecture, as mentioned above, was given by Van Schoor. Thereafter a regular schedule of activities followed, usually advertised and subsequently reported on in the *Cape Standard*, where debates were often described as 'keen'.

One of the earliest engagements, indicating the direction in which the young leaders wanted to take the NEF, was a debate organised between the Cape Literary and Debating Society and the NEF at the Liberman Institute on 8 November 1937.

An interesting historical coincidence was that 8 November was 'Rose Day', inaugurated in the United Kingdom in 1863 in honour of the arrival of Princess Alexandra of Denmark before her marriage to Edward VII. A parade was held every year on that day in Cape Town, with the proceeds in 1937 going to 'organisations serving the poor'.[22] The *Cape Standard* carried a report about an unusual intervention: 'Mrs N Abdurahman and her daughter Mrs L Gool' deliberately took 'coloured' children into the 'beautiful Rose Day procession of gaily-dressed, laughing European children'. Mrs Abdurahman said: 'My daughter and I immediately collected the children from the street – there are hundreds of them – and with placards hurriedly scrawled, which read: 'US CHILDREN'S DAY', 'WHY ARE WE NEGLECTED?', 'WE WANT TO GO TO SCHOOL' [they joined the parade]. 'It is time Cape Town had an ocular demonstration of this kind.'[23]

The motion on the table at the Liberman Institute that day was 'The non-European intellectuals are pulling their weight in the community'.[24] At issue, essentially, was the question of the 'coloured' political elite and their role in the social development of the 'coloured' community. For the motion were people such as Christian Ziervogel, the librarian at the Liberman Institute, who 'cited the many Coloured organisations that had the interests of the community at heart'. Goolam

NEW ERA FELLOWSHIP.

(Revised Constitution ,

as adopted at a Special General Meeting, on 15th April,I
1939.)

I. NAME: That this Society shall be designated "The New Era Fellowship".

2. MEMBERSHIP: Shall be open to all persons satisfying the Fellowship as to
their sympathy with aims specified under clause 3 (i).

3. SCOPE OF THE FELLOWSHIP:
(i) That members shall be pledged to fight, both within the
Fellowship and in their private capacity, for (a) the spread of enlightenment with regard to matters political, educational and religious; (b) the
unity of the oppressed peoples of South Africa, both European and Non-European, for the removal of racial and class prejudices.
(a) shall include lectures by competent members or non-members, debates
and the formation of Study Circles.(b) shall include public meetings &pamphlets
(ii)that the activities of the Fellowship shall include entertainments
(dances, social evenings, musical evenings, smoking concerts) and sporting
activities.
(iii) That the Fellowship shall make contact with visitors in sympathy
with the aims of the Fellowship specified under clause 3 (i).

4. ADMINISTRATION: (i) That the Executive Committee shall consist of a President, and
a Chairman, Vice-Chairman, General Secreary, Organising Secretary,Treasurer
and additional members representing each Study Circle, not more than one
member to be elected from each Study Circle. All such officers , except the
representatives of the Study Circles, shall be elected at a General Meeting,
shall hold office for one year, and shall be eligible for re-election. The
The representatives of the Study Circles shall be elected by each Study Cirel
e, shall hold office for one year and shall be eligible for re-election.
(ii) That the Annual General Meeting shall be called for the elect
ion of officers, when two duly appointed auditors shall present a financial
statement; two such auditors to be elected from the general members of the N
N.E.F. i.d. outside of the Executive Committee.
(iii) That the Exec. Com. shall call special general meetings at
the request of one-third of the paid-up membership.
(iv) That the Exec. Com. shall meet at least once monthly.
(v) That the nearest whole numbernabove ½ of the total Exec.Com.
shall constitute a quorum for an Exec. Com. meeting and for a general meeting one-third of the paid-up membership.

5. FINANCE:(i) That each member shall be required to, pay an entrance fee of
2/6 in addition to a monthly subscription of 6d., except that Training
College and High School students be exempt from paying the entrance fee.
(ii) Thata all monies shall be left on deposit at the Post Office
(iii) That all duly authorised withdrawals shall require the
signatures of the Chairman and Treasurer.
(iv) That the Study Circles are to be financially independent.
(v) That Study Circles shall be empowered to levy subscriptions.

6. CONSTITUTION:
(i) That any alteration to the constitution shall require a
two-thirds majority of all paid-up members.
(ii) That any such proposed alteration to the constitution shall
be handed in to the General Secretary two weeks before the General Meeting.
(iii) That voting may be effected by proxy.
(iv) That any member who conducts himself or herself in such a
manner as to bring discredit on the Fellowship, shall be liable to suspensio
n or expulsion, such powers tobe vested in a General Meeting, which such
member shall be entitled to attend.

ooooooooooooooooooooooooooooooooooooooooooooo

1

Revised constitution of the New Era Fellowship (NEF), 15 April 1939. This is the earliest
record of its founding principles; the original constitution from the organisation's inception
in 1937 is not available.

Courtesy of the Tabata Collection, UCT Libraries

2
Dr Abdullah Abdurahman (1872–1940), founder of the African People's Organisation
Reprinted with permission of Independent Media

3
Municipal election poster, 1931. The candidate for election, Dr Ismail Abdurahman, was Abdullah Abdurahman's brother.
Courtesy of the Abdurahman Papers, UCT Libraries

4

Above: The Stakesby-Lewis Hostel, Canterbury Street, Cape Town, the site of many of the cultural, social and political activities of the NEF in the late 1930s and the 1940s.

Clipping from The Cape Standard, 12 March 1940. Courtesy of the NLSA

Below: The hostel building in 2018

Photographer Jenny Hallward

5

Baruch Hirson (1921-1999), author of *The Cape Town Intellectuals* and contributor of many articles to *Searchlight South Africa*

Photographer Adine Sagalyn

6

Adv Zainnunisa 'Cissie' Gool (1897-1963), a leader of the National Liberation League and the Non-European Unity Movement. As the representative for District Six she served on the Cape Town City Council from 1938 to 1951. She was the daughter of Abdullah Abdurahman.

Courtesy of the Abdurahman Papers, UCT Libraries

7

Goolam H Gool (1905-1962), medical doctor and one of the founders of the NEF, who served on the executive committee of the All-African Convention. He was also one of the founding members, in 1943, of the Anti-Coloured Affairs Department (Anti-CAD) movement and served for a short time as vice-president of the NEUM. Cissie Gool was his sister-in-law and Abdullah Abdurahman his father-in-law.

Courtesy of the Gool Family Papers, UCT Libraries

8

Janub 'Jane' Tabata (née Gool) (1902-1996), sister of Goolam Gool and, like him, an active political figure in the All-African Convention and the Anti-CAD movement in the 1930s and 1940s. She was also one of the founding members of the NEUM. Banned in 1961 after helping to found the African People's Democratic Union of South Africa, in 1963 she fled to Zambia with her husband, Isaac Tabata.

Courtesy of the Tabata Collection, UCT Libraries

9

Isaac Bangani Tabata (known as I B Tabata) (1909-1990), leading NEUM intellectual and theoretician and author of *The Awakening of the People*

Courtesy of the Tabata Collection, UCT Libraries

10

From left to right: Nathaniel Honono, I B Tabata and Jane Gool. Honono was a founding member of the NEUM having served as a leading member of the Transkei Organised Bodies, an organisation which sought to build unity across colour and political lines in the early 1940s.

Courtesy of the National Heritage and Cultural Studies Centre, University of Fort Hare

11

March for Freedom and Equality, Cape Town 1940. Cissie Gool and Yusuf Dadoo of the
Communist Party of South Africa are in the front row.

Courtesy of the NLSA

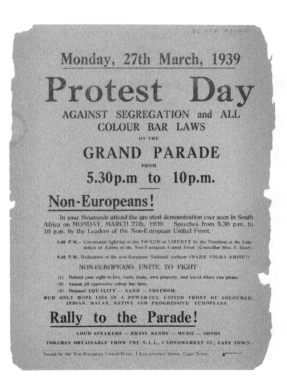

12

Poster advertising a Protest Day on Cape Town's Grand Parade, 27 March 1939. It was one of many protests organised around the formation of the Non-European United Front, which was an attempt to unite different alliances and organisations with one voice against increasingly oppressive and discriminatory laws.

Courtesy of the Abdurahman Family Papers, UCT Libraries

13

Dora Taylor (1899-1976), an immigrant from Aberdeen, Scotland, was a member of the Lenin Club and became an active participant in the cultural life of the NEF in the late 1930s. Her contribution to the field of literary criticism in South Africa was immense and her lectures always well attended.

Courtesy of the Tabata Collection, UCT Libraries

14

Benjamin Magson Kies (1919-1979), activist, lawyer and chairperson of the NEF. He was also one of the founder members of the NEUM.

Reprinted with permission of Independent Media

15

Johnny Gomas (1901-1979), Stalinist, member of the Communist Party of South Africa and a prominent voice in the National Liberation League in the late 1930s. He and Goolam Gool differed over approaches to 'race' and 'class'.

Reprinted by permission of Liz Bracks on behalf of the Gomas family

16

Spring School in Simon's Town, 1950. Among the participants were I B Tabata, Jane Gool, Dora Taylor and Alie Fataar. The schools, organised by the NEF, were political education forums for young people.

Courtesy of the Tabata Collection, UCT Libraries

17

Richard Owen Dudley (1924-2009), legendary educator and mentor of many young activists during a teaching career of almost 40 years, which included the position of deputy principal of Livingstone High School. As a social activist his profound influence and leadership made him a prominent figure in the Teachers' League of South Africa, the NEF, the NEUM and the Anti-CAD movement. He was co-founder of *The Torch* and was made Life President of the New Unity Movement.

Photograph by George Hallett, courtesy of the RO Dudley Papers, UCT Libraries

Non-European Unity Movement

MASS MEETING

HELD UNDER JOINT AUSPICES OF ALL AFRICAN CONVENTION (W.P. COM.),
NATIONAL ANTI-C.A.D. COMMITTEE AND CAPE INDIAN CONGRESS.

TO INAUGURATE

Unity Campaign of all Non-Europeans

FOR FULL CITIZENSHIP RIGHTS !

IN THE

CITY HALL

WEDNESDAY, 26TH JANUARY, 1944

AT 8 P.M.

THEIR PARLIAMENT HAS OPENED!

What does it mean to all Non-Europeans?

Come and Protest Against Further Colour Bar Laws !

1. DEMAND ABOLITION OF PASS LAWS!
2. AWAY WITH THE SEGREGATIONIST COLOURED ADVISORY COUNCIL!
3. DEMAND THE REPEAL OF THE INDIAN PEGGING ACT!

Demand EQUAL RIGHTS in the land of your birth!

Down with Segregation!   Come in your Hundreds!

CHAIRMAN : MR. I. B. TABATA
SPEAKERS :
Messrs. S. A. Jayiya, M. Bangani, J. S. Mbuqe, M. A. Barmania, Abe Desmore, E. C. Roberts, A. Fataar,
E. Ernstzen, C. I. Amra, A. E. Abdurahman, Mrs. Z. Gool, Councillor A. Ismail, Rev. A. J. C. Abrahamse,
Rev. D. Wessels, Rev. E. Jason, Rev. E. A. Lawrence, Dr. G. H. Gool.

Secretary : S. A. Jayiya, 80 Harrington Street, Cape Town.

18

Poster advertising a meeting at Cape Town's City Hall on 26 January 1944, with invitations extended to all to form a united front and campaign against segregation in the country and the laws enforcing it. I B Tabata was in the forefront of the national effort.

Courtesy of the Tabata Collection, UCT Libraries

CAPE ANTI-C.A.D. COMMITTEE

NOTHING LESS THAN FULL CITIZENSHIP
NOTHING LESS THAN 10 PT PROGRAMME

MASS MEETING

IN THE

EAST YORK HALL, 6th AVENUE, KENSINGTON

Tuesday, 8th May, 1945

AT 7.30 P.M.

HEAR ANTI-C.A.D. POLICY & PROGRAMME!

Down with Coloured Locations !

AGAINST RACE-HATRED AND FOR RACE-UNITY

Speakers—Rev. D. M. Wessels,   Mr. E. C. Roberts,
Mr. Duckitt,   Dr. G. H. Gool,   Mr. A. Fataar,
and others.

Secretary: Miss H. Ahmed, Constantia Road, Wynberg.

19

The Anti-CAD movement kept up a rigorous campaign of events, discussions, meetings and protests from its inception in 1943. Just prior to the mass meeting advertised in this poster, on 4 January 1945 in the same banqueting hall Ben Kies had delivered the second of his three key addresses, 'The Basis of Unity'.

Image courtesy of Yunus Omar

UMANYANO LWEZIMA-MHLABA
"UMANYANO YINKULULEKO"

Ingxikela Yentlanganiso
E-BANQUETING HALL (CITY HALL)
E-KAPA
NGE-CAWA 10TH MAY, 1959
ngo - 2 p.m. entloko

● Silwa:
  IZITHANGANA (BANTUSTANS)
  OOMAZIPHATHE NOONDABA-ZEBALA
● Silwa:
  OOSINGA-MFUNDO   NOOSINGA-KHOLEJI
● Silwa:
  AMAPASI NOOMAKATSHA NAMASAKA
★ Sifuna:
  AMALUNGELO OBUNTU APHELELEYO
  IPALAMENTE YABANTU BONKE
★ Sifuna:
  IMFUNDO EFANAYO NELINGANAYO
  KUBANTU BONKE
★ Sifuna:
  INKULULEKO EF EZEKILEYO

Umgcini-siblalo: Dr. A. C. JORDAN
Izithethi:
Mr. W. M. TSOTSI (Umongameli)
Miss J. GOOL
Mr. L. L. SIHLALI (Usiba-lukhulu Wengqungquthela, A.A.C.)
Mr. A. FATAAR (Us ba-lukhulu Wombutho Weetitshala Zebala,
T.L.S.A.
Mr. N. HONONO (Umongameli Wombutho Weetitshala
Zama-Afrika, C.A.T.A.)
Mr. ENVER HASSIM (Unonxhowa Wengqungquthela, A.A.C.)

Ovuke Emini Wofika Kungasekho Ndawo!
Imanywa yi-N.E.U.M., P.O. Box 3475, Cape Town.

20

Invitation in isiXhosa to an event hosted by the NEUM at Cape Town's Banqueting Hall, 1959. Among the speakers listed are Alie Fataar and Jane Gool.

Image courtesy of Yunus Omar

CAPE TEACHERS' FEDERAL COUNCIL
(Cape African Teachers' Association—Teachers' League
of South Africa)
—★—
● Calling all Parents, Teachers and Students to
A PROTEST
MEETING
Against UNIVERSITY APARTHEID
in the
CITY HALL, CAPE TOWN
on
SUNDAY, 7th APRIL, 1957
at 2.30 p.m.

Chairman:
Mr. W. P. VAN SCHOOR.
Speakers:
Dr. A. C. JORDAN, Mr. B. M. KIES, Mr. A. FATAAR

● WE DEMAND THAT ALL
UNIVERSITIES BE FREELY
OPEN TO ALL!!

Issued by the Federal Council, A. Fataar, Secretary
"Eothen," Dale Street, Landsdowne.

21

The Cape Teachers' Federal Council of the Cape African Teachers' Association call for a protest meeting against university apartheid, April 1957. The association played a pivotal role in the fight against Bantu Education in the early 1950s

Image courtesy of Yunus Omar

Gool opposed the motion. In his argument he provided the first public airing of the kind of thinking that was circulating inside of the NEF (and implicitly the WPSA) on the social structure. There was 'no intellectual class among non-Europeans', if intellectuals were to be 'found chiefly among the leisured classes. *All non-Europeans were workers*, with only an upper educated stratum which chiefly consisted of teachers. These, if they were the intellectuals, had come from the working class.' What Gool was doing was conflating race and class. Black people, in this analysis, were decidedly members of the working class. Class, in these terms, provided them with their primary identity. The motion was defeated 9 to 34.

Analyses of the social formation would develop inside of the NEF beyond this early rhetorical flourish. They would gain nuance and sophistication. There was a foretaste in a lecture announced in the *Cape Standard* on 31 January 1938: 'On Sat. 8.15pm New Era Fellowship lecture by Mrs. Dora Taylor. "Modern Writers in Relation to Modern Society" at Stakesby-Lewis Hostel.'[25]

Taylor is described by Corinne Sandwith as 'a Scottish immigrant, who developed affiliations with Trotskyist groups in South Africa, such as The Lenin Club and the Workers' Party, and who later became involved with the work of the Non-European Unity Movement'.[26]

In this lecture Taylor gave notice of the precocity of the young intellectuals in the NEF by articulately delivering one of the earliest deconstructions in the country's literary history of how discourse produces ideas of superiority and inferiority.

Shortly after this lecture, another, on 'Liberalism in South Africa', was given by Margaret Ballinger. Dr D Maurice also spoke. William Ballinger, Margaret's husband, the representative of the Friends of Africa, London, followed with a lecture on 'The Silent Masters of Civilisation', who visualised 'a solution for three main problems: 1) settlement of surplus populations, 2) demand for colonies, and 3) access to essential raw materials – as a Commonwealth of Nations'.[27] He also discussed the failure to relate production and consumption to the problems of economic distribution. His economic analysis pivoted on the dominance of the great industrial powers and their buying power. This power, the ability to consume, did not exist in the colonies, he argued, because the colonies subsisted on the exploitation of cheap 'native' labour.

All of these were major issues young people related to. Interest in the debates increased and attendance grew. The Stakesby-Lewis venue began to fill up.

Regular debates took place between the different cultural clubs. On 6 December 1938 the *Cape Standard* reported that the Sixth Annual Debate had taken place between the Cape Literary and Debating Society and the University of Cape Town Debating Society. To this came, it reported, 'prominent citizens, Coloured and European, [who] debated, lectured and attended the society's meetings throughout the year'.[28]

An inter-club debate was organised between the NEF and the Cape Literary and Debating Society at the end of 1938. The motion for the debate, proposed by an 'eloquent' Mr Yusuf, was that 'liberalism is a spent force in South Africa'. The opposers failed to convince the audience that liberalism was still alive in South Africa: 'Mr. B. Kies, M.A., in a witty summing up, exploded all the arguments of the opponents and left them without a leg to stand on.'[29] What Kies actually said was, unfortunately, not reproduced, but apparently Yusuf's contribution provided the occasion with its highlight. He said that 'the liberal element in South Africa served only to delude the masses'.

On 28 January in 1939 Peter Abrahams gave a lecture entitled 'The Rise of the Negro Poets' at the NEF Art Circle. On 15 February 1940 Mr Lewis H Maurice lectured on 'Sculpture Today and Epstein' at the Stakesby-Lewis Hostel, which was open to the public and held under the auspices of the NEF Art Circle.[30]

As these issues were being aired in the NEF, the National Liberation League (NLL) first and the Non-European United Front (NEUF) later were continuing to mobilise the people of Cape Town. Two weeks after Taylor's lecture, on 7 February 1938 Cissie Gool addressed a large demonstration of about 700 people in the Liberation Hall. It was followed by a march.[31] Apart from increasing segregation, the Aliens Act had been recently passed to restrict the flow into the country of Jewish Europeans escaping fascism. At the beginning of 1939 there was a significant protest about the price of bread. There was also the Protest Day on the Grand Parade on Monday 27 March 1939 about the need for organisations, in the spirit of the united front, to protest against their political situation: 'NON-EUROPEANS TO UNITE TO FIGHT' read an NLL pamphlet. The protest was held in the evening and torches for the march were offered at the NLL office.[32]

These activities energised the NEF politically and encouraged it to present itself more publicly. It began to assume a more distinct political identity and soon more radical programmes emerged out of the Stakesby-Lewis Hostel. On 15 April 1939 the revised NEF constitution was adopted at a special general meeting.[33]

* * *

The events of the late 1930s, particularly the beginning of the Second World War, were determinative for the agenda of the NEF. The period also saw the migration of many people into District Six. Pushed into people's faces, whether they liked it or not, was the question of drafting people who were not white into the war effort. This was captured in a banner headline of the *Cape Standard* on 16 May 1939, just a few months before war was declared: 'Coloureds and Future War, Participation Would be Inevitable'. Happening alongside this, which helped to bring clarity to the question of the participation of blacks in the war, was the development of the NEF's specialised cultural circles. Interestingly, the NLL started its own study circles – one of these was in Athlone – and organisations such as the Communist League of South Africa (CLSA) (later to become Fourth International of South Africa – FIOSA) also started their own cultural clubs and forums.[34]

The draft was an explosive issue. Ultimately, it was what caused the collapse of the NEUF. Chairperson Cissie Gool argued for 'coloured' and African people to join the effort on the grounds that the Soviet Union, which was then under attack from the Germans, should be defended. A discussion on the issue took place under the auspices of the NEF. Underlining just how important this discussion was, it was adjourned to 27 May 1939, with the whole evening to be made available for the topic. The discussion was led by 'Mr. S. Maurice. Mr. J. A. La Guma [who] believed that war was inevitable . . . but should the non-European participate?' The issue was a divisive one. While La Guma believed that all conscripts should be given equal treatment, the NEF felt otherwise. They called for non-participation. Not everyone from the previous discussion in May was present, the *Cape Standard* reported.[35]

The main questions debated were: '[What would] the attitude of the NEF be if South West Africa were attacked by Germany? And whether the non-Europeans would abide by a decision not to take part in a war when Conscription laws were enforced.' Maurice 'felt that it was the duty of the intelligent class to influence the rest, lest they took the wrong step by enlisting in time of war'.[36] He argued that if the 'non-Europeans had any rights worth defending they would be perfectly justified in going to war. At the moment the Coloured man would merely fight to defend imaginary rights . . . If the European races wished to blot each other out, the Coloured man should stand aloof.' The discussion placed the choices in sharp focus and eventually a resolution was unanimously carried. The NEF would call for non-participation.

On 17 June, in a subsequent discussion on the 'Non-European and War', sponsored by the NEF and held at the Stakesby-Lewis Hostel, the NEF members made their appeal for non-participation. The *Cape Standard* reported on 20 June 1939: 'The New Era Fellowship was totally opposed to voluntarily taking part in any war ... Mr. E. Erntzen suggested that the word imperialist be inserted [into the resolution], since a refusal to fight savoured of pacificism. No one would say that people should not fight for their rights.'[37]

It was during this time that the NEF Literary Circle was established. In its own way it came to contribute significantly to the deepening of thinking inside the NEF. A number of important discussions took place under its auspices. Cumulatively these assisted considerably in sharpening the NEF's understanding of race. In the context of the decision to agitate for non-participation in the war all these debates and discussions helped to clarify its agenda and refine its thinking. In these meetings the culture of the NEF was being laid down. The policy and practice was 'that members read papers upon various books, fictional or otherwise', after which rigorous discussion would follow. Peter Abrahams, author of *Tell Freedom*, gave an address to the Literary Circle on 'Non-European Literature in South Africa' in 1938. Abrahams sided with Johnny Gomas rather than his friend Gool.[38]

The important thread of discussion on race and class, which had been initiated by Gool and Gomas in November 1937, would continue to be debated over 1938 and into 1939. It was ventilated twice in 1938. In June the NEF debated the Livingstone Past Students' Union. Mr F Joshua led and Isaac Tabata seconded. Tabata pointed out that the Coloured people were predominantly workers. Mr F Grammer also supported the opposition, who won the debate – the outcome being that 'the Coloured man's vote is useless in South Africa'.[39]

The discussion was continued in a lecture given by Dr J Marais on the identity of 'the Coloured man' and 'the political history of the Coloured man'.[40] Marais had published, in 1937, a book called *The Cape Coloured People*. At the time it was regarded as the authoritative text on the history of the 'coloured' people. His general approach, as he admitted, was to understand the 'backwardness and apathy' of 'coloured' people. He, like Margaret Ballinger before him, would not have been tolerated in a later time. Marais said that 'there were signs that the remaining political rights of the Coloured would eventually be taken away'. In a similar discussion in 1939, Gomas said 'that the intellectuals were pulling their weight in the wrong direction'.[41]

A more significant development in this early history of the NEF was shaped in a series of lectures that took place in the middle of 1939. These provided the opportunity for NEF members to begin a more theoretical consideration of the question of race. They also served to put on a new level the questions of consciousness and the role of the intellectual elite in relation to consciousness development. Implicit within these discussions were the early signs of the psycho-social direction the NEF's analysis was taking.

It was a number of literary review evenings that inaugurated the turn. On 24 May 1939 at the Stakesby-Lewis Hostel, Kies reviewed *Black Girl in Search of God* and a Mr Stoppard reviewed Sarah Gertrude Millin's *God's Step-children*.[42] This was followed on 7 June by M S Hurwitz reviewing *Fascism and Big Business* by Daniel Guérin and Mr L Rosenberg talking about *The Black Jacobins* by C L R James.[43] A deeply significant discussion on race in literature took place later that month as a result. A Miss O Rosenberg (it is not clear who she was) read a paper on *Half-Caste* by Cedric Dover and Mr S M'lambo read a paper on *Salvation of a Race* by Steven Oliphant.[44] A discussion on the two books, as was usual, followed.

On Tuesday, 4 July 1939, under the heading 'No Half-Castes in the World', the *Cape Standard* carried Rosenberg's review.[45] 'Colour prejudice originates from economic fear. Colour prejudice denies that the concept of prejudice is an inborn racial instinct.'

Cedric Dover provided the young NEF intellectuals with a great deal of food for thought. Rosenberg paraphrased what Dover had to say:

The writer goes to tremendous lengths to ridicule the pseudo-scientific case against miscegenation: he contends 'Both radical and related miscegenation are more extensive than is commonly supposed, not only between white and Coloured populations, but also between the Coloured people themselves.'

The millinia [sic] over which the processes of fusion have spread, resulting in so inextricable a mixture of racial elements, that it is no longer possible to speak with precision of pure and hybrid populations. Today there are no half-castes in the world, because there are no full-castes . . .

He continues to expose the fallacy of biological objection to miscegenation by showing the futility of legislation against it, the essential hybridization which must have produced even 'the so-called pure races', and the groundlessness of the assertion that miscegenation produces inferior individuals as compared with 'pure' ones.

Of our glorious fatherland, especially the Cape, Mr Dover has a few interesting remarks to make . . . More interesting still is the Cape Coloured which the writer describes as the 'stewpot into which all the ethnic left-overs of the Union will eventually find their way'.[46]

Rosenberg closed her presentation with this searing insight of Dover's: 'Cedric Dover denies that the concept of prejudice is an inborn racial instinct. A newly born child knows no racial or colour prejudice and will continue to know none if they are not instilled into the minds of ignorant propagandists.'[47]

Another significant opportunity arose when A J B Desmore's book *Elements of Vocational Guidance*, which had recently been published, formed the subject of an address on 11 November 1939 by Mr Rahim, who was a member of the juvenile advisory board, at Stakesby-Lewis Hostel.[48] A big debate ensued. The *Cape Standard* mentions 'mud-slinging' and Mr Desmore's book was defended in a Letter to the Editor.[49] Ben Kies, who had chaired the session, had said in his opening remarks that 'if anyone came because of an expectation that some mud-slinging was to take place, then he or she would not be disappointed'. Some were disappointed that there was too much mud-slinging. On 28 November 1939 in his own Letter to the Editor, Kies questioned why Desmore did not refer to non-European teachers' special problem. He attacked the previous letter and said that 'this merely shows how a slave can learn to think like his master'.[50] Mr Rahim issued a challenge in the same issue, saying that most agreed with him and [explaining to the readers] 'that he was approached by the N. E. F. representative to review the book, and [his] mind was not made up in one way or the other at that stage. He came to the conclusion that Desmore had side-tracked the real and burning issue and to a great extent that was the situation of the Coloured child.'

What was the situation of this 'coloured' child? Unfortunately, there is little in the archive about how the debates were managed in these lectures. What we can ascertain, though, is that the production of consciousness of the child was in the forefront of many minds. The debates contained the most immediate and direct moves that were being made in the NEF towards a psychological analysis of how the social is constituted. Dover's provocation was to build on the earlier provocation of Lancelot Hogben. Race was a fiction, Hogben had said. Here Dover was pushing the discussion into realms that had not been broached before, that prejudice is socially produced. We do not know what Kies's approach to Millin's extremely contentious work, God's Step-children, was, only that he reviewed it on one of these platforms. In challenging Desmore, Kies gave some sense of the kind of discussion that was percolating within the circles of the NEF.

What, more poignantly, was the responsibility of the political class to this child? An ongoing discussion, in the context of this question, was taking place about the political elite.

Flowing out of the NEF's literary circle debates were signs of new directions in thinking on the question of race. Not only did these discussions attract the best minds in the small intellectual community of black Cape Town, they also sharpened their analytical skills. This insight was in evidence when a discussion began on Gandhism. Rahim, mentioned above, made the argument that 'passive resistance' was 'the only weapon left' for winning equality for black people.[51] 'Mr. S. M. Rahim spoke in favour, and moved "that the Indians of South Africa should adopt Passive Resistance", and Goolam Gool opposed.' The discussion continued over a number of sessions. On 1 August 1939 the *Cape Standard* reported: 'Non-Europeans favour "Non-violence" struggle'. This decision was reached at an inter-club debate at the Liberman Institute where many views were put forward. Rahim advocated unity and the dropping of differences between 'Bantu, Coloured and Asiatic' and the need to stand together. He advocated a 'passive resistance campaign against their oppressors'.[52] Mr Maurice felt that this would require the activation of religious feelings and he favoured a strong force. Mr R Hoedemaker suggested the holding of a 'black fast' on 1 December 1940 where no one should go to work. Mr A Ismael agreed that all should unite and that passive resistance as a method of struggle was obsolete. Mr J Paulse said the coloured people had never tried anything to prove that they have power. The NEF decided that members were free individually to support Mr J A La Guma in the Ward 7 municipal contest. Members were asked not to support Dr Abdurahman.[53]

A break with the past was being foreshadowed.

One of the criticisms of the young radicals was that they were arrogant and this accusation probably carried some truth. In the milieu and the times in which they found themselves they stood out. But the significance of the social analysis they were making in these discussions, particularly for understanding the complexity of the South African situation, should not be overshadowed by their vociferousness. The experience of being in each other's presence in the generative space of Cape Town – educated and uneducated, the relatively privileged intelligentsia and the large numbers of really poor people around them – undoubtedly created difficulty and tension. There was tension in families, tension between generations and tensions within the wider community. But everybody was aware that times were changing. There were new radicals in town.

By the beginning of 1940 evidence of the shift in the approach of the broader community of 'coloured' people was no longer in doubt. This shift was the result of several stock-taking occasions stimulated by the NEF. The first instance of this was signalled at an 'Interesting Lecture at the N. E. F.' at the end of January 1940.[54] The lecture was given by Mr Sisam, who discussed 'the Coloured man since 1938'. Mr A C Yusuf presided. Mr Sisam discussed imperialism and also reflected on the anti-segregation meeting that had taken place on the Grand Parade the previous year, on 27 March. He applauded how the 'coloureds' had stood together and religious differences were forgotten.

The editorial article pointed to the interesting discussions that were happening under the auspices of the NEF. More lectures were held. Kies gave two lectures on 'Educational Segregation, 1652–1939', which had been the subject of his BEd thesis at UCT.[55] This was followed by a review by Messrs W Parry, Awerbach [sic], Tabata and Dr Gool at the Stakesby-Lewis Hostel on Saturday 23 March 1940.[56] The title of that lecture was 'A Review of the Period between March 1938–1940'. On 14 June 1941 Tabata gave an NEF Lecture on the AAC.[57]

It was almost predictable that the NEF would become embroiled in debates about the question of race. Many of the important theoretical positions in the organisation would be foreshadowed during these searing discussions. Although answers did not emerge fully articulated, they were there in outline. The view had always been there that the struggle in South Africa was a class struggle, but how one explained race in relation to itself and in relation to class was still fully to be worked out. The dominant explanation doing the political rounds was that race was a divide-and-rule tactic. Beyond this explanation, what race actually was and how it worked was not firmly grasped. There were early perceptions that race had to be explained *in relation* to class but by the end of the 1930s that intellectual water was still muddy.

Significant about the circle of these intellectuals is that they came to the discussion of race as a consequence of the debate about the national question, their personal positions and locations in society, and the place – specifically, Cape Town – in which they lived. The framing of the national question would have them split over and constantly re-aligning around the two-stage and Permanent Revolution alternatives. Race was not, in the beginning, the focus of their discussions. But its relevance for thinking through the practicalities of managing the exigencies of making the alternative socialist society they desired forced them to give greater attention to the question of who they were. In thinking about this question, they had the provocative positions of the feminists, among them Olive Schreiner, who were themselves very aware of the struggle for racial equality and who were making the argument of the fundamental commonality, biologically, of men and women, and, critically of the anti-eugenicists. And they had discovered Cedric Dover.

5 | The Road
to Emancipation, 1940–1953

The New Era Fellowship (NEF) was born against a backdrop of extraordinary global and local upheaval. Its early years saw a second wave of carnage and barbarism engulfing the world in the Second World War. People were dying on the battlefields of Europe. German Panzers drove across the landscape of the Low Countries and France, impelled by the idea of Aryan supremacy. Six million Jews, gypsies, homosexuals, communists and non-conformists were systematically murdered.

While this was happening subjugated people of colour around the world were stirring. Within less than a decade the people of China and India would assert their sovereignty over their countries.

In South Africa people of colour were simultaneously being coaxed into making themselves available for the war effort and forced to cede what little freedoms they had.

How to make sense of this was what the young leadership of the NEF understood their task to be. The stock-taking exercise they undertook at the end of the 1930s and the beginning of the 1940s was deeply important. Out of it would come their first major theoretical statements about the social, and the beginnings of the making of a political and social agenda would be seen. The agenda was carried on the wings of the innovative social analysis, which was the result of the systematic and carefully explored programmatic questioning enabled by the NEF. Deep and meaningful reflection on the meaning

of and process for building the unity of oppressed people preoccupied them at every level of their lives. The agenda took its direction
from the thinking of Ben Kies, who produced three key documents in
this period: *The Background of Segregation* in 1943, *The Basis of Unity*
in 1945 and finally, in 1953, the magisterial 'The Contribution of the
Non-European Peoples to Civilisation'.

From early beginnings in 1943 it took just over a decade for the
ranks of the left to shift towards a clear anti-race position. One sees
through the progression of the three Kies papers a working out of
the idea of race. The process begins and continues until the end of
the 1940s with the idea of race relatively intact, but then rapidly
tips over conceptually to another space where the idea is completely
rejected.

The role of the NEF changed during this period. Where it constituted
the primary locus from which the anti-Stalinist left in South Africa moved
in the period from 1937 to about 1943, from the time of the establishment
of the Anti-CAD movement and the Non-European Unity Movement
(NEUM) it became, distinctly so, the intellectual nursery for those organisations. Kies was not alone in thinking through the problems in front
of him. In his company were other extremely important South African
intellectual-activists – members of the Workers' Party of South Africa
(WPSA) and of the NEF, Isaac Tabata, Dora Taylor and a small but
significant collection of intellectuals: Dick Dudley, Alie Fataar, Edgar
Maurice, A C Jordan, Willem van Schoor, Goolam Gool, Hosea Jaffe,
Enid Williams, Joyce Meissenheimer, Ernie Steenveld, Tom Hanmer,
Stella Pietersen, Victor Wessels, Polly Slingers, and a whole clamour of
young and eager-to-learn students.

As forums like the NEF began to strain under the weight of surveillance, Taylor took her efforts into what were perceived to be safer
outlets. She wrote weekly reviews and columns for a literary journal,
Trek, where, consistent with the precociousness of her comrades, she
produced a corpus of some of the most progressive literary commentary

the country had seen. To illustrate the point, in 1942 she wrote a review of South African novels written between 1920 and 1936:

> For the most part, their works reflect the ideology of their class as in a mirror. When they admit an African or a Coloured into the pages of their books in more than a menial or decorative capacity . . . they write as members of a dominant white caste looking from afar at some almost sub-human species. When he is not a mere victim, an object of humanitarian pity, he is a Problem, a menace, a threat to white purity and white civilisation. Sometimes the work has an air of impartiality, almost of scientific objectiveness. But it turns out to be a fraud. Race prejudice falls like a blight on nearly every approach to the non-European, and art is born of intellectual dishonesty.[1]

A C Jordan's work, too, deconstructed the canon in brilliantly incisive ways. The NEF had become, during this period, the most progressive intellectual, and even scholarly site of critical thinking in the country. Later on, in the late 1950s, lectures given by Kenny Jordaan, Cosmo Pieterse and others in a group of young intellectuals with incisive and enquiring minds, were significantly in advance of much of what was being taught at the major universities in the country at the time. The epistemological break was being made. It shook the debating and cultural circles of Cape Town to the core. It was unfortunate that it did not reach significantly beyond these spaces.

* * *

The beginning of the 1940s in South Africa was characterised by an essential changing of the political guard across a whole range of political organisations. In the African National Congress (ANC) the old leadership was displaced by a rising generation of young leaders, led by Anton Lembede, A P Mda and, around them, even younger activists like Nelson

Mandela, who would establish the ANC Youth League. In the socialist movement, especially in the Cape, the young leaders were required to both take over from the elders inside their own organisational structures, and outside of them, assume a public presence against an older and much more conservative generation. In the ranks of the NEF these were 'the three musketeers' and Kies, who began taking much more decisive, confident and assertive roles of leadership.

The most compelling issue in NEF circles was the increasing intensity of racism. As Mohamed Adhikari explains:

> Official discrimination gathered momentum in the 1930s, growing to a veritable flood of segregatory measures by the end of the decade. State interference in the labour market intensified throughout the 1930s and the opportunities for upward occupational mobility by coloureds became increasingly circumscribed . . . For the coloured elite by far the most menacing episode in the relentless advance of segregation during the 1930s came in March 1938, when Smuts announced the government's intention of implementing residential segregation for coloureds . . . The controversy over the segregation of beaches followed in the summer of 1939 . . . In addition, the *Report of the Mixed Marriages Commission*, which recommended the prohibition of inter-racial marriages and severe penalties for sex across the colour line, appeared in 1939.[2]

These measures traumatised what Adhikari describes as the 'coloured elite'. This was the context in which the NEF deepened its organisational culture. It became clear to the leadership, and this was evidenced by the disdain they showed in many public debates at the end of the 1930s, that the existing political structures in South Africa were either fatally compromised or were not going to play the public political role that was needed. In the mid-1930s already they had decided that the existing political structures were irredeemable.

This can be seen in Baruch Hirson's cameo of a gathering at Hamid Gool's home in 1934 where Gool's wife Cissie publicly castigated her father, the elder Abdurahman.[3] The newer attempts to build a united front, first with the National Liberation League (NLL) and then the Non-European United Front (NEUF), came to naught. The NLL split during 1938 and 1939, firstly over the question of mobilisation and the role of education, and then over the question of whether white people could occupy leadership roles in the organisation.[4] The NEUF had a short life. It would burn brightly for a few years before being absorbed into the collaborationist tactics of the Communist Party of South Africa (CPSA).

It is important to focus briefly for a moment on the young leaders' rejection of the older collaborationist generation. As Adhikari has explained: 'The deteriorating circumstances facing the coloured elite during the 1930s . . . politicized the [teaching] profession as a whole.'[5] These, he says, 'roused many teachers' and led to the accelerating growth in Teachers' League of South Africa (TLSA) membership into the 1930s and 1940s. It also had the effect in the TLSA of precipitating a shift away from the older leadership and their perceived accommodationism. Radicalism was in the air.

It was in this climate that the NEF leaders decided to take over the leadership of the TLSA, although there had been signs much earlier of their dissatisfaction. At the 1938 annual conference of the TLSA, they had made their presence felt: 'It was manifested as a small but vociferous group of younger teachers at the back of the hall. BJU, a regular columnist in the *Sun*, remarked of the 1938 conference that the radicals were "full of complaints as youngsters usually are, noisy, persistent and heedless of the feelings of the older ones. They are at conference today with grievances, many of them vital ones."'[6]

One issue that provoked them at that conference was a motion in the TLSA calling for stricter segregation between coloured and African teachers. The Young Turks would not yet be able to take over the organisation but by 1939 they had captured the Livingstone

High School branch and had a strong presence in the Cape Town, Salt River, Maitland, Bellville and Wellington branches.[7] At the next TLSA national conference, in 1939, the young leadership of the NEF was able to mobilise enough support within the organisation to be elected to the national executive: 'Three young radicals in the persons of Ben Kies, Alie Fataar and Willem van Schoor first entered the Executive at this conference. The League which had been a model of "moderation" and a paragon of "respectability", was never to be the same again.' Kies was the vice-chairperson of the NEF at that time.[8]

The point to emphasise about these developments, to take up the issue referred to above with respect to the deepening of the organisational culture of the NEF, was that the young leaders did not have a public political home. None of the political structures in the circumference of their ambitions and goals was sufficiently credible or legitimate.

Sarah Mokone, writing in the *Educational Journal* many years later, was at pains to emphasise the location of these intellectuals within their broader radical milieu (possibility in reaction to later charges of elitism): 'They were not freaks born out of their time but a vanguard articulating an awareness and a mood that was already widely felt and was growing, even though as 1942 came to an end, passivity and demoralisation seemed to hold the political organisations of the oppressed, such as they were, in a choking grip.'[9]

In this 'choking grip' the NEF, it could be argued, came to provide both the form and the substance of what they needed – a political vehicle. In the absence of such a vehicle its members went into the public domain, into structures such as the TLSA. Inside these structures they behaved as they would have behaved as members of a political party. This was already clearly evident in the national conference of the NEUF in April of 1939 where Kies and Eric Erntzen carried themselves as mandated delegates of a political party.[10] Their participation at this meeting was not only visible but forceful. They were pushing very distinct political positions. They were no longer operating under the mentorship of their elders. They were political leaders in their own right.

The political atmosphere in South Africa during the war years was marked by an upsurge in state surveillance of radical organisations. The number of cultural events at the Stakesby-Lewis Hostel was if not brought to a halt, certainly reduced. The NEF's firm position that people of colour should not participate in the war effort had generated some publicity, and this might also have been part of the reason. In any event, for a time it seemed that the forum was forced to behave as a clandestine organisation. In 1943 members would meet in Constantia Road, Wynberg, at the Gools' residence.[11]

At the same time the CPSA, which, from June 1941, supported participation in the war, enjoyed somewhat more political freedom.[12] It established the Friends of the Soviet Union, which met at the People's Club at 61 Commercial Street, and enjoyed a brief period of popularity as a uniting front.

* * *

The period between 1940 and 1943 was decisive for the direction of the progressive left. The circumstances that forced the NEF into a semi-underground position gave its leaders the opportunity to think deeply. This was to be made clear in the landmark lecture given by Kies on 29 May 1943 entitled 'The Background of Segregation'. Kies spoke reflectively in this lecture about the analytic stock-taking that had been taking place in the NEF: 'While it is true to say that the Coloured People [sic] have learned more in the past three years about their rulers than they have learned during the past thirty years, it is a grim necessity that we should recognise the fact that we are only at the very beginning of things, and that there is much, very much to learn and to do before we can consider ourselves anywhere near the road to emancipation.'[13] The 'road to emancipation' would be strewn with difficulties, but the NEF took on the responsibility for the commitment that was required from the left to walk the long road.

The year 1943 was a critical one. One issue, in particular, the one that brought matters to a head, would prove to be a catalyst of immense significance.

The intention of the Smuts government was to have a Coloured Affairs Department similar to the Native Affairs Department, but its official establishment was still some years away (this would happen in 1958). In the meantime the signals were clear. In early 1943 Jan Smuts and his Minister of the Interior, Harry Lawrence, set up the Coloured Advisory Council (CAC) to advance the establishment of a distinct administrative department for people classified as 'coloured'.[14] It caused an uproar of consternation, anger and protest and would lead, later in the year, to the formation of the NEUM.

The first protest action, however, was the establishment of the Anti-CAD movement. The force behind it was the NEF. Kies gave a lecture on 'The C.A.D. – the New Fraud' at the Stakesby-Lewis Hostel. On 23 February the NEF convened a meeting at the same venue.[15] Significantly, the invitation was to 'all the organisations of the oppressed'.[16] In this wording the NEF was signposting that it had moved on from the open debating forum – a forum 'for the enlightenment' of people – it had been at the beginning of its life.

Doreen Musson described the occasion: 'The meeting at the Stakesby-Lewis Hostel was the largest ever attendance by the NEF since its inception in 1937. Gomas was sharing the rostrum with Ben Kies, Alie Fataar and Isaac Tabata . . . . Gomas [attacked] the CAD, CAC and CCPC [Cape Coloured Permanent Commission] . . . [These were], said Gomas ". . . a perpetuation of the white labour policy as announced by Hertzog in 1928."'[17]

A range of people came to the meeting and out of it came the Anti-CAD committee, whose composition is an interesting reflection of the times: Kies, Goolam Gool, Jane Gool, Tabata, Saul Jayiya, Dudley, Rev Viljoen, Rev Wessels, Alie Fataar, Edgar Maurice, Cissie Gool, Gomas and Sonny Abdurahman.[18] The committee issued a statement headed 'The C.A.D. The New Fraud'.

Public meetings throughout the Cape Province followed and a national conference on 28 May was held in the Cape Town Banqueting Hall. The gathering attracted 200 delegates representing organisations such as the African People's Organisation (APO), NEUF, NLL, Fourth International of South Africa (FIOSA), trade unions, churches and civic organisations. Mokone described the coming together of the organisations as 'the biggest conference in the history of the Coloured sector of the oppressed'.[19]

The committee issued a pamphlet in which it stated its position:

WE ARE STRIVING FOR FULL DEMOCRATIC RIGHTS. When we say this we mean that we struggle for:

(i) FULL AND EQUAL POLITICAL AND CIVIC RIGHTS FOR ALL THE PEOPLE OF THE UNION . . .

WHY EVERYONE MUST OPPOSE THE CAD AND THE CCPC.

Do not fool yourself that the CAD is 'not your concern'. It is very much your business whether you are Coloured, African, Indian or White . . .

So we must all realise that while these proposals are aimed at one section of the non-European oppressed, they are the direct and vital concern of all NON-EUROPEANS, for an injury to one limb is an injury to the whole body. We must not fall into the trap of being artificially divided into three groups, oppressed Africans, oppressed Coloured, oppressed Indian – segregated even in suffering.[20]

The Anti-CAD committee committed itself to boycotting the apparatus and the entire supportive network of the CAC. Shortly thereafter, despite attempts on the part of collaborators in the APO and other organisations such as the TLSA to persuade the so-called Coloured community otherwise, a movement was started. A massive boycott was inaugurated:

By then the ferment had worked through the whole Coloured section of the population and every family and certainly every organisation had declared or was busy declaring itself on the question of the CAC and the CAD. The decision was a massive one in favour of the Anti-CAD. Every single CAC man was opposed and boycotted by at least some of his immediate relatives; it was literally brother against brother and children against father. The majority of CAC men were reduced to a miserable minority even in their own families.[21]

The Anti-CAD explained in its *Bulletin* what the boycott meant: 'Don't have any social or personal intercourse with them. Don't greet them. Don't have any conversation with them. Don't visit them and don't invite them to your home. Don't meet them, even if it's necessary to cross over to the other side of the street. Don't see them, even if you come face to face with them.'[22]

These were intense times. In the middle of 1943 the moderates abandoned the TLSA. Even though they had won two-thirds of all the votes cast – largely through proxy votes – at the TLSA's annual conference in Kimberley, 'the extreme passion that the Anti-CAD campaign unleashed amongst the radical activists . . . tore the organization apart' and the moderates threw in the towel.[23] What had particularly incensed the radicals was that three prominent members of the TLSA had made themselves available for the CAC. Gavin Lewis provides a graphic description of what purportedly happened at the meeting: 'The Kimberley TLSA conference collapsed into chaos from the moment it started, as Anti-CAD teachers drowned out the mayor's address and shouted down all attempts to discuss the conference agenda, demanding the ousting of the CAC men. For three days, the deadlock continued.'[24] The conservatives decided to leave the League and formed the Teachers' Educational and Professional Association: 'In their eyes the League had been irretrievably compromised by the behaviour of the radicals. They felt that nothing constructive could any longer be achieved in cooperation with the radicals in the name of the League.'

Leading the radicals was Ben Kies. Lewis's description of Kies is revealing:

> Although Dr. Gool played a more visible leadership role than Kies, with the latter preferring to work behind the scenes, there is little doubt that Kies was the more influential of the two. Of considerable intellect and some arrogance, Kies shaped the ideological views of his young contemporaries, and indeed a whole generation of leaders well into the 1970s. Hence the importance of his speech to the 1943 conference. His supporters faithfully followed the strategy he had mapped out, with the result that the flaws in his armour, such as the leading role of the teachers in the liberation struggle, greatly affected the Anti-CAD movement's capacity to attract mass support. It became increasingly apparent as time wore on that Coloured teachers did not share the intimate links with the aspirations of the black workers that Kies had envisaged. And Kies's argument also provided a convenient excuse for those Coloured radicals who had no wish to become involved in the arduous and often dangerous task of working among the rank and file to gain mass support.[25]

Lewis's distillation of the criticisms heaped on Kies is important to note. It pivoted on the criticism activists such as Gomas had directed at activists like Gool – that they were remote from the people. Although there may have been an element of truth to this, it was certainly not what people like Kies intended.

Kies's *The Background of Segregation*, first delivered at the first national Anti-CAD conference on 29 May 1943 was critical in setting out the programmatic position of the NEF activists. Evidence of racial thinking, as Adhikari has remarked, was still there. The vocabulary Kies used was not very different from that of his liberal counterparts. He was perfectly comfortable with terms that later would become very problematic, such as 'Natives', 'coloureds', 'whites' and so on.[26] Kies said:

> When we speak of a united front of ALL non-Europeans we do not mean lumping all non-Europeans holus-bolus together and fusing them all together in the belief that, since ALL are non-European oppressed, the African is a Coloured man, the Indian is an African, and a Coloured man is either Indian or African, whichever you please. Only those who are ignorant of both politics and history can believe in this nonsensical type of unity. When we speak of the unity or the united front of all non-Europeans, we simply mean this: they are all ground down by the same oppression; they have all the same political aspirations, but yet they remain divided in their oppression ... When they have thrown off their chains, then they can settle whatever national or racial differences they have, or think they have.[27]

It is on the basis of this speech that Adhikari argues that non-racism had not always been an article of faith for the organisation and its successor organisations: 'Generalised assertions that the NEUM was non-racist ... are exaggerated. And do not reflect the intricacies of its ideology.'[28]

There was a great deal more to Kies's address, however. Out of it came the basic theoretical and strategic positions that would inform the anti-Stalinist socialist movement for the next 60 years.

Kies explained the NEF's purpose, which was to give a 'sober picture of the factors we are up against and also to show clearly how we will have to face up to these realities'.[29] The focus was the social first and foremost. The 'basic principle upon which the British Empire is founded,' he explained, 'is that of "divide and rule". The plainer name is Segregation. And this principle works right through the Empire, from the Statute of Westminster to the Constitution of the NRC [Natives Representative Council] or the CAC; from the creation of a white working-class aristocracy in South Africa to the stoking up of Hindu-Moslem feuds in India.'

The Background to Segregation was also where Kies began to lay out a theory of race, to locate it within a larger class analysis and to emphasise how significantly race was an instrument of imperialism. 'They intend to reduce us all to the same low level of slavery,' he argued, 'but to keep us segregated even in subjection . . . but each group is always to think that its chains are different. Already the names – African, Coloured and Indian – are practically out of date; they no longer correspond to reality.'[30] What was the reality? 'The reality,' he said, was that 'in South Africa there are only white and non-white'. Subjection was possible, he maintained, because

> the bitter truth is that white South Africa still dominates because it has been able to enslave the mind, the ideas of the non-European. It is a known historical fact that in any society, the prevailing ideas, manners and customs of even the oppressed section, are the ideas, manners and customs of the ruling class . . . The Herrenvolk of South Africa have nothing to learn from Dr. Goebbels, for their vicious racial myths have bitten deep into the life and ways of the non-Europeans.[31]

Adhikari's criticism does not take this insight into account. George Hull, reading the Kies lecture critically, argues that Kies had begun in this talk to 'deplore the vicious racial myths', 'the myths of racial hierarchy'. To criticism made of his address that 'said that the Coloured People would "lose their identity" if taught alongside "pupils from other racial groups", he replied, "the sooner the Coloured man loses his identity the better off he will be"'.[32]

A conceptual corner was being turned. Changing this situation, Kies recognised, would not be easy. Two moves were needed. The first was to build a united front of oppressed people. 'A REAL United Front,' Kies said, and here he had in mind the failures of the All-African Convention (AAC), the NLL and the NEUF, 'cannot suddenly be called up or created, but it has to be BUILT. And it can only be BUILT UP from below . . . This is the first condition for a REAL United Front: it must have a mass base.'[33] The purpose, he said, was not to stir up race hatred: 'It is for the purpose of uniting ALL non-European oppressed, so that they may bring the white working-class to its senses . . . It may seem . . . that all the whites are living on milk and honey. That is not so . . . They are exploited all the same.'[34]

The second move that needed to be made was coming to terms with the fact that practical leadership always came from the intelligentsia: 'The workers and peasants have always been so exhausted and bowed down by arduous toil that they have never had time to study and look deeply into the why and wherefore of their miserable condition.'[35] The 'non-European' people, Kies argued, did not have a leisured class, but it was certainly lucky to have an intelligentsia, 'and we are luckier than that, because our intelligentsia has sprung straight from the loins of the working class. They do not have to go to the people. They belong to the people and the people are all around them.'[36]

In this he was repeating the conflation of race and class developed by Goolam Gool before him. Their positioning produced, he argued, a special role and obligation on the part of teachers and especially the TLSA. Referring to the radicals moving into the TLSA, he said: 'This augurs very well for the future. It means that the intellectuals are realising the role that they have to play.'[37] In closing he urged: 'WE MUST TURN OUR FACES TO OUR PEOPLE AND WE MUST BE AMONG THEM AND WITH THEM AND OF THEM, TEACHING AND LEADING THEM.'[38]

Kies's speech was much acclaimed. It would become a classic for the NEUM. The literature of the NEUM's successor structure, the New Unity Movement (NUM), described the moment as the birth of a new school: 'The NEUM critique of racialism was started collectively by a School of students of Language, History, Biology, Economics, Social Anthropology and Medical Science, including Genetics, inside South Africa.'[39]

The Kies speech took the organisation back to the position that Gool had been holding fast to in his argument with Gomas. It marked out, and in a programmatic way for the first time, what was going on sociologically in the country and how this sociology of superiority and inferiority could be approached tactically and strategically. The turn-around that had been foreshadowed in the NEF's stock-taking at the beginning of the 1940s was brought here to a point of clarity. An agenda for action was put on the table. At the heart of that agenda, to drive it, were teachers, the core of the intelligentsia among the oppressed. The teachers, Kies maintained, were best placed to do this:

> And so I wish to turn for one moment to the young men and women teachers, and I wish to say to them: 'We have a very responsible task, within and without the classroom. We are not pioneers in this field, for many men and women teachers in other parts of the world have gone before us. We walk in their tradition, and *our* generation of teachers is the pioneer in this country ... It is the duty of the true teacher to pull off the mask and scrape off the scales of ignorance that blind the youth. It is the duty of the true teacher to give his pupils knowledge so that they may KNOW the world, and so that they may CHANGE the world. For it is not enough for them to know; they must also change things for the benefit of humanity. And, more than this, the true teacher's duty does not end with the pupils. He has a vital and active part to play in the liberation of the people. He has to help to educate the people in the struggle. He has to help to lead them along the right road. We are all in chains, teacher and worker: We can never throw them off individually. But if we *both* play our part to the full, we will break those bonds.[40]

The way to get teachers to this level of struggle, Kies continued, was to make sure that they 'fit [themselves] ... for the task': 'The ignorant can never lead. We must see to it that we study the problems of the people and that we understand them clearly. Liberation is never achieved by raving or passing violent resolutions. It is only achieved by those WHO KNOW. Second, we must practice what we teach our students and our

127

people . . . In other words, it is only the unity of theory and practice which can produce sound leadership.'[41]

The words would become close to dictum. They would come to give the NEF and its sister organisations their basic frameworks and vocabularies.

The difference between where these socialists were in the middle of the 1930s and where they found themselves in the first half of the 1940s was that they now had the promise of organisational vehicles to advance their practice. Valuable and innovative as the cultural sphere was, it was no longer a case of only working through cultural activities.

It is perhaps useful (and appropriate) to reflect briefly here on how this social analysis dealt with the gender question. In reflecting on approaches to gender in the NEUM, with which he became involved in the 1950s, Neville Alexander said in an interview in 2006 that discussions were essentially philosophical.[42] While the gender question might not systematically have been chased down, people in the NEF were not completely unaware of it. Kies certainly was aware of it. Writing under the pseudonym Fandum in the *Sun* in a column he regularly penned, he offered, as Sandwith tells us, a view that was 'out of kilter with his times'.[43] He offered 'an explanation for the usual dominance of men in political discussion and the effects of gender differences by illuminating the primary economic logic that forces women to adopt postures of the "winsome and coy in order to persuade some egoistic brute to condescend to marry them"'. He went further. He began to construct an argument about the triple oppression women faced. Race, class and gender were the building blocks, he said, of oppression.

Interestingly, similarly Phyllis Ntantala, the wife of A C Jordan, spoke of how her husband 'was growing too. He was becoming less conservative, thanks to our moving to Cape Town. It was here that he shed a lot of his conservative ways. This was thanks also to his best friend, I.B. Tabata, an advocate of women's rights, who helped A.C. embrace the new ways and attitudes.'[44]

In light of testimonies such as these, clearly an awareness of the struggle for women's equality did exist, but the issue was not placed on the public agenda and it did not enjoy the attention that was given to race and class. And it would not be pursued, either by Kies himself or anybody else in the movement, for another couple of decades.

* * *

The major item on the agenda for action of the anti-Stalinist socialists was the establishment of an organisation that would bring South Africa's oppressed people together. A debate took place at the Anti-CAD conference around how such an organisation should be structured. Van Schoor argued for a structure based on individual membership. This was rejected in favour of a federal type organisation. A national campaign was launched to draw the major political groupings of the oppressed into the process. The support of the AAC was quickly obtained. Its leadership at that point was dominated by Tabata, Tsotsi, Gool, Kies and Jayiya.[45] The South African Indian Congress (SAIC) also agreed to participate but on terms that were later deemed to be suspicious. The AAC issued 'The Clarion Call – A Call to Unity',[46] which led, in December 1943, to the Preliminary Unity Conference 'where a 10-Point Programme was adopted as the basis for unity. The Non-European Unity Movement was formed'.[47] The 10-Point Programme consisted of minimum demands:

1. The franchise, ie the right of every man and woman over the age of 21 to elect and be elected to Parliament, Provincial Councils and all other Divisional and Municipal Councils.
2. Compulsory, free and uniform education for all children up to the age of 16, with free meals, free books and school equipment for the needy.
3. Inviolability of person, of one's house and privacy.
4. Freedom of speech, press, meetings and association.

5. Freedom of movement and occupation.
6. Full equality of rights for all citizens without distinction of race, colour or sex.
7. Revision of the land question in accordance with the above.
8. Revision of the civil and criminal code in accordance with the above.
9. Revision of the system of taxation in accordance with the above.
10. Revision of the labour legislation and its application to the mines and agriculture.[48]

The road to unity was not straightforward, however. A central issue was the structure of the federal body. Should it acknowledge or reject the country's racial sensibilities? The decision was taken that the federation, in acknowledgement of the reality of racial thinking, would consist of the representatives of the three recognised racial groups in the country – the AAC would represent the African section, the Anti-CAD the 'Coloured' and the SAIC the Indian. This was not, the point was made repeatedly, an acceptance of the racial divisions in the country. Significantly, the ANC had refused the invitation to participate and in the next few years the SAIC would withdraw in favour of an alliance with the ANC.[49]

In the public arena, particularly in Cape Town, initially there was hostility to the idea of unity. The 'In my Tower' column in the *Cape Standard* reported on 11 January 1944: 'Last week, the Anti-CAD Conference received, quite unexpectedly, a fair amount of publicity in the daily press. This was all the more significant, in view of the fact that during the past ten months' campaigning, the daily press was loath to open its columns to the views and activities of the Anti-CAD movement. Adverse criticism, however, was splashed on every occasion.'[50]

The public response, however, started to shift. In January H Ahmed wrote a Letter to the Editor of the *Cape Standard* promoting the cause of the Anti-CAD.[51] The discussion rapidly turned to the road to unity and more support for the Anti-CAD programme.[52] 'In my Tower' distinctly reported that a shift away from negative publicity about the

Anti-CAD movement was under way, and on 11 January 1944 the paper's headline was 'The Road to Unity'.[53] The declaration of unity at the Bloemfontein conference of the Anti-CAD executive was aired prominently over two pages. The headline article reported that 'a militant note was struck in the resolution which proposed that the Anti-C.A.D. Movement should inaugurate its Unity Campaign on the day of the opening of Parliament by holding joint mass meetings with African and Indian organisations throughout the Union'.

A not insignificant dynamic in the meeting was the subtle tension between the educated and the less-educated members of the gathering. The *Cape Standard* reported that a Mr M D Arendse 'made one of the best speeches of the Conference when this question [of the impact of the CAC and CAD upon the status of Coloured workers in trade unions] arose. He was particularly anxious that the anti-CAD Bulletins should be written in more simple language and should touch on matters which might interest the mass of the people.'[54]

Discussions about the idea of unity in and among the oppressed continued in the cultural and debating circles of Cape Town. A motion was considered at the Fourth International Club, 'that th[e] Conference considers [the] fight for full democratic rights inseparable from the fight against Imperialist domination . . . [in] support [of] the fight for self-determination for all oppressed Colonial people'.[55] This led to lively discussion and in the end the motion was passed with one dissident. The People's Club similarly took up the issue. It issued an invitation to a mass meeting to be held at the club in Commercial Street up the road from the Stakesby-Lewis Hostel.[56] The invitation was an indication of possible signs of unity between the opposing socialist positions.

On 24 January 1944 the *Cape Standard* announced that the launch meeting of the NEUM would take place in the City Hall on 26 January under the banner 'Unity Campaign of all Non-Europeans for Full Citizenship Rights'.[57] The meeting would be chaired by Tabata.[58] This was followed by a flurry of nationwide attempts to mobilise oppressed people. Tabata was at the forefront of the national effort, while Goolam Gool continued to preside over the Anti-CAD movement.[59] Even Cissie Gool came out in support. She 'urge[d] all Non-Europeans to unite and smash segregation once and for all.'[60] By mid-February, at a mass meeting in Langa, Africans came out in support of the Unity movement programme and Tabata's tireless journeys into the country started to bear fruit. The Kimberley Anti-CAD Committee inaugurated its Unity Campaign,[61] pointing out that there was 'one law for the White man and one for the Black'.[62] On page 7 of the same issue of the *Cape Standard*, 29 February 1944, there was talk about the 'Democratic Rights struggle'; and the De Aar Anti-CAD meeting was discussed on page 4. On 7 March it was reported that the Anti-CAD committee had been elected. There was also a march that month in Worcester and a meeting in Somerset West.[63] In all of these meetings the discussion turned increasingly to the colour bar.[64]

Significantly, in the midst of the delivery of a number of lectures on issues ranging from the war in China to the bombing by the Americans of Hiroshima and Nagasaki, it was in the NEF that the debate was examined most assiduously. On 1 April 1944 a lecture was given by Mr D Singh, President of the Indian League. The lecture was of great importance. It elicited a response from Hosea Jaffe, at that point a member of FIOSA, in an article titled 'Racial Sectarianism or Non-European Unity'.[65] He challenged Singh's position, which was that separate organisations should remain, that the move to complete unity was premature. Failure to unify, Jaffe pointed out, would harm the struggle. Tabata gave a lecture on Saturday 10 April on 'The African This Session' at the Stakesby-Lewis Hostel about the state of the African people, in which he explained the land question, describing how the Africans had been forced off the land and the legal machinery that had been used to do this.[66]

It was in the course of these discussions that Kies gave the second of his three key addresses, *The Basis of Unity*. It was delivered at the Third Unity Conference of the NEUM at the Banqueting Hall in Cape Town on 4 January 1945. This address was critical in advancing the argument that Kies had begun in *The Background of Segregation*. One cannot make the claim, of course, that the positions advanced in this lecture were the products of the debates that were taking place in the NEF, but Kies and his comrades, in giving expression to the commitments made in the founding of the NEUM, were well aware of the need to use all the legal media and events under their aegis to promote the cause of building the consciousness of the people. In this, and this is the key observation to make, they had effectively proliferated and multiplied the spaces and places where the function of the NEF when it came to educating the people could take expression. The NEF remained the nursery but the outlets for the message of the movement were significantly diversified. The socialists began to use the TLSA's *Educational Journal*, for example, whose readership was the teaching profession, and they also established a popular newspaper, *The Torch*. A cadre of intellectuals was set to work to write for both publications. Through this they developed a distinct pedagogical register.

What did *The Basis of Unity* say that was different from what Kies and his colleagues had said before? In what way did it advance the argument?

In assessing this contribution it is important to note that it remained within the logic of race and racial groups. Kies had not yet advanced to the point of rejecting the idea of race, but he came to a key moment in the analysis when he said: 'We have to declare upon the Segregationists and other reactionaries within our own organisations and within our own particular racial group.'[67] He was beginning to recognise the need for a theory of race. That recognition, it needs to be remembered, had earlier been intimated by Gool but Kies was to state it much more emphatically. 'Your political theory,' he said, 'means the way you sum up things, where you consider the interests of the oppressed to lie.' He continued: 'The Programme does matter. Theory is important.'[68]

Kies's theory began at a point where Gool and Gomas had already been in 1937, that race was artifice, a thing made up: 'The recognition that Segregation is an artificial device of the rulers, and an instrument for the domination of the Non-European, is at the same time a recognition that the division, strife and suspicion amongst the Non-European groups themselves is artificially fostered by the ruling class.'[69] The advance Kies made to this thinking was to explore the deep discursive hold race had on people's minds. 'The agencies of the White rulers,' he maintained, '. . . will go out of their way to use the Unity Movement to increase the existing racialistic feelings between black and white workers; they will spread the poison that we are anti-White, that we want to replace the White Herrenvolk by a Black Herrenvolk. But the more they do this, the more we must insist and the more we must show in practice that we are not racialist: we are not anti-White, but anti-Segregationist.' Kies concluded by claiming that 'all these points . . . together comprise a whole outlook, a *new outlook*'.[70]

That Kies was onto the breakthrough – turning the focus onto the artifice of race – is clear. He understood how it required a whole new outlook on life. He understood how the material and the ideological came together. He did not articulate this relationship theoretically in the way that a theoretician such as the great Italian Marxist Antonio Gramsci had come to understand positionality or in the way that the French deconstructionist philosophers, such as Michel Foucault, explained discourse, but he was primed around the question of the operation of dominance. He understood that the subjects of capitalism were caught in a vice grip of subservience. They were mental slaves. Their whole outlook on life, their sense of self, their explanations of their relationships with each other, their aesthetics and their consequential political takes on power were all configured by the outlook imposed on them and assimilated by them. They were in the grip of hegemony. Without using the words, Kies was making the argument that dominant discourse infiltrated the mind and the body. How he put what was needed, which 'was a complete change of orientation in the present and not at some future and unknowable date,' was incisive.[71]

Kies and his colleagues would continue to hone the argument around race and its operations. Reflecting these developments in June

1948 Tabata sent a public letter to Nelson Mandela on 'the problem of organisational unity in South Africa'. In the letter he criticised the ANC for not shedding its tribalist outlook.[72]

To clarify: while Tabata continued to use the expression 'we the African people', there was in this a clear awareness and a sense of the authenticity of his African past. It was not something he would want to wish away. It was part of who he was. It was already in his mind, not something that he wore on his skin. It was cultural. He was deeply conscious of white denigration of the culture of the African people.

Alongside him, more prescient, in a sense, were the reflections of his colleagues on culture and alienation. Kies had written in 1941 about English as a 'world language', as something that did not belong to the English.[73] Taylor had already begun to develop an analysis that challenged patrimonial and essentialist ideas about race and culture. Jordan, by 1950, was beginning to claim Western culture as the inheritance of all people: '[It is as if] this civilization sprang out of the brain of the white man in the same way as the Goddess, Pallas Athene, sprang out of the brains of Zeus.' The direction in which Jordan was heading was reflected in the publications and statements of members of the wider NEUM family.

There were a few opportunities for this incipient anti-racist position to take clearer expression. One came from a process of public consultation initiated by the Eiselen Commission into 'the formulation of the principles and aims of education for natives as an independent race, in which their past and present, their inherent racial qualities, their distinctive characteristics and aptitude, and their needs under the ever-changing social conditions are taken into consideration'.[74] The process saw people who took exception to the idea of human beings being classified into separate races comimg forward. A Mr Ntantile, a teacher from the Cape (his affiliations were not given in the evidence record), exemplified this view. In response to a question from one of the Eiselen commissioners about the racial characteristics of African people, his reply was that there was only one human race.[75]

A submission was made by the TLSA in which it similarly rejected the racial tendentiousness of the commission: '[It represents] an attitude which cannot find any scientific support at all, but it is a manifestation of a mentality peculiar to Nazism and "thinking with one's blood".'[76] These were significant statements being made in the public domain about the sociology of race.

Some years later, in 1953, Dora Taylor gave another of her lectures to students. This one was titled 'The Function of Literary Criticism' and in it she profoundly engaged the power of social and literary analysis in the most de-essentialised and deconstructive form one could find anywhere.[77] She de-ontologised identity in racial terms, bestowing on *all* human beings, irrespective of where they came from, the capacity and power to interpret the world. Tabata's lectures continued too; one, at an NEF gathering in 1951, was headed 'Landlessness is a Means of Exploitation'.

An argument was developing. Although there is not enough in the archive that is available to give an idea of the detail of all the steps it took to get to this point, it would come to full bloom with Kies's third major speech, 'The Contribution of the Non-European Peoples to Civilisation', in 1953.

The period after the establishment of the NEUM, however, was marked by a process of putting in place the wherewithal for educating the people. The NEF would have continued its activities, but it would have ceded to the formal political organs around it some of the functions it performed before their establishment. As Sandwith outlines, the *Bulletin* and *The Torch* became the 'principal focus of the young radicals, with the numerous fellowships maintaining their function as a "sorting house of ideas" and a conduit for a new black intelligentsia'.[78] The *Bulletin*, published from 1943 until the early 1950s, consisted of either single- or doubled-paged inexpensive handouts: 'Typewritten, without photographs or graphics of any kind, and with authorship kept anonymous, the *Bulletin* was designed purely for dissemination of information . . . Ben Kies, however, is the likely author of many if not all of the *Bulletins*. Because it was a weekly, it was afforded the opportunity of summarizing a week's worth of events in an intensely intellectual fashion.'[79]

A young member of the Anti-CAD remembered how the *Bulletin* was distributed and received: 'I was at Trafalgar High School at the time, and these *Bulletins* used to be distributed at the Trafalgar High School . . . We used to [presumably after he himself became a teacher] put these *Bulletins* in the desks of students.'[80] The *Educational Journal* of the TLSA, similarly, took a great deal of the socialists' attention. These outlets would build up a strong cadre of contributors, many writing under pseudonyms. The constant in all of them was Kies himself. He wrote prolifically and influentially. It was in the course of this intense engagement that he found opportunity to think of the questions of race and the nation. He developed in the process the capacity to shift his scale of analysis between the local and the international and to connect the dynamics on the ground in South Africa to global forces.

Christopher Joon-Hai Lee suggests that Kies produced a genre of writing in the process that stood in comparison with Gramsci:

Much like his ideas, this body of thought was antifascist and spoke to a specific historical moment, though also attempting a deeper and wider-ranging social analysis. If Gramsci's *Notes on Italian History* sought to describe a 'passive revolution' of bourgeois hegemonic development in Italy, Anti-CAD and later NEUM literature sought to expose the passive revolution of segregation and white *Herrenvolk* hegemony being constituted in South Africa . . . The *Bulletins* sought to promote, conceptually, and universalize a common, subjected condition of 'Non-Europeans', similar to Gramsci's 'subaltern' classes.[81]

The intimations were there in the *Bulletin*. They were brought together with incisive clarity by Kies in 1953.

* * *

On 29 September 1953 Kies gave the second A J Abrahamse Memorial Lecture in Cape Town. The lecture was part of a schedule of activities organised by the TLSA. It was titled 'The Contribution of the Non-European Peoples to World Civilisation' and its focus was on the 'myth' of 'race'.[82] Kies sought systematically to demolish the idea of 'Western Civilisation', and a 'Western man' with a 'Western soul', a 'Western philosophy', a 'Western science' and a 'Western way of life'.

The particular significance of this speech was the seemingly unproblematic couplet of 'race' and 'civilisation'. It extensively addressed how the world of the 1940s and the 1950s, despite the horrors of the Holocaust and the Second World War, continued to be constructed upon the discredited science of racial-biology. Kies said:

> The creed of the new myth requires the changing of only one word in the Nordic gospel, and it reads: 'In Westernkind the world once more its weal will find.'[83] The peoples of Asia and Africa are regarded as belonging to 'backward' or 'child' 'races', whose 'inherent inferiority' is patent from their numbers, skin colour, queer customs, heathen gods, laziness, treachery, primitive methods of farming, irresponsibility, fatalism and disregard for the sacredness of human life. In so far as it is admitted that the peoples of Asia have made any contribution to civilisation, it is conceded that they stumbled upon certain discoveries without appreciating their worth or developing them in a way from which society could benefit . . . As far as Africa is concerned . . . [it is] the home of permanently child 'races'.[84]

Kies proposed that 'one of the more important tasks of our time is to dissect this myth . . . and to give our reply to it, on the level of ideas and in the field of practice'.[85] The task needed to begin, he said – and this is key for our discussion – with placing the use of the term 'Non-European' under scrutiny. 'Non-European', he declared with emphasis, was nothing more than a geographical term. It could refer to people of 'any skin-colour, height, hair texture, skull or nose shape who live outside of the Continent of Europe'.

The moment is worthy of comparison with Biko's clarification of the meaning of the term 'black',[86] but the perspicacity of Kies's work, as an ontological route-marker for the movement he represented, was of profound importance. It came from an engagement with the historical, scientific canon long before this kind of writing appeared in the work of the world's most significant anti-racist scientists such as Stephen Jay Gould, Ashley Montagu, Paul Gilroy, David Goldberg and Robert Miles. Not only was Kies familiar with the latest anthropology of the 1950s, the work, for example, of Gordon Childe on the history of the early hominids, of the Leakeys at the Olduvai Gorge in East Africa but also of the emerging work of South African anthropologists such as Raymond Dart and Robert Broom, who were beginning to talk of the southern African region as being the cradle of humankind. Kies continued with this line of thought to acknowledge:

We are in no position at the present time to pronounce upon the weight of the evidence thus far produced by the newer line of research. It is *sufficient* for our purpose to say that we, the so-called 'children of Ham', together with Messrs D.F. Malan and Eric Louw derive from the same stock, *homo sapiens*, as Dr. L.S.B. Leakey and the Mau Mau whom he is now so bitterly fighting . . . The human race is now, as it was when *homo sapiens* evolved, one biological species, with the same number and formation of bones, the same brain and nerve structure, the same internal organs, the same four types of blood groups . . . and the same capacity, in fact propensity, for interbreeding . . . Geographical dispersal, isolation and diet have not made the slightest difference to the biological unity of man as a single species, and provide no scientific basis for a division into what are popularly mis-called 'races'.[87]

Shifting his gaze to Europe and the sites of the famous origins of civilisation, he said that in none of those sites 'was [there] any sign of a "pure race" . . . so-called Caucasoids lay mixed with the Negroids and Mongoloids in a way which admits of no way of telling whether one of them had invented a dolichocephalic harness, or another a brachycephalic wheel or still another a mezzocephalic alphabet.'[88]

Kies then turned his attention to the ways in which consciousness was formed. In this he began to articulate in the most developed terms for his time the social psychology of human development:

> As we advance nearer to man, however, so the purely instinctive recedes and we approach the level of human consciousness and self-consciousness. But in no matter how primitive a stage we find man, however, we find, too, that the culture which is coincident with him has had as an important social element what Julius Lippert called the 'care for life' (Lebensfürsorge), 'as a cultural principle'. It is necessary to stress this at the very outset, as an answer to those who, like T H Huxley in the nineteenth century, represent primitive man as living a life 'continual free fight', and who, in the face of all the evidence produced by the past 75 years of archaeology and anthropology, would elevate this error to an ethic to rationalise their treatment of the so-called 'Children of Ham'. Thus it is popular with certain South African university defenders of the *status quo* – who often seem willing to accept that Non-Whites are 'superior apes', while they themselves are fallen angels – to depict 'white Christian civilisation' as coming in the nick of time to save the !Ke, Khoi-Khoin and Bantu from extermination by one another.[89]

It appears that Kies had assimilated completely what the best and most current science was saying about the factuality of race. His speech still contained offensive terms, such as the word 'Bantu', but his explanations of what was going on sociologically and culturally were as sophisticated as could be found anywhere. Interestingly, at that time, South Africa's leading palaeontologist, Phillip Tobias, was still measuring skulls to classify them racially. Christa Kuljian describes this in her book *Darwin's Hunch*:

> [Phillip] Tobias inherited the Raymond Dart Gallery of African Faces which included over 600 life masks and 800 death masks. Just as with the skulls and skeletons, Dart had developed a system of categorising the masks, describing them according to racial type based on anatomical features. Tobias inherited this way of describing the masks, which he did annually with his students . . . For much of the 1950s, Tobias's research focused on the study of living human beings and human measurement was a major aspect of his career, which included decades of research in the Kalahari and with other peoples of southern Africa.[90]

It is not clear if Kies was specifically aware of Tobias. He certainly was aware of how the disciplines of anthropology, archaeology and palaeontology were being taught and what was being taught. In this he was extremely critical of the South African academy and its leading professors. They stood miles apart from each other. The target of Kies's thinking was a society which he and colleagues such as Tabata saw as a 'complex social structure in which the ordinary class divisions (which are easily observable as the pattern of society in Europe) are complicated and obscured by multiracial distinctions, constituting a veritable maze of conflicting interests, both real and apparent'.[91]

A further dimension of Kies's insight was his deconstruction of culture and its relation to the body. He distanced himself from the race-culture homology, and its iconicisation with 'functionless architecture, literature that does not sell'. In so doing he was advancing the theoretical position his colleagues had regularly taken. This position, exemplified in the work of Tabata, challenged white hegemony in South Africa and the ways in which the race-culture homology was perpetrated. It essentially argued that the racist state 'bolsters up the myth of itself as the master-race, a Herrenvolk, the idea being that the progenitors of this country, in some mystic past, must have issued from the lips of Brahma, while the black masses originated from the grosser parts of his anatomy.'[92] Kies, in explicating the power of all people to make civilisation, defined culture 'as the measure of man's [sic] control over nature, a control exercised through experience shared among social groups and accumulated through the ages. It is [in] deepening and extending the scope of this control that man has added so immeasurably to the potentialities of his life.'[93]

Kies brought this argument to a conclusion by saying that 'it is from his culture . . . that man derives his humanity, and begins his social history'.[94] Critically, in emphasising the significance of the slow process of 'trial and error' in history – the first cultural stage through which every society goes – he made clear how important to the discussion of the idea of a common humanity was the reality that the first processes of domestication of animals and the cultivation of plants took place outside of what is understood as Europe today. Europe, in this sense, was the inheritor of many important cultural and technological discoveries. In this argument, he anticipated Dipesh Chakrabarty's landmark postcolonial text, *Provincialising Europe*, by more than 50 years.

The use of irony in this text aside, a key feature of this approach, giving its identity framework its distinctive character, was the belief, as Tabata explains, that the world they sought to create was not 'something bloodless, static and lifeless . . . What we want is a dynamic approach depicting a living body in a state of motion, capable of adjusting itself to the play of forces around it and in turn interacting with them.'[95] The belief in the power of the human mind and body and its universal capacity for agency is the leitmotif of Kies, Tabata and their colleagues.

The impact of this lecture was profound. It significantly advanced the theoretical discussion of what race was and how it could be understood historically and sociologically. For the first time since Olive

Schreiner and Hogben, an explanation of how to locate the concept in relation to the politics of difference was being provided. 'With few exceptions,' observes Jaffe, 'colonial-liberation movements . . . fell into the trap of "races", "ethnic groups", and used these to classify the oppressed themselves.'[96] This politics, Kies made clear, had been constructed around an ideology of superiority and inferiority 'as a weapon in a global war fought mainly for the re-distribution of spheres of economic interest inhabited by the lesser breeds without the myth'.[97]

Jaffe gives Kies's analysis a strong political economy framing. Explaining racialism 'right into the present late 20th century', he describes it as 'the ideological cement for slavery and subsequent forms of colonial super-exploitation and oppression'. He continues:

> It has served the real purpose of separating the European and later also the North American colonialists from their Non-European colonial victims and prey. It has served the real material role of preserving cheap docile, slave-mentality super-profit-producing colonial labour . . . It has been the psychological balm and opium of the Europeans to justify these economic, social and political means and ends and a garotte to strangle the cry of freedom among the colonial peoples. It generated hate by Europeans and fear and later also hate among Non-Europeans. But racialism itself was generated not by hate but by the global real material interests of Euro-American capitalism.[98]

Where the politics of the early anti-Stalinists socialists was constructed around a theory of racial equality, which placed them in the same conceptual orbit as their Stalinist opponents, these grown-up socialists had come to the startling awareness that the idea of race could no longer be sustained at all.

What the NEF had begun in 1937 as an intuition culminated sixteen years later in 1953 in a distinct and autochthonous theory of social differentiation. The socialists had developed their own theory. They had come to break with their colleagues around the world: 'Marxists of renown, [who] accepted as given the existence of different, albeit equal, human "races"'. Where, until then, terms such as 'coloured', 'African', 'Indian' and 'European' were used easily and without hesitation, people in the NEF circle began to realise the implications of their facile reproduction. Jaffe himself, almost 60 years later, would mount a scathing review of the 'Eurocentric' capitulation of socialist analysis to racism.[99] It was this sociological innovation that their political opponents could not see. Richard van der Ross, for example, who would argue that none of the NEF's members had sufficient sociology,[100] would have seen, had he looked properly, an attempt, open to criticism as it was, to enter at a profound level the not-yet-opened space of sociology and psychology. Inherent in Kies's arguments was an appreciation of how social groups acquired individual and collective identity. Social Psychology as a discipline was still to emerge properly. It was evoked here vividly.

In bringing this assessment of Kies and the NEF to a close, it is necessary to point out that the NEUM continued to manage its federal structure on the basis and acceptance of three distinct racial groups within the 'Non-European' community. But its members increasingly began to shed their language of its instinctive racial inflections. They refused, furthermore, to carry and present themselves as 'coloureds'. 'Coloured' became an epithet of disgust and contempt. They would no longer be 'coloureds'. They were human beings first and foremost. If they were to accede to a political identity at all, it was that of 'South African'. Their whole outlook had changed. The task to follow was to take that outlook into the country.

6 | A Cauldron of Conflict

The closing lines of Ben Kies's A J Abrahamse Memorial Lecture, *The Contribution of Non-European Peoples to World Civilisation*, embodied a *cri de cœur* that would ring for decades in the ears of the socialist movement in South Africa. He said: 'In the eyes of the South African *Herrenvolk*, segregation or *apartheid*, curfews, locations and the South African laws may represent civilisation, and the liberation from them a relapse into barbarism. But we, together with the majority of mankind who have seen the hateful, degenerate cannibalism to which these defenders of "Western", "European", "Christian" civilisation have in fact brought civilisation in the West, we think otherwise.'[1]

The period in which Kies made his speech was in the early days of apartheid. It was neither the urbane Jan Smuts nor the intellectual descendants of a confused British ruling class that the progressive movement had to deal with, but an obdurate community of white supremacists for whom South Africa was the last remaining hope for white 'civilisation'. The historical irony was that as Kies was bringing the thinking on race among the Cape Radicals to an apogee seen almost nowhere else on the globe, at almost the same time, the Malan-Verwoerd axis, the inheritors of Francis Galton and the eugenics movement, were putting in place the architecture and the apparatus for the world's most devastating racist project – apartheid.

There they were, the consummate theoreticians of non-racism, in the hall of St George's Cathedral in Cape Town and not even a hundred metres away in South Africa's iconic colonial Houses of Parliament were the world's most stubborn race recidivists. Two 'culture-beds' brought to their most fecund states.[2] One a hothouse of nurturance, the other a laboratory of disrespect, pretentiousness and hauteur.

Within a few years of coming into power the National Party, the victors of the 1948 white election, instituted a battery of laws. As Sarah Mokone writes:

> In the first session of the Parliament of the 1950s the Malanzis wasted no time in making it clear that in that decade they were determined to mould, in accordance with their Apartheid philosophy and the master-race ideology, a South Africa in which each ethnic group would live in a geographically demarcated area, separate from all other groups: only persons of white descent would sit and be represented in the law-making institutions of the land and other ethnic groups would be excluded from the body politic.[3]

These laws began to be introduced in 1948, first enforcing apartheid on trains and, in quick measure, included the Prohibition of Mixed Marriages Act of 1949, the Population Registration Act of 1950, the Group Areas Act of 1950, the Suppression of Communism Act of 1950, and a slew of other punishingly restrictive laws.

The NEF had served the purpose, in the period before the apartheid onslaught, of bringing the progressive movement to a point of significant theoretical clarity. What did it do with this clarity in the 1950s? With its new tools of analysis, how did it respond?

As Mokone has remarked, the new apartheid order made the development of a total strategy a central part of its plans. Central to this strategy was the process of 'obliterat[ing] for all time from [the minds of the oppressed] *any idea at all* of equality in a free South Africa'.[4] They saw 'the solution to this problem in a system of schooling that would indoctrinate the new generations of the oppressed into an unquestioning acceptance of their inferior position in South Africa'. Thus, Mokone continues, was 'spawned the monster of Bantu Education, under the control of the government Department of Native Affairs. With doctrines of Christian-National (CNO) "eiesoortigheid" (own kind) and "andersoortigheid" (otherness) it was intended to crush forever all aspirations for freedom on the part of the majority section of the oppressed.' Its object, wrote Mokone, was to lay the foundations of the architect of apartheid, Hendrik Verwoerd's 'grandiose schemes . . . [for] the South African White Nation that he so fantastically visualised'.

The response of the socialists was to mobilise. Hundreds of meetings and rallies were organised around South Africa. While the African National Congress (ANC) sprang into action, the Non-European Unity Movement (NEUM) sought to distinguish itself from the ANC by emphasising its policy of non-collaboration: 'The struggle against *Herrenvolkism* could be won,' writes Mokone, 'only if waged on the basis of the Unity of all the oppressed and by their refusing to become involved in the machinery of their own oppression. The strategy of struggle had to be Non-Collaboration in any form of oppressive machinery.'[5]

The NEUM made a point of focusing on the question of consciousness and in 1951 it put out a statement, 'A Declaration to the People of South Africa'. The statement opened with an analysis of consciousness, then expanded: 'We know that the *Herrenvolk* are waging relentless war upon us and aim at crushing us as a people and reducing us to a soul-less, will-less ambition-less chattel slavery. Yet we go about as if we *did not know* either the cause of our suffering or the remedy for it.'[6]

The point the declaration was making was that of understanding, consciousness, *knowing*. It pivoted its attack on hegemony by rejecting in total what it described as '*Herrenvolk*' ideology. To that ideology it presented its own understanding of South Africa:

Who are the people to whom we are addressing this declaration? Who constitutes the South African nation? The answer to this question is as simple as it would be in any other country. The nation consists of the people who were born in South Africa and who have no other country but South Africa as their mother-land. They may have been born with a black skin or with a brown one, a yellow one or a white one. They may be long-headed or round-headed; straight-haired or curly-haired; they may have long noses or broad noses; they may speak Xhosa, Zulu, Sotho, English or Afrikaans, Hindi, Urdu or Swahili, Arabic or Jewish, they may be Christians, Mohammedans, Buddhists, or any other faith. So long as they are born of a mother and belong to the human species, so long as they are not lunatics or incurable criminals, they all have an equal title to be South Africans, members of the nation, with the same rights, privileges and duties.[7]

To a contemporary ear elements of this declaration are problematic, but the basic issue, to which Kies had spoken forcefully in his *Contribution of Non-European Peoples to World Civilisation* in 1953, was the construct of race. To be South African all one needed was to be a member of the human race. To win the war, the declaration concluded, required sacrifice and discipline: 'Even without arms, with the only weapon at our disposal – Non-Collaboration – we can win. But in order to achieve victory, We have got to build the Nation.'[8]

* * *

Ralph Bunche and many other scholars have argued that the intellectuals in the National Liberation League (NLL) and its successor organisations, like the NEF, had difficulty in communicating their message to ordinary people.[9] Isaac Tabata was later to cite this as a reason for forming the Society of Young Africa (SOYA). Again, this may be partially correct, but the truth of the matter was that the anti-Stalinist socialists used what they had learnt. They embarked during the 1950s on an intense educational programme.

This campaign involved the establishment of structures all over South Africa and putting out as much writing as they could. It remains unclear how the disciplinary structure of the anti-Stalinists operated. While unverified sources suggest that the Workers' Party of South Africa (WPSA) ceased to exist in 1953 (this could have been related to the Suppression of Communism Act of 1950, of course), it must be assumed that it continued to operate behind the scenes after it went underground in June 1939.[10] Its influence, through the NEUM, was evident in the deliberate strategy that was embarked on in the 1950s, of establishing education and cultural fellowships in the major suburbs and townships of the Cape and in encouraging the brightest young people in the schools to become teachers.

Although the Teachers' League of South Africa (TLSA) was a major site for the development of the ideas of the NEF, it is also important to emphasise that so, too, was the Cape African Teachers' Association (CATA). CATA played a major role in the fight against Bantu Education in 1952 and 1953 throughout the Cape. Led by Leo Sihlali in the 1950s, its members fought for their children, against the ANC policy to boycott Bantu Education, to stay in their schools but not to participate in the structures, such as the school boards and school committees, which had been set up to run the schools.[11]

This saw an entire generation of gifted young intellectuals deliberately moving into high schools and taking leadership positions: Edgar Maurice at Harold Cressy, Ernie Steenveld and Polly Slingers at Trafalgar, Richard Dudley at Livingstone and Tom Hanmer at Trafalgar and then at Wesley College. At Cressy Maurice would be succeeded by Victor Ritchie, Peter Meyer and Lionel Adriaan. Their colleagues included the peerless Helen Kies, Dickie Williams, Maureen Adriaan and a talented cadre of loyal TLSA colleagues. Trafalgar at its height had Steenveld, Slingers, Solly Edross, Hassan Bavasah and a whole string of young teachers who profoundly influenced a generation of younger leaders. There they developed almost legendary status. Harold Cressy became one of the University of Cape Town's (UCT's) top five feeder schools. The historian Ciraj Rassool said that approximately 30 of the 35 students in his matriculation class landed up at UCT.

Sedick Isaacs described the succession of teachers who '[came] over the years to try and teach us about Democracy, Oppression, and the History of the Struggle against discrimination . . . We read about revolutions in other parts of the world and the story of Djamila Bopacha of the Algerian resistance against the French impressed us greatly . . . There were great teachers at Trafalgar High School like Slingers and Steenveldt [sic] and Cosmo Pieterse.'[12]

Marcus Solomon, who, along with Neville Alexander, was a member of the National Liberation Front and was imprisoned on Robben Island as a member of the Yu Chi Chan, spoke at the funeral of Polly Slingers on 17 October 2017. He remembered having been changed by him: 'My daughter said to me the other day, "Your body language changes in his presence."' In his tribute he said: 'I came to Trafalgar High School from Grahamstown. He was my senior teacher. I spent two years in his class. He changed my life . . . He didn't just teach through books. It was through example. Our children today see only a bunch of hypocrites.'

The environments into which these teachers came were fraught, to say the least. A school such as Trafalgar, for example, was, at its peak, a cauldron of conflict. Alongside the progressives, and they came in many stripes, were also many conservatives. Fakier Jessa, who was at Trafalgar in the 1960s, spoke of the presence of conservative and 'religionist' teachers at the school who 'rammed the syllabus down our throats'.[13] It should also be remembered that a number of teacher-activists, including Ben Kies, were banned in the 1950s. Kies was banned in 1956 'because of his political views and subsequently became a lawyer, with Dullah Omar, and later an advocate'.[14] The times in which they worked were marked by increasing state surveillance. People were watched, subjected to harassment and their careers brought to an end. Victor Wessels was banished to the Northern Cape. Dudley was banned; he was not permitted to attend meetings of the NEF. A whole cadre of NEF products, including people such as Kenny Abrahams who, with Neville Alexander, was instrumental in the establishment of the South West African People's Organisation, were subjected to years of cruel torment by the apartheid state.

In this atmosphere fellowships were established on the Cape Flats, the South Peninsula, in Langa, Paarl and the Northern Suburbs. They developed active identities of their own and constituted direct sites of connection and engagement with the communities in which they were set. Alexander remembered how, as a young student in his late teens, he and fellow students – Fikile Bam was one – were drawn into the fellowships and societies that had grown around the NEF, such as the Cape Peninsula Students' Union and SOYA, a deliberate alternative to the ANC Youth League. 'We read a lot, discussed a lot, socialized a lot to raise funds. We never got together socially for fun. We were reading, novels, Russian, even Afrikaans.'[15] These traditions and practices persisted into the heady days of the 1970s and the 1980s. Speaking at the opening session of the annual conference of the New Unity Movement (NUM), in Cape Town, on 17 December 2017, Allan Zinn – an important member of the NUM – remembered how he was inducted into the Cape Flats Education Fellowship (CAFEF) in the early 1970s:

I came into CAFEF as a 19 year old. The chair was Gerald Fife. People thought that CAFEF was Fife. The security police were on his neck all the time. At one point the caretaker of the venue where we were supposed to meet was kidnapped. We then met at a family member of Ian Viljoen. These family members were white and lived in a white area. Seven of the people there at those meetings were from the union movement, including the Cape Town Municipal Workers' Union. The way these fellowships worked is that you prepared for a lecture in groups of five and one person was selected to prepare especially for giving the lecture. The others were prepared to lead the discussion from the floor. It took a year before I was invited to another level, a higher level. The older members spent time with us. Preparing us . . . These cultural societies also got you into big trouble. The police came after you. (I remember the network that they came to constitute.) I had moved to the Eastern Cape and we started there, in Grahamstown, the Phoenix Cultural Society. This Phoenix Cultural Society linked Cape Town with Gaborone. The police asked us, 'What is this Phoonix?' I had a pamphlet sent to me from Cape Town from Doolie Desai on Kies. It was the time of Kies's death. It was written by one of the people here in the room today and Vutela.

These interventions were experienced by some as class-producing projects. Fakier Jessa remembered the South Peninsula Education Fellowship (SPEF), in not so pleasant ways:

The upper strata of the coloured group found it admirable to be a NEUM member as it suited both their political and class positions. The NEUM teachers at Trafs [Trafalgar] High encouraged scholars to join their youth wing, i.e. the South Peninsula Education Fellowship (SPEF) and there, on Sunday afternoons, literature was discussed and introduced in a fashionable way. SPEF, a middle class 'grooming' school, acutely inward focused, encouraged their members to accumulate knowledge and to join the ranks of the intelligentsia, to speak 'good' English in order to sustain their self-absorption and self-admiration through the accumulation of Marxist-Leninist reading.[16]

Jessa's experience was not all negative, however. Critical though he was, he would also remark about how much he had learnt.

SOYA in this broad narrative was an important initiative. It was established, as Allison Drew explains, at the prompting of Tabata, and had branches all over the country:

[It was a] response to the increasing numbers of African workers in towns and mounting pressure from NEUM youth for more township activity. It was also an attempt to counter the growing influence of the ANC among students and urban youth. To compete with the ANC Youth League SOYA began as an African-only youth grouping geared especially to the political education of working class Africans. Its membership became non-racial in the 1950s, including coloureds and Indians.[17]

SOYA was challenged from within the NEUM. Hosea Jaffe took a particularly critical attitude towards it. It became affiliated, as a result, with the All-African Convention (AAC) rather than with the NEUM itself. It had a distinctly Africanist orientation. Phumi Giyose, a prominent NUM leader, was a member of SOYA. He called himself a 'child of the NEF' when he spoke at an open session of the national conference of the NUM in Cape Town on 16 December 2017. He said that he joined SOYA

> . . . at the end of 1951 at the AAC Conference in Queenstown. Jabavu, at the end of the AAC Conference announced that all were invited to spend one more day in Queenstown to discuss the AAC programme. The flower of the youth who became leaders remained behind, Cameron Madikizela, Victor Wessels, the Wilcox girls. Tabata outdid himself. He asked the youth of the land to come together to form a new organization to build a new outlook throughout Africa. All of us would do well to revisit that document (which he delivered that day) . . . Many harkened to the words of Tabata. SOYA grew like a wild-fire, it started branches at the University of Fort Hare, Healdtown, St. John's College in Umtata. Chris Hani, many in the ANC, Thabo Mbeki, began their life in SOYA, to build a new outlook and a new soul of the people.

Phyllis Ntantala describes SOYA as a major cultural organisation of the early 1950s, whose slogan was 'We Fight Ideas with Ideas'.[18] It had been launched, she explains, under the auspices of the All-African Convention . . . to counter the rabid racism of the Youth League with its slogan 'Africa for the Africans'. SOYA spread rapidly throughout the African colleges, schools and townships and brought logic and reason to the South African situation. SOYA taught young people that it was not the whites who were the enemy of the blacks, but the capitalist system which exploited both black and white workers; that white workers had been coopted through concessions and made to think that they were not exploited and their place lay with the white owners of capital; however, the day was not far off when white workers would know that their comrades-in arms were the exploited African workers.[19]

Jaffe was influential in the establishment of the new fellowships that sprang up around Cape Town and elsewhere in the country. An illustration of the work that was going on in these structures is evident in the lectures delivered at CAFEF in 1955 on the French Revolution. Reference flowed frequently to the significance of the French Revolution for the South African struggle. The lectures included talks by Smith and Leitch on 'France in 1848 and 1871', Mr J de Beer on 'France in the 20th Century', Mr N Greeshof on 'The Literature of the French Revolution' and an illustrated lecture on 'Music and the French Revolution' by Mr Pulvermacher from UCT's College of Music. Significantly, from the socialists came a lecture by Jaffe titled 'An Outline of the French Revolution', another by Dr N A Murison on 'The Philosophes of the French Revolution', another by Victor Wessels on 'Some Comments on the Great French Revolution', and one by Cosmo Pieterse titled 'The Napoleonic Era: Aftermath of the Revolution'.[20] The lectures, which sparkled with erudition, were characterised by their attention to the craft of writing.

Another structure that was established at that time was the Cape Peninsula Students' Union (CPSU). Frank van der Horst, who became a president of the South African Council on Sport in the 1980s and who was a member of the CPSU, described the time in which it operated as 'critical'. To it came the leading intellectuals of the NEF, people such as Kies and Dullah Omar, who opened a 'new outlook on our lives' and 'taught us how to live under fascism'. 'We discussed revolution. But we had to do so underground . . . The WPSA and the NEF, led by people like Burlak, provided the guiding light,' he said.[21]

The impact of these interventions was powerful. Young people were formed by them. They came to imbibe 'the new outlook'. Even though, as Alexander commented, there was a somewhat Eurocentric bias in the selection of topics and issues, a level of critical scholarship was achieved in these forums and political circles that was not in any sense the inferior of anything emerging out of the academic world.[22] Rereading the CAFEF lectures of 1955 almost 35 years later, Jaffe remarked that they anticipated and preceded the 'monumental' contributions of the post-structuralists by decades.[23]

The TLSA also took the decision in the 1950s, contrary to the ANC, which decided, especially on the East Rand, to start its own schools, to keep its members within the schooling system. Linda Chisholm, writing about the pedagogical significance of this period, makes the following observation:

> Many commentators and critics have lambasted the Movement for its petty-bourgeois social base and the dominance of teachers within its organizational structures.[24] To this is ascribed its failure to organize a mass base, to move beyond the realm of education and ideas. What is seen in one context by some writers as a weakness or a failing can, in another, be perceived as its strength. An ambiguous and contradictory strength, but a strength nonetheless; the creation of a disciplined, critical and oppositional culture in

schools and cultural life which placed a heavy emphasis on the subversive and liberating capacities of education.

Certainly this emphasis on education by a mainly teacher base was both its strength and its failing. Its strength can be measured in an examination of the origins of the political leadership of the Western Cape today. As Neville Alexander, himself a dissident product of this movement, has written somewhat sweepingly but not without a grain of truth: 'Hardly any young intellectual in the Western Cape entered political life [between the 1940s and the 1970s] but through the portals of the NEUM. Even its opponents and rivals . . . could not escape its all pervasive influence.'[25]

The point of taking the movement to the schools was to change the 'whole outlook' of the people. In this welter of activity, some of the most critical of the NEUM's texts were written. In 1952, Mnguni (the pseudonym used by Hosea Jaffe) published *Three Hundred Years* under the direct auspices of the NEF and Nosipho Majeke (pseudonym for Dora Taylor) published *The Role of the Missionaries in Conquest*. Tabata produced *The Awakening of the People* in 1958 and went on to write *Education for Barbarism* in 1959.

Three Hundred Years and *The Role of the Missionaries* were constructed as deliberate attempts to take the learning of the socialists since 1935 to the people. They were published deliberately in 1952 to offer South Africans a perspective on the country's 300-year-long history. This history was celebrated through the Van Riebeeck celebrations in 1952 which, as Ntantala explains, the National Party government went out of its way to make a success.[26] The NEF and its sister organisations played a large role in persuading the people of Cape Town to boycott the occasion. On 4 April the NEF organised a rally on the Grand Parade. On the platform were Kies, Jane Gool, Tabata, Saul Jayiya and Ntantala. Ntantala spoke to the topic 'We Have Nothing to Celebrate'. Related to 'the position of African women, the exploited workers in the cities and the widows of the reserves', she said: 'I was not at a loss for words.' The words came too in Jaffe's milestone *Three Hundred Years*, which put into the South African debate about history and its making a completely new reading. Its introduction outlines its aims:

> The purpose of this history is to expose the process of conquest, dispossession, enslavement, segregation and disenfranchisement of the oppressed Non-Europeans of South Africa, in order that the oppressed as a whole will understand better how to transform the status quo into a society worth living for and worth living in. The present South Africa, the status quo did not drop from the heavens. It was man-made. It can be transformed by man [sic] ... To understand these forces of liberation and reaction and the contemporary struggle between the two, we must understand how both came into being. For we cannot know a phenomenon without knowing its history.[27]

The urgency of understanding history and its complexity was even greater in *The Role of the Missionaries*. Taylor, as Majeke, drawing on more than 15 years of rigorous thinking, used the opportunity of the history to show how discourse worked – the discourse of mental enslavement: 'The Mission-school, then, feeds the Black child on inferiority and starves him [sic] educationally ... It is possible to indoctrinate the youth with the desired ideas, to insinuate into his mind all the habits of thought that will make him accept his inferiority.'[28]

These works were deeply influential. Arthur Wheatley, a student of Tom Hanmer's, a member of the TLSA and the NEUM, would write to Hanmer in March 1957:

> Dear Mr Hanmer,
>
> Thank you for initiating the process by which the scales were finally removed from my eyes. I am now partly aware of the issues that we are faced with today.

> When I read the book [*The Role of the Missionaries*] . . . it
> reminded me of the series of interesting lectures you gave in the
> History of Education.[29]

Tabata's continued publication of books and speeches was influential. He insistently sought to put the worlding process into clear perspective. His *Awakening of the People* put the experience of the Second World War into context:

> With the end of the war in sight, the Herrenvolk, strong in their
> sense of security, proceeded with their plans in respect of the
> Blacks on the assumption that they could establish their old mas-
> ter and servant relationship. It did not seem to occur to them that
> a war had intervened – a war which had a revolutionizing effect
> on established ideas and habits of mind amongst all the oppressed
> throughout the world. The Blacks in South Africa, too, were no
> longer prepared to accept the old relationship . . . faced with the
> various oppressive schemes . . . the Blacks determined to fight
> back. The Coloured people replied to the segregatory measure, the
> C.A.C. [Coloured Advisory Council] by forming the National Anti-
> Coloured Affairs Department . . . It swiftly gathered the Coloured
> people together and boycotted the Coloured Advisory Council as
> an institution . . . The intensive campaign against the new meas-
> ure, the holding of meetings and the dissemination of pamphlets
> all led to a rapid heightening of political consciousness . . . Every
> day brought its political lessons . . . They realized that their fate
> was indissolubly bound up with that of the other sections of the
> oppressed, the Africans and the Indians . . . They were beginning to
> understand that the battle of the African is the battle of *all* [empha-
> sis in the original] in South Africa.[30]

Tabata's *Education for Barbarism* was a stinging critique of Bantu Education.[31] Tabata showed how its central purpose was the preservation of white supremacy and how much it depended on the propagation of the idea of 'clans' and tribes, which he described as ludicrous anachronisms.

The significance of this whole corpus of writing and organisation was that it brought, over a period of 20 years, the discussion about race and identity to a pitch that was distinct and certainly in advance of much that was taking place elsewhere in the world. The talks organised by the NEF would stimulate a lot of thought and ideas would be developed as the years passed. The NEF armed the youth. Precocious young intellectuals would continue to emerge out of the school of the movement. They in turn would begin to take issue with their elders and with each other.

It was almost inevitable that a split would come. On 23 March 1951, Tabata wrote in his diary: 'Good Friday/Full moon. On this day SOYA was formed in Athlone' and early the following year, on 17 January 1952, on a Thursday: 'N.E.F. met to discuss inter alia "me" – the meeting was adjourned.'[32]

Tabata felt the NEF was not attracting enough young African students and so he wanted to create a new platform. At the time he was writing under the pseudonym B Ywaye. When the hostel closed in 1952 he and Jane Gool moved into a house in Malan Street. He was banned in 1956 and at the end of his banning order in 1961 he left the organisation to start the African People's Democratic Union of Southern Africa (APDUSA). The debate, pitting what were called the 'Jaffeites' on one side and the 'Tabata Group' on the other, began around point 7 of the 10-Point Programme, the point about land.[33] The effects of the split were destructive. Comrades were no longer comrades. A culture of vituperation entered the movement. Issues of personality were brought into the arena. Expulsions and counter-expulsions came to characterise organisational life. The SOYA national executive committee, for example – and it is unclear who the people were – reported from its national conference in Pietermaritzburg in 1959 that the 'bogus AAC' leadership 'was on the basis of evidence manufactured by its so-called credentials committee, henceforth, expelling the following organisations from the All-African Convention:- The New Era Fellowship, the Cape Flats

Education Fellowship, the Langa Education Fellowship, and the Wits branch of the SOYA.'[34]

Split as the movement may have been, the core ideas retained their poignancy. This was in startling evidence when Kenny Jordaan responded to the Communist Party of South Africa's (CPSA's) Lionel Forman's reopening of the 'National Question'. In April of 1954 Forman wrote an article titled 'Discussion of South Africa's National Question', in which he examined the question of the term 'nation' and why it mattered.[35] In response to this discussion groups convened a special debate on the issue. In the book *A Trumpet From the Housetops: The Selected Wrtings of Lionel Forman*, Jordaan's participation in this 'intense debate' is referred to but, strangely, the passage contains no detail.[36] Jordaan's response to Foreman is captured in Drew.[37]

Jordaan, a brilliant theoretician, who was actually associated with the Fourth International of South Africa (FIOSA) group but would go on to develop close relationships with comrades in the NEUM, generated a new theoretical position, which equated to a theory of combined and uneven development.[38] The insight of this thinking, insights that Jordaan would return to repeatedly in his writing on the 'Land Question', was that there were no stages in the revolution. There was no first stage of national self-determination. Pre-colonial Africa was no longer a viable goal towards which to strive or to recreate. South Africa, after colonialism, was deep into modernity. The struggle was that of the workers against capitalism.

The ethos that had been planted in the movement was of taking the nation to school. 'Fight Ideas with Ideas' said the front cover of the SOYA publication *SOYAN* in February 1959.[39]

* * *

The visibility of the NEF shifted decidedly in the third and final phase of its existence in the 1950s. It did not have that front-of-stage presence it had enjoyed before the establishment of the Anti-CAD and the NEUM.

Before these organisations came into existence it had to double up as the political base and the cultural school for the anti-Stalinist socialist community. It operated off a discipline that saw comrades having to account for themselves. Once these organisations came into being the NEF took on the role that its founders – Goolam Gool and Ben Kies in the main – had projected for it. It became a space for debate and intellectual discourse. Dick Dudley said of this phase of its development that the NEF had been passed on to the younger members of the socialist movement for looking after. He 'and Helen Kies ... took more of a leadership role because their "elders" were busy with their involvement with other political organizations – the Non-European Unity Movement and the transformed Teachers' League of South Africa'.[40]

Where it had been a sorting-house in the beginning, a space where ideas and issues were cleared up, from the late 1940s and 1950s the NEF indisputably became the political school of the left. As a school it developed distinct features and rituals, recruiting promising students from the schools in which its members taught and from the university. New youth organisations were established, such as the Non-European Students' Association, which deliberately prepared new members for entry into the NEF and to go through the training of working on the ground, distributing pamphlets and disseminating the ideas of the movement.

7 | Legacy

Any discussion of the impact and significance of the New Era Fellowship (NEF) is almost indissolubly bound up with the Non-European Unity Movement (NEUM). The NEUM has been examined and written about in some detail by the major historians and commentators on the Cape Radicals and their period.[1] Separating that critique out from what the NEF achieved is not easy.

What is indisputable about the NEF is that it seeded into South Africa's political and intellectual life a relatively small but deeply important legacy. In the 1940s and well into the 1960s its members established, especially in the Western Cape but also in the Eastern Cape – the heartland of what is now too automatically described as African National Congress (ANC) territory – structures that engaged powerfully with local communities. These structures were unashamedly about ideas. The leadership of the NEF was, as Ciraj Rassool has put it, intent on 'taking the nation to school'.[2] Their signature was of the intellectual-activist. It was not sufficient that people mobilised behind an idea; it was critical that they came to own it and to live it.

The attitude of the members of the NEF and its sister organisation – the NEUM – to their work was that it was necessary continually to seed ideas into people's minds to counter the racist and divisive ideology of the everyday. In 1943 Ben Kies had been very clear about this: 'We must turn our faces to our people and we must be among them and with them and of them, teaching and leading them.³ The Cape Radicals had many remarkable qualities but above all of them was the fact that they were intellectuals. Epistemology and the science of ideas were their tools of trade. They were people who una- shamedly espoused and encouraged in people around them the desire to think. But they were also proponents of the idea that one had to live one's beliefs. The personal was political. Being fully human and demonstrating this humanness consumed them. They cultivated attitudes about relationships between people, about sex, about children, about social obligation.

This work was difficult, involving, as it did, more than simply win- ning political allegiance or proselytising in a narrow sense. The teach- ing and learning demanded self-reflection in relation to their country's history and the ways in which it was used for the purposes of building racial identity. In its formative dimensions their work required a cog- nitive engagement, which for many was not easy. The entire mode of address and deportment of the NEF was pedagogical. The political was pedagogical. This was clearly on display wherever they assembled, in forums and meeting places, to debate and argue around the project of emancipation in South Africa. It was in all of their writings. Rassool's description of how the NEF operated is succinct:

> Together, these constituted a long-range project in public education, with features resembling state-like rituals and practices. Through an analysis of power in society and the conditions of resistance and collaboration, a system of representation was created, com- plete with its own vocabulary, framing categories, nouns, verbs, activities and procedures through which the nation was defined, the 'enemy' named and conceptualised, and through which a moral code of behaviour was counter-posed to that of the 'enemy'.⁴

The movement, wrote Rassool, possessed a knowledge-producing impe- tus, which took expression in leaflets, pamphlets, newspapers and books. It was taken into a range of public institutions, inside the system and outside of it. Inside the system, a strategic decision having been taken to 'collaborate' with the formal structures of education, a long history of culture building was initiated in schools. The schools where the NEF's members were able to enter became the most important sites of public education in the country. Generation after generation of extremely important South Africans were products of these institututions.

In their prime schools such as Trafalgar, Livingstone, Harold Cressy, South Peninsula, Athlone, Alexander Sinton and Belgravia, to name a few, developed educational practices and values that made them, at the height of apartheid, the leading places of learning in the country. Young people taking their education there would have been given the opportunity, irrespective of their social backgrounds and origins, to explore the full limits of their capabilities.

The story of Anthony Figaji is instructive. Speaking, in 2012, at the launch of Mohamed Adhikari's biography of Harold Cressy, he described how he grew up in a simple working-class home and was raised by a single mother. The support he received from the Harold Cressy teaching community, and particularly, he said, from Helen Kies, had been life-affirming. He was encouraged and assisted to go to the University of Cape Town (UCT), where he graduated as a medical doctor. From there he went on to become an internationally recognised paediatric neurosurgeon.

Outside the formal system, the network of fellowships and cultural associations that were established under the aegis of the NEF produced many outstanding individuals in different spheres of excellence and examples of outstanding critical thought. Critical about these institutions, as Dick Dudley noted, was that they subsisted in a relatively independent intellectual arena.[5] Out of an almost autonomous discursive space emerged many of the country's key dissident scholars, some of whom would go into the academy.[6] This was something critics like Leonard Thompson never understood about the NEF. The NEF did not require the approval or sanction of dominance. It did not measure itself against the prescripts of excellence determined in the spaces of dominance. Subjectivity and identity, as the key figurative tropes of the dominant racialised society against which it set itself, were major objects of its practice. Rassool has projected this impetus as one defined by the imperatives of 'identity formation'.[7] In some ways it was more than that.

Without wanting to reduce the complexity of the experience, there were clear ontological dimensions. The NEF brought an urgency to its work, which is well described in Alan Wieder's 2008 biography of Dudley. This involved deep preparation, particularly for public engagements, such as making a speech or making an input to a gathering or, more intensely, when giving a formal talk. In an interview in 2007 Neville Alexander described how in its detail this meant that one's verbal references, one's quotes, the context against which one was invoking an allusion, had to be not only absolutely correct, but also pertinent.[8] There was a fastidiousness about those in control of the shaping process in demanding of the individual an almost complete re-imagination of his or her identity as a human being. One had in effect to be asking more of oneself – what it meant to be a full, active and self-fulfilling human being. They were consummate modernists in their thinking and projection, but modernists who also held each other and themselves to demanding standards. Psychoanalytically, there is much that one can make of this in the South African context of race.

The NEF required of its members and followers an explicit but perhaps under-articulated level of quality. This demanded that one should exceed and even efface one's own 'raced' history and the multiple caricatures of one kind or another projected onto it. In objectivist terms one could be tempted to describe this as race suicide, but the point was that they began their argument with the proposition that, actually, there was nothing in the notion of race in the first place. In the 1950s they reached a point where, in describing themselves, they explicitly discarded any racial identity. There was an acknowledgement of the cultural resources that oppression sought to delegitimise, such as Isaac Tabata's invocation of his Africanness, but they refused to turn this into a racial property. For them race was a vacuous concept.

At the same time they remained powerfully aware of the ideological grip race had on the popular imagination and the effects it induced. It was this ideological grip that they targeted. In their comportment they required of each other the disposition of modernism but, more importantly here, one that was purposefully 'post-racial'. This ideal was insistent. It took its urgency from the contexts in which they worked, where constructions of identity and their modes of description were only available in debased racial frames. The burgeoning language of apartheid and its insistent attempt to fill in coloured and African identity in the pejorative vocabulary of drunkenness, lewdness and, most pointedly, that of loss of self-control, would have been especially offensive to them.

The preoccupation with self-control undoubtedly produced tensions and contradictions. These notwithstanding, and they are reflected upon below, the question of subject formation as a project in the NEF and its sister structures is important. Producing a 'non-racial' person was their goal. How this was articulated is important for an assessment of the work of the movement and the distinctive contribution it made. Clearly, as Rassool has explained, its distinctiveness can be found in the NEF's attempt to chart a different route to modernity.[9]

Modernity, as Tabata, one of the movement's founding theoreticians, argued, is accepted in this world view as an 'inescapable fact . . . that is rapidly taking place in their mode of living, with all its hardships, and in [the African people's] habits of thought . . . For the worker the machine and the factory dictate a new set of relationships and attitudes, and outside the factory too, also a new set of social and economic needs.'[10] At the heart of this approach was a socialist understanding of what the world had become: 'Capitalism has not simply changed the habits of the tribalist and the feudalist. It has created a new man [sic].'

Tabata and his colleagues did not have Dipesh Chakrabarty and Saurabh Dube's word – 'worlding' – but it was exactly this process to which the Cape Radicals applied their minds.[11] Capitalism was worlding a 'new man'. This new person, however, was deploying knowledge and information to 'barbarous intent'. Tabata described it thus: 'The discovery of the limitless power of atomic energy is turned to the creation of diabolical instruments of devastation and destruction. The ways of progress are devious and growth is painful; the mechanical inventions of man [sic] have outstripped his social evolution and moral values.'[12]

The new person the NEF envisaged was someone else. And in the South African context this 'new man' had to be distinctly *more*. Similarly, this was also the case in the Soviet Union and China, the two great experiments of ontology playing out in the world. The new person had to undergo a complete renovation of their world view. They needed to take a particular form to cope with the new complexity of capitalism. It was for this reason that in the South African context even more was asked for. At the heart of the NEF's project was a robust individualism explained and described entirely in the language of Enlightenment perfectibility: 'Each member [of society] must be armed with the necessary equipment to play his part to his utmost capacity.'[13]

Critically, in South Africa it had to be so on the basis of a new non-racial spirit.

Universalist as the foundational language of the NEUM was, it remained, significantly, acutely conscious of the specificity of the local setting. Its empirical methodology for deepening this awareness was complex. While unambiguously Marxist, it sought to ground itself in the conditions of the local. Tabata's methods of data gathering were based on his travels into the countryside. As Rassool described it, 'Tabata's rural tours were a type of spatial practice of research, of "travel encounters", of doing surveys and collecting data for later dissemination.'[14] The NEUM sought to produce a deep cognitive engagement with the conditions of the local for the purpose of understanding how to move beyond it. For Tabata, understanding the conditions of the local was vital.

It was this interest in the relationship of the local to the wider global order that people like Richard van der Ross have misunderstood. The

NEF's project was a great deal more searching than Van der Ross's interpretation of it as concerned with racial identity. The NEF and the NEUM came to pose the question of social identity in a way that engaged with, in the first instance, the social change that South Africa was going through. They examined identity and citizenship in profoundly insightful ways. Like Tabata, Alexander also drew deeply from this well.

The particular value to be drawn from the intervention of the NEF and the NEUM is their deep interrogation of dominant historiographies. In particular they examined these historiographies' weaknesses, especially with regard to the issues of race and class. Unfortunately, the challenge that Ben Kies, Alexander and others working in this tradition constituted is regularly by-passed; it has in effect remained a closed book to mainstream history, sociology and politics. The truth is that they developed a counter-narrative to the racialised script that, even in its radical versions, was already firmly embedded in South African historiography. It is time that their work is given the recognition that is due.

It is the *originality* of these intellectuals' work, less than the work itself, that needs reassessing. The question of the work's indigeneity and its contribution, as autochthonous theory, should not be in dispute. What the NEF was developing, without having the terminology for it, was classic 'Southern Theory'.[15] This originality was not sustained beyond the 1960s, however, inside the main body of the tradition and its organisational manifestations. The reason for this is complex. The argument by the critics is that it had much to do with the strategy of the organisation's 'non-collaboration' stance, which inhibited its capacity to mobilise.

There is a more conceptually interesting discussion, however. As emphasised above, the important point to make with respect to this expositon is that it is not per se a discussion of the political history of this group of socialists. Rather, its focus is on what it was that made them intellectually distinctive. The political theory of non-collaboration, which was the hallmark of their practical engagement and the reason why, largely, they have been ridiculed by mainstream politicians and scholars, is not what is under the microscope. It is their approach to race and identity that needs to be highlighted. The question that needs to be posed in this context is: did they get it right?

The work of Ashis Nandy, one of India's most insightful post-colonial scholars, is helpful here.[16] Interpreting the significance of Gandhi's large oeuvre for thinking and acting in the colonial struggle against Britain, he comments that Gandhi is amenable to be read in the narrow racialised lexicon of subjectivisation. In this a kind of quintessential Indianness can be discerned. Available in *Hind Swaraj*, however, is a statement about *learning* to act in and through history. This learning – 'the right state of mind' – 'is not a private cultural or psychological experience, and . . . not a secret defiance but a public ethic and a political program'.[17] Read as a statement about the self as a project, Nandy says, the aim is self-actualisation. He argues that Gandhi offered 'an alternative language of public life and an alternative set of political and social values, and he tried to actualize them as if it was the most natural thing to do'.[18]

One can say much the same about the thinking of the NEF. That it was developing a counter-hegemonic alternative can certainly be claimed – but did it get it right? Did it get the actualisation right? Did it understand the deep challenge of reworlding the time and space in which it found itself?

Two preliminary considerations are offered here. Both require a great deal more discussion. The first is that their analysis of consciousness and how it was constructed and constituted was extremely insightful. Through a considered process of political and scholarly reflection, the NEF radicals evolved a theory of how people come to think as they do. The act of thinking about questions such as identity and race has nothing to do, they concluded, with one's physiognomy. Thinking is a social act. The analytic corollary of this is of how that thinking is instantiated. The NEF came, correctly, and long before sociology would explicitly arrive at this conclusion, to understand that this thinking could be explained and accounted for in the structures of domination. They saw that ideology was learnt.

Race, in this accounting, was insidious. Rejecting it totally was essential.

The second consideration is more controversial. It has generated a great deal of criticism. This is the sociological deconstruction of power in mid-twentieth-century South African society. The theoreticians of the NEF, essentially, like the Black Consciousness community, parsed the structure of South Africa into two parts – Europeans and Non-Europeans, or, in the language of the Black Consciousness theorists, into Black and White. In both explanations these were not racial descriptions. They were descriptions of power and subjectivity. Whiteness or Europeanness produced the material realities of enfranchised whites and disenfranchised blacks.

Possibly within the NEF there was a misreading of the complexity of power, and possibly its leaders did not sufficiently locate themselves in their material relationship to power. Where black professionals fitted into this analysis was problematic, however. Many of these young leaders were professionals. More specifically, many were members of the teaching profession. In this, objectively they were privileged; in how they regarded themselves (their subjective orientations), they were privileged. At the same time they were the organic intellectuals of the class out of which they came – the working class. With their first-generation proximity to their working-class parents, they did not doubt their affinity to the working class.

While this connection might well have been there in the beginning, and they did not waver from their ideals, the economic system of production in the country already set them apart from the direct producers, the workers. And as a consequence of changing times, politically and economically, as apartheid took hold, further separation would have caused gaps to widen. The NEF did not sufficiently problematise their ideological locations – what Pierre Bourdieu calls habituses. Perhaps they underestimated the seductions of these habituses.

Their modes of socialisation, the structuring of solidarities, and their ways of pulling people towards forms of individualism – all of these things would have set these Cape Town intellectuals apart. The cultural disjunction between where they found themselves and where they might have come from must have been intensely challenging. This would have been especially so in the rapidly changing class structure of the 1930s and 1940s.

The challenges were intersectional. Teachers were in a complex position. They were disadvantaged in some respects and advantaged in others. If teachers were to be in the vanguard, how might they be trained to manage the challenges of disjunctive habituses? How did they manage their contradictions of class and of their racial positioning? How, specifically, did they manage the world of their parents?

The viscerality of positioning needs to be explored in greater depth. One hopes that a path can be opened for a discussion about how the powerful ontological and epistemological breakthrough the NEF undoubtedly made did not succeed in being seeded into the wider social universe. Critics cite a variety of reasons for this. One of these is the NEF's tendency to the dogmatic. Also put forward are their position of non-collaboration and their boycott tactic, which required detaching themselves from the heat of political struggle. These points are valid, but they evade the deeper question. The question that needs to be more usefully explored is that of the fundamental sociological framing of the teachers, these intellectual children of the working class.

By the 1940s teachers were already complex social subjects. They were no longer simply the children of their parents. They had moved structurally into new class positions. Society had advanced so dramatically that an accompanying theory of class formation, and not simply race formation, is called for. What is not in doubt is that in the theory of non-racialism the Cape Radicals produced globally leading thinking.

Tasking teachers with taking on the responsibility of re-educating the children was not in itself misplaced. A powerful insight was in play when the leadership of the NEF came to the conclusion that hegemony had recruited the education system for maintaining its dominance. Race was a powerful educational weapon and teachers were the most potent agents of the idea of race. But teachers had to be turned to the struggle. Was putting them in the vanguard a sociological miscalculation? The knock-on consequences for political mobilisation and political education were enormous. The teachers could take the nation to school, but could they lead its children to the barricades? Whose interests would they be defending?

There are many reasons why the Cape cultural revolution struggled to grow into the mass movement the NEF hoped it might be, but what should not be in dispute is that it turned Cape Town into a global centre of progressive knowledge production. It was in its most feverish moments both provocative and productive. From it came the most advanced thinking on race almost anywhere in the world. That that thinking emerged in the small interstices of relatively small privilege is in itself a significant psycho-social fact of a space defined by racist hubris. That the Cape Radicals embodied in their lives the reality of an anti-racist alternative needs to be acknowledged. And the tantalising possibility they offered – that a 'new era' was attainable – cries out to be recognised for the gift it was. The example that these extraordinary men and women set and the ideals they passed on to their contemporaries and the generations that followed needs to be acknowledged as the significant contribution it was to South Africa's history.

Notes

Introduction

1 Joe Rassool, 'Notes on the History of the Non-European Unity Movement in South Africa, and the role of Hosea Jaffe', *Revolutionary History* 4, no. 4 (1993), electronic supplement, accessed 5 December 2018, https://www.marxists.org/history/etol/revhist/supplem/rassool.htm.

2 See the following by Baruch Hirson: 'The Black Republic Slogan – Part II: The Response of the Trotskyists', *Searchlight South Africa* 1, no. 4 (1990); 'Bunting vs. Bukharin: The "Native Republic" Slogan', *Searchlight South Africa* 1, no. 3 (1989); *The Cape Town Intellectuals: Ruth Schechter and Her Circle, 1907–1934* (Johannesburg: Wits University Press, 2001); 'Colour and Class: The Origins of South African Trotskyism', *Revolutionary History* 4, no. 4 (1993); 'A Short History of the Non-European Unity Movement: An Insider's View', *Searchlight South Africa* 3, no. 4 (1995); 'A Question of Class: The Writings of K A Jordan', *Searchlight South Africa* 1, no. 2 (1989); 'The Trotskyist Groups in South Africa, 1932–48', *Searchlight South Africa* 3, no. 2 (1993).

3 Richard van der Ross, *The Rise and Decline of Apartheid: A Study of Political Movements among the Coloured People of South Africa, 1880–1985* (Cape Town: Tafelberg, 1986), 247.

4 Saurabh Dube, 'Presence of Europe: A Cyber Conversation with Dipesh Chakrabarty', in *Postcolonial Passages: Contemporary History-writing on India*, ed. Saurabh Dube (New Delhi: Oxford University Press, 2004), 245.

5 Dube, 'Presence of Europe', 247.

6 Phumi Giyose, with Cameron Madikizela and Sefton Vutela, *The Return of Spartacus: Silhouettes of Revolutionary Fighters*, mimeograph (Uitenhage: New Unity Movement, n.d.), 2.

7 Van der Ross, *Rise and Decline of Apartheid*, 243.

8 I was present at a commemorative event for the establishment of the South Peninsula Education Fellowship (SPEF) in honour of its founder Dawood Parker in the late years of the first decade of the 2000s. In paying tribute to

SPEF some of the female speakers spoke of the gendered division of labour in the organisation and especially about how they were automatically expected to help in the kitchen.

9   Neville Alexander, *Language Policy and National Unity in South Africa* (Cape Town: Buchu Books, 1989).

10 Van der Ross, *Rise and Decline of Apartheid*, 235.

11 Richard Dudley was called 'Dick' by people who knew him well, 'RO' by his students and 'Richard' on formal occasions.

12 Terence Ranger, 'The Invention of Tradition in Colonial Africa', in *The Invention of Tradition*, ed. Eric Hobsbawm and Terence Ranger (Cambridge: Canto, 1983).

13 George McCall Theal, *History of South Africa under the Administration of the Dutch East India Company* (London: Swan Sonnenschein, 1897), 254.

14 Crain Soudien, 'A Hundred Years of South African Thinking against "Race"' (unpublished address to Andrew Mellon Colloquium on 'Race', Haarlem, Netherlands, May 2017).

15 Saul Dubow, *Scientific Racism in Modern South Africa* (Cambridge: Cambridge University Press; Johannesburg: Wits University Press), 1995; Ann Vogel, 'Who's Making Global Civil Society: Philanthropy and US Empire in World Society', *The British Journal of Sociology* 57, no. 4 (2006).

16 Keith Breckenridge, *Biometric State: The Global Politics of Identification and Surveillance in South Africa, 1850 to the Present.* (Cambridge: Cambridge University Press, 2014).

17 The point needs to be made here that this book focuses on the intellectuals of Cape Town. It is about the Cape Town face of the NEF. It does not tell the story of the NEF's work and influence outside of Cape Town and its production of important individuals outside of that city, such as Phumi Giyose, Fikile Bam, Dennis Brutus, Reg Feldman and many others. That work remains to be done.

18 Fakier Jessa, *Echoes: Tales from District Six* (Cape Town: Fakier Jessa, 2016), 95.

19 Bill Nasson, 'The Unity Movement Tradition: Its Legacy in Historical Consciousness', in *History from South Africa: Alternate Visions and Practices*, ed. Joshua Brown (Philadelphia: Temple University Press, 1991), 190.

20 Van der Ross, *Rise and Decline of Apartheid*, 247.

21 Van der Ross, *Rise and Decline of Apartheid*, 243.

22 Tom Hanmer in Alan Wieder, *Teacher and Comrade: Richard Dudley and the Fight for Democracy in South Africa* (Albany: State University of New York Press, 2008), 27.

23 Allison Drew, *South Africa's Radical Tradition: A Documentary History, Vol. 1* (Cape Town: University of Cape Town Press, 1996), 165; Phyllis Ntantala,

A Life's Mosaic: The Autobiography of Phyllis Ntantala (Johannesburg: Jacana Media, 2009).

24 Steve G Lofts, 'Translator's Introduction: The Historical and Systematic Context of *The Logic of the Cultural Sciences* by Ernst Cassirer', in *The Logic of the Cultural Sciences* by Ernst Cassirer (New Haven: Yale University Press, 2000), xxxv.

25 Ernst Cassirer, *The Logic of the Cultural Sciences* (New Haven: Yale University Press, 2000), 65.

26 Ibekwe Chinweizu, *Decolonising the African Mind* (Lagos: Pero Press, 1987).

27 Van der Ross, *Rise and Decline of Apartheid*, 235.

28 Edward H Carr, *What is History?* (Harmondsworth: Penguin, 1964).

29 Carr, *What is History?*, 30.

30 Ranger, 'Invention of Tradition'.

31 Neville Alexander, 'Non-Collaboration in the Western Cape', in *The Angry Divide: Social and Economic History of the Western Cape*, ed. Wilmot G. James and Mary Simons (Cape Town: David Philip, 1989); Saul Dubow, *A Commonwealth of Knowledge: Science, Sensibility and White South Africa, 1820–2000* (Oxford: Oxford University Press, 2006); Saul Dubow, *Racial Segregation and the Origins of Apartheid in Twentieth-Century South Africa, 1919–36* (London: Macmillan, 1989); Dubow, *Scientific Racism*; Robert Miles, *Racism* (London: Routledge, 1989); Michael Omi and Howard Winant, *Racial Formation in the United States: From the 1960s to the 1980s* (New York: Routledge and Kegan Paul, 1986); Soudien, 'Hundred Years'; Crain Soudien, *Realising the Dream: Unlearning the Logic of Race in the South African School* (Cape Town: HSRC Press, 2012); Crain Soudien, 'South Africa: The Struggle for Social Justice and Citizenship in South African Education', in *The Palgrave International Handbook of Education for Citizenship and Social Justice*, ed. Andrew Peterson, Michalinos Zembylas and James Arthur (London: Palgrave, 2016); Derek Hook, *(Post)Apartheid Conditions: Psychoanalysis and Social Formation* (Cape Town: HSRC Press, 2014).

32 Miles, *Racism*, 42.

33 Aletta Norval, *Deconstructing Apartheid Discourse* (London: Verso, 1996); Derek Hook, *Critical Psychology* (Cape Town: University of Cape Town Press, 2004); Hook, *(Post)Apartheid Conditions*; Garth Stevens, Norman Duncan and Derek Hook, eds., *Race, Memory and the Apartheid Archive* (Johannesburg: Wits University Press, 2013).

34 Soudien, 'South Africa'.

35 Soudien, 'Hundred Years'. The term 'culture-bed' is from Breckenridge, *Biometric State*, 20.

36 Parker's library became the focus of some conflict among the Cape Radicals in the 1990s as the New Unity Movement began to remobilise. This library is currently in storage.

37 Hosea Jaffe, *Abandoning Imperialism* (Milan: Jaca Books, 2008).

38 Allison Drew, *South Africa's Radical Tradition: A Documentary History, Vol. 2* (Cape Town: University of Cape Town Press, 1997), 164.

Chapter 1

1 Keith Breckenridge, *Biometric State: The Global Politics of Identification and Surveillance in South Africa, 1850 to the Present* (Cambridge: Cambridge University Press, 2014), 20.

2 Dora Taylor, 'Introduction', in *The Awakening of the People* by I B Tabata (Nottingham: Bertrand Russell Peace Foundation for Spokesman Books, 1974), vii.

3 Richard Dudley, 'Forced Removals: The Essential Meanings of District Six', in *The Struggle for District Six: Past and Present*, ed. Shamil Jeppie and Crain Soudien (Cape Town: Buchu Books, 1990), 30.

4 Hosea Jaffe, *European Colonial Despotism: A History of Oppression and Resistance in South Africa* (London: Kamak House, 1994), 162.

5 Baruch Hirson, 'Colour and Class: The Origins of South African Trotskyism', *Revolutionary History* 4, no. 4 (1993), 72.

6 Raashied Galant, 'The Life and Times of Helen Kies: A Brief Examination', accessed 31 December 2017, https://www.academia.edu/1079361/The_life_ and_times_of_Helen_Kies?auto=download.

7 *The Cape Standard*, 14 November 1939, 4 (Cape Standard (1936–1947), National Library of South Africa, Cape Town Campus, MP1217).

8 *The Cape Standard*, 12 March 1940 (Cape Standard (1936–1947), National Library of South Africa, Cape Town Campus, MP1217).

9 Christopher Saunders, *The Making of the South African Past: Major Historians on Race and Class* (Cape Town: David Philip, 1988).

10 Leonard Thompson, in Saunders, *Making of the South African Past*, 138.

11 Saunders, *Making of the South African Past*, 137.

12 Hosea Jaffe, ed., *The Great French Revolution* (Cape Town: New Unity Movement, 1989), xiii.

13 Christopher Joon–Hai Lee, 'The Uses of the Comparative Imagination: South African History and World History in the Political Consciousness and Strategy of the South African Left, 1943–1959,' *Radical History Review* 92 (2005), 33.

14 Thomas Karis and Gwendolen M Carter, eds., *From Protest to Challenge, Volume 2: Hope and Challenge, 1935–1952* (Stanford: Hoover Institution Press, 1973); Rob Davies, Dan O'Meara and Sipho Dlamini, *The Struggle for South Africa: A Reference Guide to Movements, Organizations and Institutions.* (London: Zed Press, 1984).

15 Isaac B Tabata, *The Awakening of the People* (Nottingham: Bertrand Russell Peace Foundation for Spokesman Books, 1974), 58.

16 Ben Kies, *The Basis of Unity* (Cape Town: Non-European Unity Movement, 1945), 10.

17 Maurits van Bever Donker, Ross Truscott, Gary Minkley and Premesh Lalu, eds., *Remains of the Social: Desiring the Post-Apartheid* (Johannesburg: Wits University Press, 2017); Premesh Lalu, 'Empire and Nation', *Journal of Southern African Studies* 31, no. 3 (2015); Peter Limb, 'The Empire Writes Back: African Challenges to the Brutish (South African) Empire in the Early 20th Century', *Journal of Southern African Studies* 31, no. 3 (2015).

18 Joe Rassool, 'Notes on the History of the Non-European Unity Movement in South Africa, and the Role of Hosea Jaffe', *Revolutionary History* 4, no. 4 (1993), electronic supplement, accessed 5 December 2018, https://www.marxists.org/history/etol/revhist/supplem/rassool.htm.

19 Gavin Lewis, *Between the Wire and the Wall: A History of South African 'Coloured' Politics* (Cape Town: David Philip, 1987); George Hull, 'Neville Alexander and the Non-racialism of the Unity Movement' (unpublished paper, Cape Town, 2018).

20 Corinne Sandwith, *World of Letters: Reading Communities and Cultural Debates in Early Apartheid South Africa* (Pietermaritzburg: University of KwaZulu-Natal Press, 2014), 168; and her discussion of the work of Ciraj Rassool, page 87, note 91 and page 168.

Chapter 2

1 M M Herries, 'The Ideological Matrix (III): Political Trends and Developments among Non-Whites since "Union"', *Educational Journal* XXXII, no. 8 (1961), 18.

2 Hobart Houghton, 'Economic Development, 1865–1965,' in *The Oxford History of South Africa, Vol. 2, 1870–1966*, ed. Monica Wilson and Leonard Thompson (Oxford: Oxford University Press, 1975), 32.

3 Nigel Worden, *The Making of Modern South Africa* (Oxford: Blackwell, 1994), 90.

4 Sarah Mokone, 'Majority Rule: Some Notes', reprinted from *Educational Journal* (1982), accessed 6 November 2018, http://www.apdusaviews.co.za/repository/Majority%20Rule%20with%20Biographical%20Note.pdf, 15.

5 Shamil Jeppie, 'Popular Culture and Carnival in Cape Town: The 1940s and 1950s', in *The Struggle for District Six: Past and Present*, ed. Shamil Jeppie and Crain Soudien (Cape Town: Buchu Books, 1990), 70.

6 Don Pinnock, 'Ideology and Urban Planning: Blueprints of a Garrison City', in *The Angry Divide*, ed., Wilmot G James and Mary Simons (Cape Town: David Philip, 1989), 164.

7 Robert Edgar, *An African American in South Africa: The Travel Notes of Ralph J Bunche: 28 September 1937– 1 January 1938* (Johannesburg: Wits University Press, 1992), 80.

8 Jeppie, 'Popular Culture', 70.

9 Amelia Lewis, 'Reflections on Education in District Six', in *The Struggle for District Six: Past and Present*, ed. Shamil Jeppie and Crain Soudien (Cape Town: Buchu Books, 1990), 186.

10 *First National Coloured-European Conference: Report of Proceedings* (Cape Town: Atlas Printing Works: 1933), 26.

11 *First National Coloured-European Conference*, 31.

12 *First National Coloured-European Conference*, 31.

13 Jackie Loos, 'Miss Jackson and Her Pupils "Sowed the Seeds" of Education', *Cape Argus*, 11 October 2000, 11.

14 Ernst Gideon Malherbe, ed., *Educational Adaptations in a Changing Society.* Report of the South African Education Conference held in Cape Town and Johannesburg in July 1934, under the Auspices of the New Education Fellowship (Cape Town: Juta & Co, 1937), iv.

15 Malherbe, *Educational Adaptations*, v.

16 *The Cape Standard*, 1 February 1944, 9 (Cape Standard (1936–1947), National Library of South Africa, Cape Town Campus, MP1217).

17 Yunus Omar, '"In my Stride": A Life History of Alie Fataar, Teacher' (PhD dissertation, University of Cape Town, 2015).

18 Alie Fataar, in Omar, 'In my Stride', 180.

19 Mohamed Adhikari, *'Let us Live for Our Children': The Teachers' League of South Africa, 1913–1940* (Cape Town: Buchu Books and University of Cape Town Press, 1993), 180–181.

20 Richard van der Ross, *The Rise and Decline of Apartheid: A Study of Political Movements among the Coloured People of South Africa, 1880–1985* (Cape Town: Tafelberg, 1986), 236.

21 Van der Ross, *Rise and Decline of Apartheid*, 181.

22 African People's Democratic Union of Southern Africa (APDUSA), 'Farewell to Comrade Minnie Gool', *APDUSA Views* (December 2005), 4.

23 *The Cape Standard*, 8 November 1937, 1 (Cape Standard (1936–1947), National Library of South Africa, Cape Town Campus, MP1217).

24 Gavin Lewis, *Between the Wire and the Wall: A History of South African 'Coloured' Politics* (Cape Town: David Philip, 1987), 144.

25 Lewis, *Between the Wire and the Wall*, 141.

26 Lewis, *Between the Wire and the Wall*, 144.

27 Lewis, *Between the Wire and the Wall*, 147.

28 W Le Grange in Lewis, *Between the Wire and the Wall*, 147.

29   Johannes Marais, *The Cape Coloured People, 1652–1937* (Johannesburg: Wits University Press, 1962).

30   Corinne Sandwith, *World of Letters: Reading Communities and Cultural Debates in Early Apartheid South Africa* (Pietermaritzburg: University of KwaZulu-Natal Press, 2014), 131.

31   Esther Wilkin, 'District 6 (Western Cape)', accessed 27 December 2017, https://jdap.co.za/roots-2/dorps-towns/dorps-towns/district-6-western-cape/.

32   Crain Soudien, 'A Hundred Years of South African Thinking against "Race"' (unpublished address to Andrew Mellon Colloquium on 'Race', Haarlem, Netherlands, May 2017).

33   Fred Hendricks and Peter Vale, 'The Critical Tradition at Rhodes University: Retrospect and Prospect', *African Sociological Review* 9, no. 1 (2005); Cape of Good Hope, 'First Report and Proceedings, with Appendices, of a Commission Appointed to Inquire into and Report upon Certain Matters Connected with the Educational System of the Colony. Presented to both Houses of Parliament by Command of His Excellency the Governor, 1891, Cape Town' (National Archives of South Africa, Cape Town, G-9-91 [CCP 1/2/1/80]); Mohamed Adhikari, *Against the Current: A Biography of Harold Cressy, 1889–1916* (Cape Town: Juta, 2012); Edgar Brookes, *A History of the University of Natal* (Pietermaritzburg: University of Natal Press, 1966); M Boucher, 'Graaff-Reinet and Higher Education: A Decade of Decline, 1875–1885', *Kleio* 7, no. 2 (1975).

34   Olive Schreiner in Liz Stanley and Andrea Salter, eds., *The World's Great Question: Olive Schreiner's South African Letters 1889–1920* (Cape Town: Van Riebeeck Society, 2014), 287.

35   Baruch Hirson, *The Cape Town Intellectuals: Ruth Schechter and Her Circle, 1907–1934* (Johannesburg: Wits University Press, 2001), 93.

36   Hirson, *Cape Town Intellectuals*, 139.

37   Eddie Roux in Hirson, *Cape Town Intellectuals*, 164.

38   Eddie Roux in Hirson, *Cape Town Intellectuals*, 167.

39   Baruch Hirson, 'Colour and Class: The Origins of South African Trotskyism', *Revolutionary History* 4, no. 4 (1993).

40   Omar, 'In my Stride'.

41   Hirson, *Cape Town Intellectuals*, 170.

42   Allison Drew, *South Africa's Radical Tradition: A Documentary History, Vol. 1* (Cape Town: University of Cape Town Press, 1996), 193.

43   Bernhard Herzberg in Hirson, *Cape Town Intellectuals*, 170–171.

44   General Secretary of the Workers' Party of South Africa in Drew, *South Africa's Radical Tradition, Vol. 1*, 166.

45   Drew, *South Africa's Radical Tradition, Vol. 1*, 166.

46   Ciraj Rassool, 'The Individual, Auto/biography and History in South Africa'
     (PhD dissertation, University of the Western Cape, 2004).

47   Omar 'In my Stride', 50.

48   Selim Gool, 'The Gools of Cape Town – A Family Memoir: A South
     African Muslim Family in Search of Radical Modernity', accessed 9
     November 2017, https://www.academia.edu/11836014/THE_GOOLS_of_
     CAPE_TOWN_-_Notes_towards_a_family_biography.

49   This is a rare reference to Ben Kies.

50   Gool, 'Gools of Cape Town'.

51   Peter Abrahams, *Tell Freedom: Memories of Africa* (London: Faber and Faber,
     1982), 322.

52   Marcus Solomon, former Robben Island prisoner, interview with the author,
     24 October 2017, Cape Town.

53   Abrahams, *Tell Freedom*, 329.

54   Edgar, *African American in South Africa*, 60.

55   Isaac Deutscher, *The Prophet Outcast: Trotsky 1929–1940* (London: Verso,
     2003), 32.

56   'The South African Question' (resolution adopted by the Executive
     Committee of the Communist International following the Sixth Comintern
     Congress), accessed 13 December 2018, https://www.marxists.org/history/
     international/comintern/sections/sacp/1928/comintern.htm.

57   Deutscher, *Prophet Outcast*, 32.

58   Baruch Hirson, 'The Black Republic Slogan – Part II: The Response of the
     Trotskyists', *Searchlight South Africa* 1, no. 4 (1990), 44.

59   Hirson, 'Colour and Class', 127; emphasis in the original.

60   Adhikari, *Let us Live for Our Children*, 180.

61   Drew, *South Africa's Radical Tradition, Vol. 1*, 25.

62   Baruch Hirson, 'A Short History of the Non-European Unity Movement:
     An Insider's View', *Searchlight South Africa* 3, no. 4 (1995), 66.

63   Drew, *South Africa's Radical Tradition, Vol. 1*, 30.

64   Drew, *South Africa's Radical Tradition, Vol. 1*, 24–26.

65   Baruch Hirson in Sandwith, *World of Letters*, 89.

66   Sandwith, *World of Letters*, 89.

67   Hirson, 'Colour and Class', 17, 41.

68   Drew, *South Africa's Radical Tradition, Vol. 1*, 25.

69   Drew, *South Africa's Radical Tradition, Vol. 1*, 25.

70   Drew, *South Africa's Radical Tradition, Vol. 1*, 26.

71   Drew, *South Africa's Radical Tradition, Vol. 1*, 27.

72   Drew, *South Africa's Radical Tradition, Vol. 1*, 187.

73   Hirson, 'Colour and Class'.

74 Hirson, 'Short History', 78.

75 Baruch Hirson, 'A Question of Class: The Writings of K A Jordan', *Searchlight South Africa* 1, no. 2 (1989), 22.

76 Drew, *South Africa's Radical Tradition, Vol. 1*, 31.

77 Lewis, *Between the Wire and the Wall*, 180.

78 Drew, ed., *South Africa's Radical Tradition, Vol. 1*, 31.

79 Mokone, 'Majority Rule', 16.

80 Drew, *South Africa's Radical Tradition, Vol. 1*, 33.

81 Naz Gool Ebrahim, with Donna Brenneis and Shahena Wingate-Pearse, *The Truth is on the Walls* (Cape Town: David Philip, 2011), 51.

82 Lewis, *Between the Wire and the Wall*, 183, 192.

83 Lewis, *Between the Wire and the Wall*, 181.

84 Doreen Musson, *Johnny Gomas: Voice of the Working Class* (Cape Town: Buchu Books, 1989), 86.

85 National Liberation League in Drew, *South Africa's Radical Tradition, Vol. 1*, 255.

86 National Liberation League in Drew, *South Africa's Radical Tradition, Vol. 1*, 255.

87 Johnny Gomas in Drew, *South Africa's Radical Tradition, Vol. 1*, 267; emphasis added.

88 Lewis, *Between the Wire and the Wall*, 134; George Hull, 'Neville Alexander and the Non-racialism of the Unity Movement' (unpublished paper, Cape Town, 2018), 6.

89 Drew, *South Africa's Radical Tradition, Vol. 1*, 282.

90 Edgar, *African American in South Africa*, 64.

91 Drew, *South Africa's Radical Tradition, Vol. 1*, 255.

92 Musson, *Johnny Gomas*, 56.

93 Bruce Baum, *The Rise and Fall of the Caucasian Race: A Political History of Racial Identity* (New York: New York University Press, 2006), 176.

94 Julian Huxley in Baum, *Rise and Fall of the Caucasian Race*, 176.

95 James Tabery and Sahotra Sarkar, 'R A Fisher, Lancelot Hogben, and the "Competition" for the Chair of Social Biology at the London School of Economics in 1930: Correcting the Legend'. *The Royal Society: Notes and Records* 69, no. 4 (2015), accessed 13 December 2018, https://www.ncbi.nlm.nih.gov/pmc/articles/PMC4650099/.

96 Baum, *Rise and Fall of the Caucasian Race*, 174.

Chapter 3

1 Allison Drew, *South Africa's Radical Tradition: A Documentary History, Vol. 1* (Cape Town: University of Cape Town Press, 1996), 330. Drew does not provide a primary source for this information.

2 Alan Wieder, *Teacher and Comrade: Richard Dudley and the Fight for Democracy in South Africa* (Albany: State University of New York Press, 2008), 44.

3 Baruch Hirson, 'The Trotskyist Groups in South Africa, 1932–48', *Searchlight South Africa* 3, no. 2 (1993), 111.

4 Robert Edgar, *An African American in South Africa: The Travel Notes of Ralph J Bunche: 28 September 1937 – 1 January 1938* (Johannesburg: Wits University Press, 1992), 331.

5 Wieder, *Teacher and Comrade*, 44.

6 Yunus Omar, '"In My Stride": A Life History of Alie Fataar, Teacher' (PhD dissertation, University of Cape Town, 2015), 175.

7 Mokone, Sarah. 'Majority Rule: Some Notes', reprinted from *The Educational Journal* 1982, accessed 6 November 2018, http://www.apdusaviews.co.za/repository/Majority%20Rule%20with%20Biographical%20Note.pdf, 20.

8 Drew, *South Africa's Radical Tradition, Vol. 1*, 252.

9 Drew, *South Africa's Radical Tradition, Vol. 1*, 253

10 Baruch Hirson, 'Colour and Class: The Origins of South African Trotskyism', *Revolutionary History* 4, no. 4 (1993), 44.

11 Drew, *South Africa's Radical Tradition, Vol. 1*, 24.

12 Drew, *South Africa's Radical Tradition, Vol. 1*, 168–169.

13 Drew, *South Africa's Radical Tradition, Vol. 1*, 164.

14 Edward Roux, *Time Longer Than Rope: A History of the Black Man's Struggle for Freedom in South Africa* (Madison: University of Wisconsin Press, 1964), 312.

15 Roux, *Time Longer Than Rope*, 312.

16 Roux, *Time Longer Than Rope*, 312.

17 Roux, *Time Longer Than Rope*, 312.

18 Edgar, *African American in South Africa*, 332; Corinne Sandwith, *Word of Letters: Reading Communities and Cultural Debates in Early Apartheid South Africa* (Pietermaritzburg: University of KwaZulu-Natal Press, 2014), 142.

19 *The Cape Standard*, 14 November 1949 (Cape Standard (1936–1947), National Library of South Africa, Cape Town Campus, MP1217).

20 Bonita Bennett, Noorunisaa Delate, Chrischené Julius, Premesh Lalu, Giorgio Miescher, Ciraj Rassool, Virgil Slade and Tina Smith, eds., *Fields of Play: Football, Memories and Forced Removals in Cape Town*, District Six Museum exhibition catalogue (Cape Town: District Six Museum, 2010), 153.

21 Bennett et al., *Fields of Play*, 153.

22 Bennett et al., *Fields of Play*, 151.

23 Marcus Solomon, former Robben Island prisoner, interview, 24 October 2017, Cape Town.

24 Drew, *South Africa's Radical Tradition, Vol. 1*, 174.

25 Letter from 'Coloured Student', in Denis-Constant Martin, *Coon Carnival: New Year in Cape Town, Past and Present* (Cape Town: David Philip, 1999), 118.

26 Martin, *Coon Carnival*, 118.

27 Shamil Jeppie, 'Popular Culture and Carnival in Cape Town: The 1940s and 1950s', in *The Struggle for District Six: Past and Present*, ed., Shamil Jeppie and Crain Soudien (Cape Town: Buchu Books, 1990), 74.

28 Amelia Lewis, 'Reflections on Education in District Six', in *The Struggle for District Six: Past and Present*, ed. Shamil Jeppie and Crain Soudien (Cape Town: Buchu Books, 1990), 190.

29 Lewis, 'Reflections on Education in District Six', 190.

30 Denis-Constant Martin, *Sounding the Cape: Music, Identity and Politics in South Africa* (Cape Town: African Minds, 2013), 122.

31 Martin, *Sounding the Cape*, 122.

32 Sandwith, *World of Letters*, 142.

33 Vivian Bickford-Smith, Elizabeth van Heyningen and Nigel Worden, *Cape Town in the Twentieth Century: An Illustrated Social History* (Cape Town: David Philip, 1999), 84.

34 Sandwith, *World of Letters*, 143.

35 Ben Kies, 'The Revolt of the Youth', in Sandwith, *World of Letters*, 144–145.

36 Sandwith, *World of Letters*, 145.

37 Wieder, *Teacher and Comrade*, 18.

38 Sandwith, *World of Letters*, 138.

39 Richard Dudley, in Wieder, *Teacher and Comrade*, 46–47.

40 Wieder, *Teacher and Comrade*, 46.

41 Neville Alexander, political activist, educationalist and academic, interview, 2 July 2006, Cape Town; Solomon, interview.

42 Richard Dudley, in Wieder, *Teacher and Comrade*, 45.

43 Sandwith, *World of Letters*, 147.

44 Keith Breckenridge, *Biometric State: The Global Politics of Identification and Surveillance in South Africa, 1850 to the Present* (Cambridge: Cambridge University Press, 2014), 20.

Chapter 4

1 Phumi Giyose, with Cameron Madikizela and Sefton Vutela, *The Return of Spartacus: Silhouettes of Revolutionary Fighters*, mimeograph (Uitenhage: New Unity Movement, n.d.).

2 M M Herries, 'The Ideological Matrix (III): Political Trends and Developments among Non-Whites since "Union"', *Educational Journal* XXXII, no. 8 (1961), 18.

3 Giyose, Madikizela and Vutela, *Return of Spartacus*, 2.

4   Sarah Mokone, 'Majority Rule: Some Notes', reprinted from *Educational Journal* (1982), accessed 6 November 2018, http://www.apdusaviews.co.za/repository/Majority%20Rule%20with%20Biographical%20Note.pdf, 20.

5   The tactics of clandestinity were a large part of the debate and assessment of the approach that had been taken by the followers of the WPSA.

6   Baruch Hirson, 'Colour and Class: The Origins of South African Trotskyism', *Revolutionary History* 4, no. 4 (1993), 32.

7   Allison Drew, *South Africa's Radical Tradition: A Documentary History, Vol. 1* (Cape Town: University of Cape Town Press, 1996), 151.

8   Drew, *South Africa's Radical Tradition, Vol. 1*, 155.

9   Hosea Jaffe, *European Colonial Despotism: A History of Oppression and Resistance in South Africa* (London: Kamak House, 1994), 160.

10 Hirson, 'Colour and Class', 35.

11 Hosea Jaffe, *The Pyramid of Nations* (Milan: Victor, 1980), 27.

12 Hirson, 'Colour and Class', 33.

13 Giyose, Madikizela and Vutela, *Return of Spartacus*, 2.

14 Leon Trotsky, 'Remarks on the Draft Thesis of the Workers' Party, 20 April 1935', accessed 6 November 2018, http://disa.ukzn.ac.za/sites/default/files/pdf_files/slfeb90.5.pdf; Drew, *South Africa's Radical Tradition, Vol. 1*, 150.

15 *The Cape Standard*, 14 November 1939, 13 (Cape Standard (1936–1947), National Library of South Africa, Cape Town Campus, MP1217).

16 W P Van Schoor, 'The Origin and Development of Segregation in South Africa'. A J Abrahamse Memorial Lecture, Cathedral Hall, Cape Town, 5 October 1950. Accessed 17 December 2018, https://www.sahistory.org.za/archive/document-51-w-p-van-schoor-origin-and-development-segregation-south-africa-j-abrahamse-memor.

17 Jaffe, *European Colonial Despotism*, 150.

18 *The Cape Standard*, March 1939 (Cape Standard (1936–1947), National Library of South Africa, Cape Town Campus, MP1217).

19 *The Cape Standard*, 7 June 1938, 9 (Cape Standard (1936–1947), National Library of South Africa, Cape Town Campus, MP1217).

20 *The Cape Standard*, 16 May 1939, 9 (Cape Standard (1936–1947), National Library of South Africa, Cape Town Campus, MP1217).

21 Jaffe, *European Colonial Despotism*, 162.

22 *The Cape Standard*, 8 November 1937, 1 (Cape Standard (1936–1947), National Library of South Africa, Cape Town Campus, MP1217).

23 *The Cape Standard*, 8 November 1937, 1 (Cape Standard (1936–1947), National Library of South Africa, Cape Town Campus, MP1217).

24 *The Cape Standard*, 8 November 1937, 1 (Cape Standard (1936–1947), National Library of South Africa, Cape Town Campus, MP1217).

25 *The Cape Standard*, 31 January 1938, 11 (Cape Standard (1936–1947), National Library of South Africa, Cape Town Campus, MP1217).

26 Corinne Sandwith, *World of Letters: Reading Communities and Cultural Debates in Early Apartheid South Africa*. (Pietermaritzburg: University of KwaZulu-Natal Press, 2014), 15.

27 *The Cape Standard*, 11 October 1938, 1 (Cape Standard (1936–1947), National Library of South Africa, Cape Town Campus, MP1217).

28 *The Cape Standard*, 6 December 1938, 1 (Cape Standard (1936–1947), National Library of South Africa, Cape Town Campus, MP1217).

29 *The Cape Standard*, 6 December 1938, 1 (Cape Standard (1936–1947), National Library of South Africa, Cape Town Campus, MP1217).

30 *The Cape Standard*, 13 February 1940, 5 (Cape Standard (1936–1947), National Library of South Africa, Cape Town Campus, MP1217).

31 *The Cape Standard*, 15 February 1938 (Cape Standard (1936–1947), National Library of South Africa, Cape Town Campus, MP1217).

32 Isaac Tabata diaries, UCT/BC925, Special Collections, Jagger Library, University of Cape Town.

33 Tabata diaries, UCT/BC925.

34 *The Cape Standard*, 15 March 1938, 7 (Cape Standard (1936–1947), National Library of South Africa, Cape Town Campus, MP1217).

35 *The Cape Standard*, 20 June 1939, 2 (Cape Standard (1936–1947), National Library of South Africa, Cape Town Campus, MP1217).

36 *The Cape Standard*, 16 May 1939, 1 (Cape Standard (1936–1947), National Library of South Africa, Cape Town Campus, MP1217).

37 *The Cape Standard*, 20 June 1939, 12 (Cape Standard (1936–1947), National Library of South Africa, Cape Town Campus, MP1217).

38 Alan Wieder, *Teacher and Comrade: Richard Dudley and the Fight for Democracy in South Africa* (Albany: State University of New York Press, 2008), 45.

39 *The Cape Standard*, 14 June 1938, 7 (Cape Standard (1936–1947), National Library of South Africa, Cape Town Campus, MP1217).

40 *The Cape Standard*, 26 July 1938, 4 (Cape Standard (1936–1947), National Library of South Africa, Cape Town Campus, MP1217).

41 *The Cape Standard*, 8 November 1939, 2 (Cape Standard (1936–1947), National Library of South Africa, Cape Town Campus, MP1217).

42 *The Cape Standard*, 16 May 1939, 9 (Cape Standard (1936–1947), National Library of South Africa, Cape Town Campus, MP1217).

43 *The Cape Standard*, 6 June 1939, 14 (Cape Standard (1936–1947), National Library of South Africa, Cape Town Campus, MP1217).

44 *The Cape Standard*, 20 June 1939 (Cape Standard (1936–1947), National Library of South Africa, Cape Town Campus, MP1217).

45 Miss O Rosenberg, 'No Half-Castes in the World', *The Cape Standard*, 4 July 1939, 12 (Cape Standard (1936–1947), National Library of South Africa, Cape Town Campus, MP1217).

46 Rosenberg, 'No Half-Castes'.

47 Rosenberg, 'No Half-Castes'.

48 *The Cape Standard*, 14 November 1939, 8 (Cape Standard (1936–1947), National Library of South Africa, Cape Town Campus, MP1217).

49 *The Cape Standard*, 21 November 1939, 12 (Cape Standard (1936–1947), National Library of South Africa, Cape Town Campus, MP1217).

50 *The Cape Standard*, 28 November 1939, 7 (Cape Standard (1936–1947), National Library of South Africa, Cape Town Campus, MP1217).

51 *The Cape Standard*, 25 July 1939, 7 (Cape Standard (1936–1947), National Library of South Africa, Cape Town Campus, MP1217).

52 *The Cape Standard*, 1 August 1939, 9 (Cape Standard (1936–1947), National Library of South Africa, Cape Town Campus, MP1217).

53 Abdurahman died later that year, marking the end of the era of petition politics.

54 *The Cape Standard*, 30 January 1940 (Cape Standard (1936–1947), National Library of South Africa, Cape Town Campus, MP1217).

55 Sandwith, *World of Letters*, 171.

56 *The Cape Standard*, 19 March 1940, 7 (Cape Standard (1936–1947), National Library of South Africa, Cape Town Campus, MP1217).

57 Tabata diaries, UCT/BC925.

Chapter 5

1 Dora Taylor in Corinne Sandwith, *World of Letters: Reading Communities and Cultural Debates in Early Apartheid South Africa*. (Pietermaritzburg: University of KwaZulu-Natal Press, 2014), 121.

2 Mohamed Adhikari, *'Let us Live for Our Children': The Teachers' League of South Africa, 1913–1940* (Cape Town: Buchu Books and University of Cape Town Press 1993), 63.

3 Baruch Hirson, *The Cape Town Intellectuals: Ruth Schechter and Her Circle, 1907–1934* (Johannesburg: Wits University Press, 2001), 171.

4 Allison Drew, *South Africa's Radical Tradition: A Documentary History, Vol. 1* (Cape Town: University of Cape Town Press, 1996), 33.

5 Adhikari, *Let us Live for Our Children*, 64.

6 Adhikari, *Let us Live for Our Children*, 69.

7 Adhikari, *Let us Live for Our Children*, 70.

8   Alan Wieder, *Teacher and Comrade: Richard Dudley and the Fight for Democracy in South Africa* (Albany: State University of New York Press, 2008), 44.

9   Sarah Mokone, 'Majority Rule: Some Notes', reprinted from *Educational Journal* (1982), accessed 6 November 2018, http://www.apdusaviews.co.za/repository/Majority%20Rule%20with%20Biographical%20Note.pdf, 23.

10 Drew, *South Africa's Radical Tradition, Vol. 1*, 308–310.

11 Isaac Tabata diaries, UCT/BC925, Special Collections, Jagger Library, University of Cape Town.

12 Allison Drew, *Discordant Comrades: Identities and Loyalties on the South African Left* (Ashgate, 2000), 233–6.

13 Ben Kies, *The Background of Segregation* (Cape Town: Anti-CAD Committee, 1943), 2.

14 Hosea Jaffe, *European Colonial Despotism: A History of Oppression and Resistance in South Africa* (London: Kamak House, 1994), 162; Mokone, 'Majority Rule', 23.

15 Jaffe, *European Colonial Despotism*, 162; Mokone, 'Majority Rule', 23.

16 Jaffe, *European Colonial Despotism*, 162.

17 Doreen Musson, *Johnny Gomas: Voice of the Working Class* (Cape Town: Buchu Books, 1989), 9.

18 Jaffe, *European Colonial Despotism*, 162–163.

19 Mokone, 'Majority Rule', 25.

20 In Mokone, 'Majority Rule', 25.

21 Mokone, 'Majority Rule', 25.

22 Gavin Lewis, *Between the Wire and the Wall: A History of South African 'Coloured' Politics* (Cape Town: David Philip, 1987), 214.

23 Adhikari, *Let us Live for Our Children*, 71.

24 Lewis, *Between the Wire and the Wall*, 218.

25 Lewis, *Between the Wire and the Wall*, 216.

26 Mohamed Adhikari, *Not White Enough, Not Black Enough: Racial Identity in the South African Coloured Community* (Cape Town, Double Storey Books, 2005), 98–100.

27 Kies, *Background of Segregation*, 12.

28 Adhikari, *Not White Enough*, 98.

29 Kies, *Background of Segregation*, 2.

30 Kies, *Background of Segregation*, 3.

31 Kies, *Background of Segregation*, 4–5.

32 George Hull, 'Neville Alexander and the Non-racialism of the Unity Movement' (unpublished paper, Cape Town, 2018), 4.

33 Kies, *Background of Segregation*, 13.

34 Kies, *Background of Segregation*, 14.

35 Kies, *Background of Segregation*, 14.

36 Kies, *Background of Segregation*, 14–15.

37 Kies, *Background of Segregation*, 15.

38 Kies, *Background of Segregation*, 16.

39 'Why Was Racialism Never Dismantled in South Africa?', *The Bulletin* 19, no. 3 (2011), 22.

40 Kies, *Background of Segregation*, 15.

41 Kies, *Background of Segregation*, 15–16.

42 Neville Alexander, political activist, educationalist and academic, interview, 1 December 2006, Cape Town.

43 Sandwith, *World of Letters*, 167.

44 Phyllis Ntantala, *A Life's Mosaic: The Autobiography of Phyllis Ntantala* (Johannesbug: Jacana Media, 2009), 118.

45 Jaffe, *European Colonial Despotism*, 163.

46 Mokone, 'Majority Rule', 3.

47 Jaffe, *European Colonial Despotism*, 164.

48 Lewis, *Between the Wire and the Wall*, 222.

49 Jaffe, *European Colonial Despotism*, 166.

50 'In my Tower', *The Cape Standard*, 11 January 1944, 7 (Cape Standard (1936–1947), National Library of South Africa, Cape Town Campus, MP1217).

51 *The Cape Standard*, 4 January 1944, 9 (Cape Standard (1936–1947), National Library of South Africa, Cape Town Campus, MP1217).

52 *The Cape Standard*, 11 January 1944, 2 (Cape Standard (1936–1947), National Library of South Africa, Cape Town Campus, MP1217).

53 *The Cape Standard*, 11 January 1944, 1 (Cape Standard (1936–1947), National Library of South Africa, Cape Town Campus, MP1217).

54 *The Cape Standard*, 11 January 1944, 1 (Cape Standard (1936–1947), National Library of South Africa, Cape Town Campus, MP1217).

55 *The Cape Standard*, 11 January 1944, 1 (Cape Standard (1936–1947), National Library of South Africa, Cape Town Campus, MP1217).

56 *The Cape Standard*, 11 January 1944, 7 (Cape Standard (1936–1947), National Library of South Africa, Cape Town Campus, MP1217).

57 *The Cape Standard*, 24 January 1944, 3 (Cape Standard (1936–1947), National Library of South Africa, Cape Town Campus, MP1217).

58 Tabata diaries, UCT/BC925.

59 *The Cape Standard*, 1 February 1944, 9 (Cape Standard (1936–1947), National Library of South Africa, Cape Town Campus, MP1217).

60 *The Cape Standard*, 8 February 1944, 3 (Cape Standard (1936–1947), National Library of South Africa, Cape Town Campus, MP1217).

61 *The Cape Standard*, 29 February 1944, 5 (Cape Standard (1936–1947), National Library of South Africa, Cape Town Campus, MP1217).

62 Tabata diaries, UCT/BC925.

63 *The Cape Standard*, 28 March 1944, 7; *The Cape Standard*, 4 April 1944, 11 (Cape Standard (1936–1947), National Library of South Africa, Cape Town Campus, MP1217).

64 *The Cape Standard*, 4 April 1944, 5 (Cape Standard (1936–1947), National Library of South Africa, Cape Town Campus, MP1217).

65 *The Cape Standard*, 25 April 1944, 3 (Cape Standard (1936–1947), National Library of South Africa, Cape Town Campus, MP1217); Ziyana Lategan, 'The Contribution of Hosea Jaffe to South African Political Thought' (paper presented at the University of Cape Town's Historical Studies Department, Historical Studies Seminar, 4 August 2016, 1.

66 Tabata diaries, UCT/BC925.

67 Ben Kies, *The Basis of Unity* (Cape Town: Non-European Unity Movement, 1945), 10.

68 Kies, *Basis of Unity*, 6.

69 Kies, *Basis of Unity*, 8.

70 Kies, *Basis of Unity*, 10.

71 Kies, *Basis of Unity*, 10.

72 Isaac B Tabata, *Letter to Mandela on the Problem of Organisational Unity in South Africa* (Cape Town: African People's Democratic Union of South Africa, 1948), 5.

73 Sandwith, *World of Letters*, 153.

74 South African Commission on Native Education. *Report of the Commission on Native Education, 1949–1951*. Report U.G. No. 53/1951, 7. Pretoria: The Government Printer, 1951. Special Collections, African Studies Library, University of Cape Town.

75 Andrew Murray Papers, memorandum 52. African Studies Centre, University of Cape Town.

76 Andrew Murray Papers, memorandum 68.

77 Dora Taylor, 'The Function of Literary Criticism' (unpublished lecture, 1953, Ronnie and Chrystal Bitten private collection). It is unclear where the lecture was given. It could have been at an NEF meeting.

78 Sandwith, *World of Letters*, 158.

79 Christopher Joon-Hai Lee, 'The Uses of the Comparative Imagination: South African History and World History in the Political Consciousness and Strategy of the South African Left, 1943–1959', *Radical History Review* 92 (2005), 42.

80 Lee, 'Uses of the Comparative Imagination', 36.

81 Lee, 'Uses of the Comparative Imagination', 45.

82   Ben Kies, *The Contribution of Non-European Peoples to World Civilisation* (A J Abrahamse Memorial Lecture) (Cape Town, The Teachers' League of South Africa, 1953).

83   Kies is referring here to Rudolf Rocker's *Nationalism and Culture*, originally published in 1937.

84   Kies, *Contribution of Non-European Peoples*, 8.

85   Kies, *Contribution of Non-European Peoples*, 9.

86   Neville Alexander, *An Ordinary Country: Issues in the Transition from Apartheid to Democracy in South Africa* (Pietermaritzburg: University of KwaZulu-Natal Press, 2002), 41.

87   Kies, *Contribution of Non-European Peoples*, 12.

88   Kies, *Contribution of Non-European Peoples*, 18.

89   Kies, *Contribution of Non-European Peoples*, 13.

90   Christa Kuljian, *Darwin's Hunch: Science, Race and the Search for Human Origins* (Johannesburg: Jacana Media, 2016), 116.

91   Isaac B Tabata, *The Awakening of the People* (Nottingham: Bertrand Russell Peace Foundation for Spokesman Books, 1974), 1.

92   Kies, *Contribution of Non-European Peoples*, 13.

93   Kies, *Contribution of Non-European Peoples*, 14.

94   Kies, *Contribution of Non-European Peoples*, 14.

95   Tabata, *Awakening*, 1.

96   Hosea Jaffe, *The Pyramid of Nations* (Milan: Victor, 1980), 27.

97   Kies, *Contribution of Non-European Peoples*, 8.

98   Jaffe, *Pyramid of Nations*, 26.

99   Hosea Jaffe, *Abandoning Imperialism* (Milan: Jaca Books, 2008), 59.

100 Richard van der Ross, *The Rise and Decline of Apartheid: A Study of Political Movements among the Coloured People of South Africa, 1880–1985* (Cape Town: Tafelberg, 1986), 235.

Chapter 6

1   Ben Kies, *The Contribution of Non-European Peoples to World Civilisation* (A J Abrahamse Memorial Lecture) (Cape Town, The Teachers' League of South Africa, 1953), 40.

2   The term 'culture-bed' is from Keith Breckenridge, *Biometric State: The Global Politics of Identification and Surveillance in South Africa, 1850 to the Present* (Cambridge: Cambridge University Press, 2014).

3   Sarah Mokone, 'Majority Rule: Some Notes', reprinted from *Educational Journal of the Teacher's League of South Africa* (1982), accessed 6 November 2018, http://www.apdusaviews.co.za/repository/Majority%20Rule%20with%20Biographical%20Note.pdf, 66.

4 Mokone, 'Majority Rule', 66.

5 Mokone, 'Majority Rule', 68.

6 Mokone, 'Majority Rule', 68.

7 Mokone, 'Majority Rule', 68.

8 Mokone, 'Majority Rule', 68.

9 See, for example, Robert Edgar, *An African American in South Africa: The Travel Notes of Ralph J Bunche: 28 September 1937 – 1 January 1938* (Johannesburg: Wits University Press, 1992); Linda Chisholm, 'Making the Pedagogical More Political, and the Political More Pedagogical: Education Traditions and Legacies of the Non-European Unity Movement', in *Vintage Kenton: A Kenton Education Association Commemoration*, compiled by Wendy Flanagan, Crispin Hemson, Joe Muller and Nick Taylor (Cape Town: Maskew Miller Longman, 1994).

10 See https://www.revolvy.com/topic/Workers%20Party%20of%20South%20Africa, accessed 19 December 2018.

11 Phyllis Ntantala, *A Life's Mosaic: The Autobiography of Phyllis Ntantala* (Johannesburg: Jacana Media, 2009), 164.

12 Sedick Isaacs, *Surviving in the Apartheid Prison: Flash Backs of an Earlier Life* (Indiana: Xlibris, 2010), 19.

13 Fakier Jessa, *Echoes: Tales from District Six* (Cape Town: Fakier Jessa, 2016), 94–95.

14 Allison Drew, *South Africa's Radical Tradition: A Documentary History, Vol. 2* (Cape Town: University of Cape Town Press, 1997), 155.

15 Neville Alexander, political activist, educationalist and academic, interview, 16 May 2008, Cape Town.

16 Jessa, *Echoes*, 94.

17 Drew, *South Africa's Radical Tradition, Vol. 2*, 164.

18 Ntantala, *Life's Mosaic*, 153.

19 Ntantala, *Life's Mosaic*, 153.

20 All the citations in this paragraph come from the foreword – with no attribution – to Hosea Jaffe, ed., *The Great French Revolution* (Cape Town: New Unity Movement, 1989).

21 Frank van der Horst, input at the opening session of the annual conference of the New Unity Movement, Cape Town, 16 December 2017.

22 Alexander, interview, 16 May 2008.

23 Hosea Jaffe, ed. *The Great French Revolution* (Cape Town: New Unity Movement, 1989), xiii.

24 Chisholm is referring to sources such as Gavin Lewis, *Between the Wire and the Wall: A History of South African 'Coloured' Politics* (Cape Town: David Philip, 1987); Roy Gentle, 'The NEUM in Perspective' (unpublished Honours

dissertation, University of Cape Town, 1978); and Neville Alexander, 'Aspects of Non-Collaboration in the Western Cape, 1943–1963', *Social Dynamics* 12, no. 1 (1986).

25 Chisholm, 'Making the Pedagogical', 242.

26 Ntantala, *Life's Mosaic*, 155.

27 Mnguni [Hosea Jaffe], *Three Hundred Years* (Cumberwood: African People's Democratic Union of South Africa), 1988, 1.

28 Nosipho Majeke [Dora Taylor] in Christopher Joon-Hai Lee, 'The Uses of the Comparative Imagination: South African History and World History in the Political Consciousness and Strategy of the South African Left, 1943–1959', *Radical History Review* 92 (2005), 48.

29 Arthur Wheatley, correspondence with Tom Hanmer, Cape Town, 21 March 1957. Crain Soudien, private collection.

30 Isaac B Tabata, *The Awakening of the People* (Nottingham: Bertrand Russell Peace Foundation for Spokesman Books, 1974), 48.

31 Tabata, *Awakening*, 15.

32 Tabata diaries, UCT/BC925, Special Collections, Jagger Library, University of Cape Town.

33 Hosea Jaffe, *European Colonial Despotism: A History of Oppression and Resistance in South Africa* (London: Kamak House, 1994), 175.

34 In Drew, *South Africa's Radical Tradition, Vol. 2*, 150.

35 In Sadie Forman and André Odendaal, eds., *A Trumpet from the Housetops: The Selected Writings of Lionel Forman* (Cape Town: David Philip, 1992), xix.

36 Forman and Odendaal, *Trumpet from the Housetops*, xix.

37 Allison Drew, *South Africa's Radical Tradition: A Documentary History*, Vol. 2 (Cape Town: University of Cape Town Press, 1997), 164.

38 Baruch Hirson, 'A Question of Class: The Writings of K A Jordan,' *Searchlight South Africa* 1, no. 2 (1989), 26.

39 Tabata diaries, UCT/BC925.

40 Richard Dudley in Alan Wieder, *Teacher and Comrade: Richard Dudley and the Fight for Democracy in South Africa* (Albany: State University of New York Press, 2008), 48.

Chapter 7

1 No Sizwe [Neville Alexander], *One Azania, One Nation: The National Question in South Africa* (London: Zed Press, 1979); Neville Alexander, 'Non-Collaboration in the Western Cape', in *The Angry Divide: Social and Economic History of the Western Cape*, ed. Wilmot G. James and Mary Simons (Cape Town: David Philip, 1989); Grant Farred, 'Meta-intellectuals: Intellectuals and Power', in *The Poverty of Ideas: South African Democracy and the Retreat of*

Intellectuals, ed. William Gumede and Leslie Dikeni (Johannesburg: Jacana Media, 2009); Maurice Hommel, *Capricorn Blues: The Struggle for Human Rights in South Africa* (Toronto: Culturama, 1981); Gavin Lewis, *Between the Wire and the Wall: A History of South African 'Coloured' Politics* (Cape Town: David Philip, 1987); Bill Nasson, 'The Unity Movement Tradition: Its Legacy in Historical Consciousness', in *History from South Africa: Alternate Visions and Practices*, ed. Joshua Brown (Philadelphia: Temple University Press, 1991); Ciraj Rassool, 'Taking the Nation to School' (unpublished paper presented at the University of the Western Cape's South African and Contemporary History Seminar, 15 May 2001); 'The Individual, Auto/biography and History in South Africa' (PhD dissertation, University of the Western Cape, 2004).

2 Rassool, 'Taking the Nation to School', 2.

3 Ben Kies, *The Background of Segregation* (Cape Town: Anti-CAD Committee, 1943), 16.

4 Rassool, 'Taking the Nation to School', 2.

5 Richard Dudley in Alan Wieder, *Teacher and Comrade: Richard Dudley and the Fight for Democracy in South Africa* (Albany: State University of New York Press, 2008), 44.

6 Christopher Saunders, *The Making of the South African Past: Major Historians on Race and Class* (Cape Town: David Philip, 1988).

7 Rassool, 'Taking the Nation to School', 3.

8 Neville Alexander, political activist, educationalist and academic, interview with the author, 6 June 2007.

9 Rassool, 'Taking the Nation to School', 16.

10 Isaac B Tabata, *Education for Barbarism: Bantu (Apartheid) Education in South Africa* (London and Lusaka: Unity Movement of South Africa, 1980), 53.

11 Saurabh Dube, 'Presence of Europe: A Cyber Conversation with Dipesh Chakrabarty', in *Postcolonial Passages: Contemporary History-writing on India*, ed. Saurabh Dube (New Delhi: Oxford University Press, 2004), 254.

12 Tabata, *Education for Barbarism*, 58.

13 Tabata, *Education for Barbarism*, 58.

14 Rassool, 'Taking the Nation to School', 18.

15 Raewyn Connell, *Southern Theory: The Global Dynamics of Knowledge in Social Science* (Cambridge: Polity Press, 2007).

16 Ashis Nandy, *Exiled at Home* (New Delhi: Oxford, 2005).

17 Connell, *Southern Theory*.

18 Nandy, *Exiled at Home*, 85.

List of Illustrations

Illustrations numbers 1-3, 6-9,12-14 and 16-18 are housed in the various collections at Special Collections, University of Cape Town Libraries, www .specialcollections.uct.ac.za

1   Revised NEF constitution, 15 April 1939
    Courtesy of the Tabata Collection, UCT Libraries
    BC925 UMSA / Tabata Collection, A 1939 mss_bc925_a_1939_001

2   Dr Abdullah Abdurahman
    Reprinted with permission of Independent Media
    Independent Media Photograph Collection va_independent_1a_001

3   Municipal election poster, 1931
    Courtesy of the Abdurahman Papers, UCT Libraries
    BC506 Abdurahman Family Papers mss_bc506_a5.3

4   Stakesby-Lewis Hostel, Canterbury Street, Cape Town.
    Newspaper clipping from *The Cape Standard*, Tuesday 12 March 1940
    Image courtesy of the National Library of South Africa, Cape Town
    The hostel building in 2018
    Photographer Jenny Hallward

5   Baruch Hirson
    Photographer Adine Sagalyn

6   Cissie Gool
    Courtesy of the Abdurahman Papers, UCT Libraries
    BC506 Abdurahman Family Papers mss_bc506_a5.17

7   Goolam Gool
    Courtesy of the Gool Family Papers, UCT Libraries
    BC1141 Gool Family Papers, F a i 001mss_bc1141_fai_001

8   Jane Tabata
    Courtesy of the Tabata Collection, UCT Libraries
    BC925 UMSA / Tabata Collection, D1.3 mss_bc925_d1.3

9   I B Tabata
    Courtesy of the Tabata Collection, UCT Libraries
    BC925 UMSA / Tabata Collection, D1.2 mss_bc925_d1.2

10 Nathaniel Honono, I B Tabata and Jane Gool
    Image courtesy of the National Heritage and Cultural Studies Centre,
        University of Fort Hare

11 March for Freedom and Equality, 1940
    Image courtesy of the National Library of South Africa, Cape Town

12 Protest Day Poster, 1939
    Courtesy of the Abdurahman Family Papers, UCT Libraries
    BC506 Abdurahman Family Papers, A3.24 mss_bc506_a3.24

13 Dora Taylor
    Courtesy of the Tabata Collection, UCT Libraries
    BC925 UMSA / Tabata Collection, D1.4 mss_bc925_d1.4

14 Benjamin Magson Kies
    Reprinted with permission of Independent Media
    Independent Media Photograph Collection, 23F bv_independent_23F_001

15 Johnny Gomas
    Reprinted with permission of Liz Bracks on behalf of the Gomas family
    Image scanned from Doreen Musson, *Johnny Gomas: Voice of the Working Class.*
        Cape Town: Buchu Books, 1989

16 Spring School in Simonstown, 1950
    Courtesy of the Tabata Collection, UCT Libraries
    BC925 UMSA / Tabata Collection, D1.5mss_bc925_d1.5

17 Richard Dudley
    Photograph by George Hallett, courtesy of the R O Dudley Papers, UCT Libraries
    BC1522 RO Dudley Papers, File A7

18 NEUM Mass Meeting Poster, 1944
    Courtesy of the Tabata Collection, UCT Libraries
    BC925 UMSA / Tabata Collection, A 1944 mss_bc925_a_1944_001

19 Cape Anti-CAD Mass Meeting, 1945
    Image courtesy of Yunus Omar

20 NEUM pamphlet, 1959
    Image courtesy of Yunus Omar

21 Cape Teachers' Federal Council call for mass meeting, April 1957
    Image courtesy of Yunus Omar

Bibliography

Abrahams, Peter. *Tell Freedom: Memories of Africa*. London: Faber & Faber, 1982.

Adhikari, Mohamed. *Against the Current: A Biography of Harold Cressy, 1889–1916*. Cape Town: Juta, 2012.

Adhikari, Mohamed. *'Let us Live for Our Children': The Teachers' League of South Africa, 1913–1940*. Cape Town: Buchu Books and University of Cape Town Press, 1993.

Adhikari, Mohamed. *Not White Enough, Not Black Enough: Racial Identity in the South African Coloured Community*. Cape Town: Double Storey Books, 2005.

Alexander, Neville. 'Aspects of Non-Collaboration in the Western Cape, 1943–1963'. *Social Dynamics* 12, no. 1 (1986): 1–14.

Alexander, Neville. *Language Policy and National Unity in South Africa*. Cape Town: Buchu Books, 1989.

Alexander, Neville. 'Non-Collaboration in the Western Cape'. In *The Angry Divide: Social and Economic History of the Western Cape*, edited by Wilmot G. James and Mary Simons, 180–192. Cape Town: David Philip, 1989.

Alexander, Neville. *An Ordinary Country: Issues in the Transition from Apartheid to Democracy in South Africa*. Pietermaritzburg: University of KwaZulu-Natal Press, 2002.

Andrew Murray Papers. African Studies Centre, University of Cape Town.

APDUSA (African People's Democratic Union of South Africa). 'Farewell to Comrade Minnie Gool'. *APDUSA Views*, special issue, December 2005. Accessed 28 December 2018, https://www.sahistory.org.za/sites/default/files/file%20uploads%20/a_tribute_to_minnie_gool.pdf.

Bam, June. 'The Development of a New History Curriculum for the Secondary Level in South Africa: Considerations Related to the Possible Inclusion of Themes Drawn from Unity Movement History'. Master's thesis, University of Cape Town, 1993.

Baum, Bruce. *The Rise and Fall of the Caucasian Race: A Political History of Racial Identity*. New York: New York University Press, 2006.

Bennett, Bonita, Noorunisaa Delate, Chrischené Julius, Premesh Lalu, Giorgio Miescher, Ciraj Rassool, Virgil Slade and Tina Smith, eds. *Fields of Play: Football, Memories and Forced Removals in Cape Town*. District Six Museum exhibition catalogue. Cape Town: District Six Museum, 2010.

Bickford-Smith, Vivian, Elizabeth van Heyningen and Nigel Worden. *Cape Town in the Twentieth Century: An Illustrated Social History*. Cape Town: David Philip, 1999.

Boucher, M. 'Graaff-Reinet and Higher Education: A Decade of Decline, 1875–1885'. *Kleio* 7, no. 2 (1975): 1–16.

Breckenridge, Keith. *Biometric State: The Global Politics of Identification and Surveillance in South Africa, 1850 to the Present*. Cambridge: Cambridge University Press, 2014.

Brookes, Edgar. *A History of the University of Natal*. Pietermaritzburg: University of Natal Press, 1966.

Cape of Good Hope. 'First Report and Proceedings, with Appendices, of a Commission Appointed to Inquire into and Report upon Certain Matters Connected with the Educational System of the Colony. Presented to both Houses of Parliament by Command of His Excellency the Governor, 1891, Cape Town'. National Archives of South Africa, Cape Town, G-9-91 (CCP 1/2/1/80).

Carr, Edward H. *What is History?* Harmondsworth: Penguin, 1964.

Cassirer, Ernst. *The Logic of the Cultural Sciences*. New Haven: Yale University Press, 2000.

Chinweizu, Ibekwe. *Decolonising the African Mind*. Lagos: Pero Press, 1987.

Chisholm, Linda. 'Making the Pedagogical More Political, and the Political More Pedagogical: Education Traditions and Legacies of the Non-European Unity Movement'. In *Vintage Kenton: A Kenton Education Association Commemoration*, compiled by Wendy Flanagan, Crispin Hemson, Joe Muller and Nick Taylor, 241–263. Cape Town: Maskew Miller Longman, 1994.

Connell, Raewyn. *Southern Theory: The Global Dynamics of Knowledge in Social Science*. Cambridge: Polity Press, 2007.

Davies, Rob, Dan O'Meara and Sipho Dlamini. *The Struggle for South Africa: A Reference Guide to Movements, Organizations and Institutions*. London: Zed Press, 1984.

Deutscher, Isaac. *The Prophet Outcast: Trotsky 1929–1940*. London: Verso, 2003.

Drew, Allison. *South Africa's Radical Tradition: A Documentary History*, Vol. 1. Cape Town: University of Cape Town Press, 1996.

Drew, Allison. *South Africa's Radical Tradition: A Documentary History*, Vol 2. Cape Town: University of Cape Town Press, 1997.

Drew, Allison. *Discordant Comrades: Identities and Loyalties on the South African Left*. Ashgate, 2000.

Dube, Saurabh. 'Presence of Europe: A Cyber Conversation with Dipesh Chakrabarty'. In *Postcolonial Passages: Contemporary History-writing on India*, edited by Saurabh Dube, 254–257. New Delhi: Oxford University Press, 2004.

Dubow, Saul. *A Commonwealth of Knowledge: Science, Sensibility and White South Africa, 1820–2000*. Oxford: Oxford University Press, 2006.

Dubow, Saul. *Racial Segregation and the Origins of Apartheid in Twentieth-Century South Africa, 1919–36*. London: Macmillan, 1989.

Dubow, Saul. *Scientific Racism in Modern South Africa*. Cambridge: Cambridge University Press and Johannesburg: Wits University Press, 1995.

Dudley, Richard. 'Forced Removals: The Essential Meanings of District Six'. In *The Struggle for District Six: Past and Present*, edited by Shamil Jeppie and Crain Soudien, 197–203. Cape Town: Buchu Books, 1990.

Ebrahim, Naz Gool, with Donna Brenneis and Shahena Wingate-Pearse. *The Truth is on the Walls*. Cape Town: David Philip, 2011.

Edgar, Robert. *An African American in South Africa: The Travel Notes of Ralph J Bunche: 28 September 1937 – 1 January 1938*. Johannesburg: Wits University Press, 1992.

Farred, Grant. 'Meta-intellectuals: Intellectuals and Power'. In *The Poverty of Ideas: South African Democracy and the Retreat of Intellectuals*, edited by William Gumede and Leslie Dikeni, 67–89. Johannesburg: Jacana Media, 2009.

Forman, Sadie and André Odendaal, eds. *A Trumpet from the Housetops: The Selected Writings of Lionel Forman*. Cape Town: David Philip, 1992.

Galant, Raashied. 'The Life and Times of Helen Kies: A Brief Examination'. Accessed 31 December 2017, https://www.academia.edu/1079361/The_life_and_times_of_Helen_Kies?auto=download.

Gentle, Roy. 'The NEUM in Perspective'. Honours dissertation, University of Cape Town, 1978.

Giyose, Phumi, with Cameron Madikizela, and Sefton Vutela. *The Return of Spartacus: Silhouettes of Revolutionary Fighters*. Mimeograph. Uitenhage: New Unity Movement, n.d.

Goldin, Ian. *Making Race: The Politics and Economics of Coloured Identity in South Africa*. London: Maskew Miller Longman, 1987.

Gool, Selim. 'The Gools of Cape Town – A Family Memoir: A South African Muslim Family in Search of Radical Modernity'. Accessed 9 November 2017, https://www.academia.edu/11836014/THE_GOOLS_of_CAPE_TOWN_-_Notes_towards_a_family_biography.

Hendricks, Fred and Peter Vale. 'The Critical Tradition at Rhodes University: Retrospect and Prospect'. *African Sociological Review* 9, no. 1 (2005): 1–13.

Herries, M M. 'The Ideological Matrix (III): Political Trends and Developments among Non-Whites Since "Union"'. *Educational Journal* XXXII, no. 8 (1961): 18–20.

Hirson, Baruch. 'The Black Republic Slogan – Part II: The Response of the Trotskyists'. *Searchlight South Africa* 1, no. 4 (1990): 44–56.

Hirson, Baruch. 'Bunting vs. Bukharin: The "Native Republic" Slogan'. *Searchlight South Africa* 1, no. 3 (1989): 51–65.

Hirson, Baruch. *The Cape Town Intellectuals: Ruth Schechter and Her Circle, 1907–1934.* Johannesburg: Wits University Press, 2001.

Hirson, Baruch. 'Colour and Class: The Origins of South African Trotskyism'. *Revolutionary History* 4, no. 4 (1993): 25–56.

Hirson, Baruch. 'A Question of Class: The Writings of K A Jordan'. *Searchlight South Africa* 1, no. 2 (1989): 21–35.

Hirson, Baruch. 'A Short History of the Non-European Unity Movement: An Insider's View'. *Searchlight South Africa* 3, no. 4 (1995): 64–93.

Hirson, Baruch. 'The Trotskyist Groups in South Africa, 1932–48'. *Searchlight South Africa* 3, no. 2 (1993): 54–118.

Hommel, Maurice. *Capricorn Blues: The Struggle for Human Rights in South Africa.* Toronto: Culturama, 1981.

Hook, Derek. *(Post)Apartheid Conditions: Psychoanalysis and Social Formation.* Cape Town: HSRC Press, 2014.

Houghton, Hobart. 'Economic Development, 1865–1965'. In *The Oxford History of South Africa, Vol. 2, 1870–1966,* edited by Monica Wilson and Leonard Thompson, 1–48. Oxford: Oxford University Press, 1975.

Hull, George. 'Neville Alexander and the Non-racialism of the Unity Movement'. Unpublished paper. University of Cape Town, 2018.

Isaacs, Sedick. *Surviving in the Apartheid Prison: Flash Backs of an Earlier Life.* Indiana: Xlibris, 2010.

Jaffe, Hosea. *Abandoning Imperialism.* Milan: Jaca Books, 2008.

Jaffe, Hosea. *European Colonial Despotism: A History of Oppression and Resistance in South Africa.* London: Kamak House, 1994.

Jaffe, Hosea. *The Pyramid of Nations.* Milan: Victor, 1980.

Jaffe, Hosea, ed. *The Great French Revolution.* Cape Town: New Unity Movement, 1989.

Jeppie, Shamil. 'Popular Culture and Carnival in Cape Town: The 1940s and 1950s'. In *The Struggle for District Six: Past and Present,* edited by Shamil Jeppie and Crain Soudien, 67–87. Cape Town: Buchu Books, 1990.

Jessa, Fakier. *Echoes: Tales from District Six.* Cape Town: Fakier Jessa, 2016.

Karis, Thomas and Gwendolen M Carter, eds. *From Protest to Challenge, Volume 2: Hope and Challenge, 1935–1952.* Stanford: Hoover Institution Press, 1973.

Kayser, Robin. 'Land and Liberty: The Non-European Unity Movement and the Land Question, 1933–1976'. Master's thesis, University of Cape Town, 2002.

Khan, Farieda. 'The Origins of the Non-European Unity Movement'. Honours dissertation, University of Cape Town, 1976.

Kies, Ben. *The Background of Segregation*. Cape Town: Anti-CAD Committee, 1943.

Kies, Ben. *The Basis of Unity*. Cape Town: Non-European Unity Movement, 1945.

Kies, Ben. *The Contribution of Non-European Peoples to World Civilisation*. A J Abrahamse Memorial Lecture. Cape Town: The Teachers' League of South Africa, 1953.

Kuljian, Christa. *Darwin's Hunch: Science, Race and the Search for Human Origins*. Johannesburg: Jacana Media, 2016.

Lalu, Premesh. 'Empire and Nation'. *Journal of Southern African Studies* 31, no. 3 (2015): 437–450.

Lategan, Ziyana. 'The Contribution of Hosea Jaffe to South African Political Thought'. Paper presented at the University of Cape Town's Historical Studies Department. Historical Studies Seminar, 4 August 2016.

Lee, Christopher Joon-Hai. 'The Uses of the Comparative Imagination: South African History and World History in the Political Consciousness and Strategy of the South African Left, 1943–1959'. *Radical History Review* 92 (2005): 31–61.

Lewis, Amelia. 'Reflections on Education in District Six'. In *The Struggle for District Six: Past and Present*, edited by Shamil Jeppie and Crain Soudien, 180–191. Cape Town: Buchu Books, 1990.

Lewis, Gavin. *Between the Wire and the Wall: A History of South African 'Coloured' Politics*. Cape Town: David Philip, 1987.

Limb, Peter. 'The Empire Writes Back: African Challenges to the Brutish (South African) Empire in the Early 20th Century'. *Journal of Southern African Studies* 31, no. 3 (2015): 599–616.

Lofts, Steve G. 'Translator's Introduction: The Historical and Systematic Context of *The Logic of the Cultural Sciences* by Ernst Cassirer'. In *The Logic of the Cultural Sciences* by Ernst Cassirer, xiii–xliii. New Haven: Yale University Press, 2000.

Loos, Jackie. 'Miss Jackson and Her Pupils "Sowed the Seeds" of Education'. *Cape Argus*, 11 October 2000, 11.

Majeke, Nosipho [Dora Taylor]. *The Role of the Missionaries in Conquest*. Cumberwood: African People's Democratic Union of South Africa, 1983. Originally written in 1952.

Malherbe, Ernst Gideon, ed. *Educational Adaptations in a Changing Society*. Report of the South African Education Conference held in Cape Town and Johannesburg in July 1934, under the Auspices of the New Education Fellowship. Cape Town: Juta, 1937.

Martin, Denis-Constant. *Coon Carnival: New Year in Cape Town, Past and Present*. Cape Town: David Philip, 1999.

Martin, Denis-Constant. *Sounding the Cape: Music, Identity and Politics in South Africa*. Cape Town: African Minds, 2013.

Miles, Robert. *Racism*. London: Routledge, 1989.

Mnguni [Hosea Jaffe]. *Three Hundred Years*. Cumberwood: African People's Democratic Union of South Africa, 1988.

Mokone, Sarah. 'Majority Rule: Some Notes'. Reprinted from *Educational Journal of the Teacher's League of South Africa* (1982). Accessed 6 November 2018, http://www.apdusaviews.co.za/repository/Majority%20Rule%20with%20 Biographical%20Note.pdf.

Musson, Doreen. *Johnny Gomas: Voice of the Working Class*. Cape Town: Buchu Books, 1989.

Nandy, Ashis. *Exiled at Home*. New Delhi: Oxford, 2005.

Nasson, Bill. 'The Unity Movement Tradition: Its Legacy in Historical Consciousness'. In *History from South Africa: Alternate Visions and Practices*, edited by Joshua Brown, 144–164. Philadelphia: Temple University Press, 1991.

Norval, Aletta. *Deconstructing Apartheid Discourse*. London: Verso, 1996.

No Sizwe [Neville Alexander]. *One Azania, One Nation: The National Question in South Africa*. London: Zed Press, 1979.

Ntantala, Phyllis. *A Life's Mosaic: The Autobiography of Phyllis Ntantala*. Johannesburg: Jacana Media, 2009.

Omar, Yunus. '"In my Stride": A Life History of Alie Fataar, Teacher'. PhD dissertation, University of Cape Town, 2015.

Omi, Michael and Howard Winant. *Racial Formation in the United States: From the 1960s to the 1980s*. New York: Routledge and Kegan Paul, 1986.

Pinnock, Don. 'Ideology and Urban Planning: Blueprints of a Garrison City'. In *The Angry Divide*, edited by Wilmot G. James and Mary Simons, 150–168. Cape Town: David Philip, 1989.

Ranger, Terence. 'The Invention of Tradition in Colonial Africa'. In *The Invention of Tradition*, edited by Eric Hobsbawm and Terence Ranger, 211–263. Cambridge: Canto, 1983.

Rassool, Ciraj. 'The Individual, Auto/biography and History in South Africa'. PhD dissertation, University of the Western Cape, 2004.

Rassool, Ciraj. 'Taking the Nation to School'. Unpublished paper presented at the University of the Western Cape's South African and Contemporary History Seminar, 15 May, 2001.

Rassool, Joe. 'Notes on the History of the Non-European Unity Movement in South Africa, and the Role of Hosea Jaffe.' *Revolutionary History* 4, no. 4 (1993), electronic supplement. Accessed 5 December 2018, https://www.marxists.org/history/etol/revhist/supplem/rassool.htm.

Roux, Edward. *Time Longer Than Rope: A History of the Black Man's Struggle for Freedom in South Africa.* Madison: University of Wisconsin Press, 1964.

Sandwith, Corinne. *World of Letters: Reading Communities and Cultural Debates in Early Apartheid South Africa.* Pietermaritzburg: University of KwaZulu-Natal Press, 2014.

Saunders, Christopher. *The Making of the South African Past: Major Historians on Race and Class.* Cape Town: David Philip, 1988.

Soudien, Crain. 'A Hundred Years of South African Thinking against "Race"'. Unpublished address to Andrew Mellon Colloquium on 'Race', Haarlem, Netherlands, May 2017.

Soudien, Crain. *Realising the Dream: Unlearning the Logic of Race in the South African School.* Cape Town: HSRC Press, 2012.

Soudien, Crain. 'South Africa: The Struggle for Social Justice and Citizenship in South African Education'. In *The Palgrave International Handbook of Education for Citizenship and Social Justice*, edited by Andrew Peterson, Michalinos Zembylas and James Arthur, 571–590. London: Palgrave, 2016.

South African Commission on Native Education. *Report of the Commission on Native Education, 1949–1951.* Report U.G. No. 53/1951. Pretoria: The Government Printer, 1951. Special Collections, African Studies Library, University of Cape Town.

'The South African Question'. Resolution adopted by the Executive Committee of the Communist International following the Sixth Comintern Congress. Accessed 13 December 2018, https://www.marxists.org/history/international/comintern/sections/sacp/1928/comintern.htm.

Stanley, Liz and Andrea Salter, eds. *The World's Great Question: Olive Schreiner's South African Letters 1889–1920.* Cape Town: Van Riebeeck Society, 2014.

Stevens, Garth, Norman Duncan and Derek Hook, eds. *Race, Memory and the Apartheid Archive.* Johannesburg: Wits University Press, 2013.

Tabata, Isaac B. Diaries. *UCT/BC925, Special Collections,* Jagger Library, University of Cape Town.

Tabata, Isaac B. *The Awakening of the People.* Nottingham: Bertrand Russell Peace Foundation for Spokesman Books, 1974. First published in 1958 by the African People's Democratic Union of South Africa.

Tabata, Isaac B. *Education for Barbarism: Bantu (apartheid) education in South Africa.* London and Lusaka: Unity Movement of South Africa, 1980 [1959].

Tabata, Isaac B. *Letter to Mandela on the Problem of Organisational Unity in South Africa*. Cape Town: African People's Democratic Union of South Africa, 1948.

Tabery, James and Sahotra Sarkar. 'R A Fisher, Lancelot Hogben, and the "Competition" for the Chair of Social Biology at the London School of Economics in 1930: Correcting the Legend'. *The Royal Society: Notes and Records* 69, no. 4 (2005): 437–446. Accessed 13 December 2018, https://www.ncbi.nlm.nih.gov/pmc/articles/PMC4650099/.

Taylor, Dora. 'The Function of Literary Criticism'. Unpublished lecture, 1953, Ronnie and Chrystal Bitten private collection.

Taylor, Dora. 'Introduction'. In *The Awakening of the People* by I B Tabata, vii–xii. Nottingham: Bertrand Russell Peace Foundation for Spokesman Books, 1974.

Theal, George McCall. *History of South Africa under the Administration of the Dutch East India Company*. London: Swan Sonnenschein, 1897.

Trotsky, Leon. 'Remarks on the Draft Thesis of the Workers' Party, 20 April 1935'. Accessed 6 November 2018, http://disa.ukzn.ac.za/sites/default/files/pdf_files/slfeb90.5.pdf.

Van Bever Donker, Maurits, Ross Truscott, Gary Minkley and Premesh Lalu, eds. *Remains of the Social: Desiring the Post-Apartheid*. Johannesburg: Wits University Press, 2017.

Van der Ross, Richard. *The Rise and Decline of Apartheid: A Study of Political Movements among the Coloured People of South Africa, 1880–1985*. Cape Town: Tafelberg, 1986.

Van Schoor, W P. 'The Origin and Development of Segregation in South Africa'. *A J Abrahamse Memorial Lecture*, Cathedral Hall, Cape Town, 5 October 1950. Accessed 17 December 2018, https://www.sahistory.org.za/archive/document-51-w-p-van-schoor-origin-and-development-segregation-south-africa-j-abrahamse-memor.

Vogel, Ann. 'Who's Making Global Civil Society: Philanthropy and US Empire in World Society'. *British Journal of Sociology* 57, no. 4 (2006): 635–655.

'Why Was Racialism Never Dismantled in South Africa?' *The Bulletin* 19, no. 3 (2011): 22.

Wieder, Alan. *Teacher and Comrade: Richard Dudley and the Fight for Democracy in South Africa*. Albany: State University of New York Press, 2008.

Wilkin, Esther. 'District 6 (Western Cape)'. Accessed 27 December 2017, https://jdap.co.za/roots-2/dorps-towns/dorps-towns/district-6-western-cape/.

Worden, Nigel. *The Making of Modern South Africa*. Oxford: Blackwell, 1994.

Index